Nuevo South

Historia USA
A series edited by Luis Alvarez, Carlos Blanton, and Lorrin Thomas

Nuevo South

Latinas/os, Asians, and the Remaking of Place

PERLA M. GUERRERO

University of Texas Press ⬥ *Austin*

Copyright © 2017 by the University of Texas Press
All rights reserved
First edition, 2017

A version of chapter 2 previously appeared, in a different form, as "Yellow Peril in Arkansas: War, Christianity, and the Regional Racialization of Vietnamese Refugees," *Kalifou: A Journal of Comparative and Relational Ethnic Studies* 3, no. 2 (216): 230–252. Passages in other parts of this book appeared in "A Tenuous Welcome for Latinas/os and Asians: States' Rights Discourse in Late Twentieth-Century Arkansas," in *Race and Ethnicity in Arkansas: New Perspectives*, ed. John A. Kirk (Little Rock: University of Arkansas Press, 2015), 141–151; and "Chicana/o History as Southern History: Race, Place, and the US South," in *A Promising Problem: The New Chicana/o History*, ed. Carlos Kevin Blanton (Austin: University of Texas Press, 2016), 83–110.

Requests for permission to reproduce material from this work should be sent to:

Permissions
University of Texas Press
P.O. Box 7819
Austin, TX 78713-7819
utpress.utexas.edu/rp-form

♾ The paper used in this book meets the minimum requirements of ANSI/NISO Z39.48-1992 (R1997) (Permanence of Paper).

Library of Congress Cataloging Data

Names: Guerrero, Perla M., author.
Title: Nuevo South : Latinas/os, Asians, and the remaking of place / Perla M. Guerrero.
Description: First edition. | Austin : University of Texas Press, 2017. | Series: Historia USA | Includes bibliographical references and index.
Identifiers: LCCN 2017015268| ISBN 978-1-4773-1364-0 (cloth : alk. paper) | ISBN 978-1-4773-1444-9 (pbk. : alk. paper) | ISBN 978-1-4773-1365-7 (library e-book) | ISBN 978-1-4773-1366-4 (nonlibrary e-book)
Subjects: LCSH: Hispanic Americans—Arkansas. | Cuban Americans—Arkansas. | Vietnamese Americans—Arkansas. | Social integration—Arkansas—History—20th century. | Refugees—Arkansas. | Immigrants—Arkansas—Social conditions. | Arkansas—Social conditions. | Arkansas—Race relations. | Arkansas—Emigration and immigration.
Classification: LCC F420.S75 G84 2017 | DDC 305.8009767—dc23
LC record available at https://lccn.loc.gov/2017015268

doi:10.7560/313640

Para mis papás por todos sus sacrificios y con mucho amor

Contents

Preface ix

Acknowledgments xi

Introduction 1

1. New South to Nuevo South: Region, Labor, and Race 27
2. Yellow Peril in Arkansas: War, Christianity, and the Regional Racialization of Vietnamese Refugees 49
3. Mariel Cubans as an "Objectionable Burden" and "Illegal Aliens" 74
4. Latinas/os and *Polleras*: Social Networks, Multisite Migration, Raids, and Upward Mobility 112
5. "Northwest Arkansas's No. 1 Societal Concern": "Illegal Aliens," Acts of Spatial Illegality, and Political Mobilizations 152

Conclusion: Race, Plantation Bloc, and Nuevo South 177

Notes 183

Bibliography 215

Index 229

Preface

In 1985 I left Guanajuato, Mexico, with my mother and brother to join my father in Pico Rivera, California. We lived there until 1996, when we moved to Fort Smith, Arkansas. As I was standing in the lunch line on the first day at my new high school, a girl asked me, "What are you?" This was my first encounter with the question, although I would hear it many more times. In an attempt to be playful, I asked her to guess. She listed Vietnamese, Laotian, Hawaiian, "Indian from India," Native American, "Eskimo," and Filipina. At first I thought she was kidding, but I soon realized her query was an attempt to complete a puzzle she could not put together on her own. Throughout my time in Arkansas I got asked that question a lot by strangers and, except in this instance, when my questioner was an Asian girl—an immigrant, I would find out later—always by white people, and often in public spaces.

I begin here because it points to the complexities in the racialization of a new group in a particular place and time. The Asian American girl tried to place me within the racial and ethnic fields familiar to her, which at that time did not include Latinas/os. Over time, as more Latinas/os settled in the Fort Smith area, we became familiar to its residents. Three years later I went to college in Conway, Arkansas, a very white city two and a half hours southeast of Fort Smith and half an hour from Little Rock, where people turned and gave me quizzical looks. In and around Conway people either thought I was white or asked, "What are you?" Again, this changed when more Latinas/os began to live and work in the area. Once there were others to compare me to, I sometimes heard, "But you're not a real Mexican like the other ones." Usually the people who told me this—including friends—meant it as a compliment; I did not take it as such, but wondered instead what constituted "real Mexicans" to them.

Arkansas changed my life because that is where I learned about racialization—depending on variables such as dress, language spoken, and peer group, people would categorize me differently in terms of my race. Later, in graduate school, I realized that southern California also taught me about racialization; after all, I had expected to be recognized as Mexican or Latina when we moved fifteen hundred miles east. But at sixteen all I knew was that I had always been constructed as Mexican, and I could not comprehend how Arkansans could not make sense of me.

My research about race in the South, about how Asians and Latinas/os are understood in the region in general and in Arkansas specifically, is a direct result of moving to this southern place. There were not a lot of Latinas/os in Arkansas when my family moved there, but as more of us arrived, we became hypervisible as we attended schools and moved into apartment buildings on the north side of Fort Smith. I lived through the shift from being an unknown to facing what became a powerful and racialized construction of my community as drug dealers, illegal aliens, and criminals. In short, our very presence was threatening, so much so that a state newspaper once declared Latinas/os as "Northwest Arkansas Number One Societal Concern." People who made an exception for me because I wasn't "a *real* Mexican like the other ones" made it very clear that people like my father were unwanted. Although I was accepted as an individual, my community was not, and that included my mom and dad—one a stay-at-home parent, the other a poultry worker, both with limited English abilities. But you cannot accept me and reject my parents and expect me to be okay with that—most, if not all, children of immigrants are not okay with that.

Acknowledgments

This project was born out of a deep desire to understand a particular historical moment. That I managed to complete this book is largely due to the support I have received from family, friends, and colleagues. The Department of American Studies at the University of Maryland, College Park, has been a wonderfully supportive environment for a young scholar. Nancy Struna, Mary Sies, Sheri Parks, and Psyche Williams-Forson have taught me so much about being an engaged scholar; Nancy and Psyche, department chairs, protected my time so that I could write, and for that I am eternally grateful. I was fortunate to have Christina Hanhardt, Randy Ontiveros, Janelle Wong, and Nancy Mirabal as colleagues and friends; I could not have asked for better or more enthusiastic supporters. I am most grateful for Julie Park, Jan Padios, and Sharada Balachandran Orihuela. When I started my job, I never imagined I would find such good friends at the university. I cherish our friendship for many reasons, but at the top of the list are their honesty, generosity, and wit. I was also fortunate to find supportive colleagues outside of UMD who have been generous with their time and have deeply engaged with my work. I thank them—Carlos Kevin Blanton, Paul Ortiz, and Julie Weise—as well as two anonymous reviewers for their feedback, which made this book much stronger. My work has also been supported by the James Irvine Foundation, the Ford Foundation, the Smithsonian Institution, and a Research and Scholarship Award from the University of Maryland, College Park. I was fortunate that Kerry Webb at the University of Texas Press supported me and this project and that the staff graciously gave me extra time when family emergencies delayed our timeline. I would also like to thank John Brenner, the copy editor for the book, who helped to polish the chapters.

A word of thanks to Shelley Blanton, archivist at the Pebley Center,

Boreham Library, University of Arkansas–Fort Smith, for supporting my project with such gusto and for digging through many collections to find sources that would help me in writing this book. Linda R. Pine, the head of Archives & Special Collections, Ottenheimer Library, University of Arkansas at Little Rock; Andrea Cantrell, the head of Research Services, Special Collections, University of Arkansas Libraries; and Frances Morgan, the manager of the Bill Clinton State Government Project, provided great guidance and support. I would especially like to thank all the Arkansans who gave so much of their time and shared part of their histories with me. I regret that I was unable to incorporate more of their voices into this book, but I want to assure them that their insights are still with me and their perspectives are integral to my second book project about Latina/o southerners.

I could not have completed this project without the great community that I found in the Department of American Studies and Ethnicity at the University of Southern California. I benefited greatly from the knowledge and mentorship of all the members of my dissertation committee. George Sánchez, my adviser, believed in this project from the beginning and helped me think through its various permutations with questions, challenges, and advice while also providing words of encouragement when needed. I learned a lot from Ruthie Gilmore's keen grasp of geography and political economy; her classes changed the way I think about the world, while her tireless work on social justice issues is humbling. Laura Pulido's work in geography and Chicano studies enriched this project and my thinking in a multitude of ways, while her commitment to fair labor and environmental practices provide an example I wish to follow. I thank her especially for giving me the opportunity to work with her on an article that gave me invaluable experience and immensely aided the path of this dissertation. Finally, Terry Seip readily agreed to join my committee, and the support and guidance he provided were indispensable. During my time in ASE, other faculty members worked closely with me as well, and my overall intellectual development is informed by each of them in ways they may not recognize but which I cherish greatly.

In graduate school I was fortunate to befriend Sharon Luk, Michelle Commander, Thang Dao, Tasneem Siddiqui, Araceli Esparza, Imani Johnson, Laura S. Fugikawa, Isabela Seong-Leong Quintana, Sionne Neely, Jesús Hernández, Nisha Kunte, Anton Smith, Micaela Smith, Carolyn Dunn, Anthony Bayani Rodriguez, Emily Hobson, Gretel H. Vera-Rosas, Wendy Cheng, Terrion Williams, Alvaro D. Marquez, and Orlando Serrano, among others who are too many to name. One of the things that made ASE such a wonderful experience was the camaraderie that often involved reading and critiquing each other's work, so I thank each person that ever read any draft of this book. Longtime friends, particularly Diem Le, Hong Vong, and Kim Kwee, were more than understanding when research, writing, and teaching got in the way of talking on the phone and spending time together. I would also like to thank Brooke and Treavor Edwards for so readily opening their home to me as I looked for an apartment in Little Rock for a year of research.

If I had never moved to Arkansas, I would be a wholly different person. I am thankful that my time there led me to my path as an ethnic studies and American studies scholar. When I was conducting research in the summer of 2012, I got involved with a social justice organization that works with Latina/o youth and attended their yearly training workshop. During the meet-and-greet, a teenage Latina came up to me and said, "Hi, I've never met anyone like you." I had never met a Latina with a graduate degree when I was in Arkansas either. I felt heavy with sadness that more than ten years after I left, this still had not changed. I also realized that part of the reason she had not met anyone like me is because it seems that many of us who are from Arkansas leave and rarely return. When I left, I was sure I would not return; I was exhausted. I was tired of seeing the social distance I felt reflected and reinforced through the absence of Latina/o history—in life we were unwanted, in books we were invisible. I am working toward establishing a history about Latinas/os in Arkansas—about Latinas/os in the South—so that future youths can see themselves in the books they read, and can see the contributions of their parents and grandparents, whether they worked in the poultry industry or building community organizations.

From the beginning, my family was the greatest source of strength, support, nourishment, and love. En los últimos quince años he tenido la oportunidad de reestablecer relaciones con toda mi familia en México y eso me hace muy dichosa. Esos viajes me han servido para darme ánimo cuando lo necesitaba y para llenarme de mucho amor—y de comida. Mi hermano Sandro siempre está ahí cuando necesito desahogarme y distraerme y lo quiero mucho. Papás, ustedes sacrificaron mucho—principalmente dejar a sus familias para inmigrar a Estados Unidos con la esperanza de darnos mejores oportunidades—motivo por el cual les doy las gracias. Pero más que nada, les doy las gracias por sus abrazos, besos, y amor incondicional. Los quiero con todo mi corazón.

Nuevo South

Introduction

Dr. Lam Van Thatch, the informal leader of the group, wore a brown tailored suit as he led seventy exhausted Vietnamese refugees from the airplane on May 2, 1975.[1] About four hundred people, including government officials and church leaders, welcomed them to Fort Smith before they were transported to Fort Chaffee, an Arkansas refugee and processing center. The Vietnamese arrivals—some without coats—stood in the rain and fifty-five-degree weather as Jack Freeze, the city's mayor, and David Pryor, the state's governor, welcomed them to Arkansas and the United States.[2] Pryor, a Democrat, explained to the refugees through an interpreter that the people of the United States, and particularly Arkansans, understood their situation: "We hope that you realize that we share the agony, pain and sorrow you have experienced."[3] Citing the benevolent nature of Americans across the country who had gathered provisions such as clothing and toys, and emphasizing Arkansans' Christian rectitude, he said, "[L]et me assure you, if I may, that the people of Arkansas are an open and friendly people. We have a long history and tradition of sharing what we have with others and using our best attempts to subscribe to the Biblical admonition, 'Do unto others as you would have them do unto you.' . . . This is the spirit and the nature of our people."[4]

Five years later, on May 7, 1980, Bill Clinton, the new Democratic governor, received news that the federal government would be reactivating Fort Chaffee as a processing center and sending a new group of refugees there.[5] He then released a statement to the press:

> The Cuban refugees who are now temporarily housed in Florida came to this country in flight from a Communist dictatorship. I know that everyone in this state sympathizes and identifies with them in their desire for

freedom. I will do all I can to fulfill whatever responsibilities the President imposes upon Arkansas to facilitate the refugees' resettlement in this country. I have ordered all appropriate state agencies to co-operate with Federal officials in working out details of the resettlement at Fort Chaffee.[6]

The statements that the governors made in response to the Vietnamese and Cuban refugees were indicative of the different receptions the groups received. Whereas Pryor reassured the Vietnamese refugees that Arkansans shared their "agony, pain and sorrow," Clinton assured Arkansans that the Cubans were in the state due to a federal imposition. In doing so, Clinton invoked states' rights, a particularly incendiary discourse in the state that had blocked the Little Rock Nine from integrating Central High School just twenty-three years earlier.

By the 1990s, another group of Latinas/os was in Arkansas. In the fall of 1994, Fabian walked into the commons area at a northwest Arkansas high school and saw "Hang the nigger and kill Mexicans" scrawled on a wall.[7] It was his first day on the job; wholly unprepared for what he saw, he walked out. But he needed the job, so he returned to the school the next day. He recalls that only one Black student and a couple of Asian students attended the school that year. But there were "a lot" of Latinas/os, he said: "Well, fifty. Some from California, many from Mexico, some Salvadorans."[8] The presence of Latinas/os marked a dramatic shift for a twelve-county area that, despite the placement of Vietnamese and Cubans at Fort Chaffee, had remained overwhelmingly white—close to 99 percent in many towns, cities, and counties—throughout the twentieth century.

Northwest Arkansas became overwhelmingly white through racial cleansing, including two vicious episodes in Harrison, Arkansas, in 1905 and 1909. These events were part of a larger pattern of state-sanctioned anti-Black violence resulting in murder, displacement, and the removal of African Americans from various places in Arkansas, Oklahoma, Illinois, and Missouri. White people ensured that northwest Arkansas remained white through racist practices such as "sundown towns." These were places where African Americans could not be present after daylight hours for fear of being beaten, murdered, or lynched.[9] In fact, Springdale and Rogers, two of the small cities that had dynamic Latina/o growth in the 1990s, had been sundown towns through most of the twentieth century. The graffiti Fabian saw on the wall might have been mere teenage bravado, but if so, it was deeply rooted in regional and local history. At that moment, African Americans and Latinas/os were both the objects of racial loathing, with some whites making explicit requests for their murders.

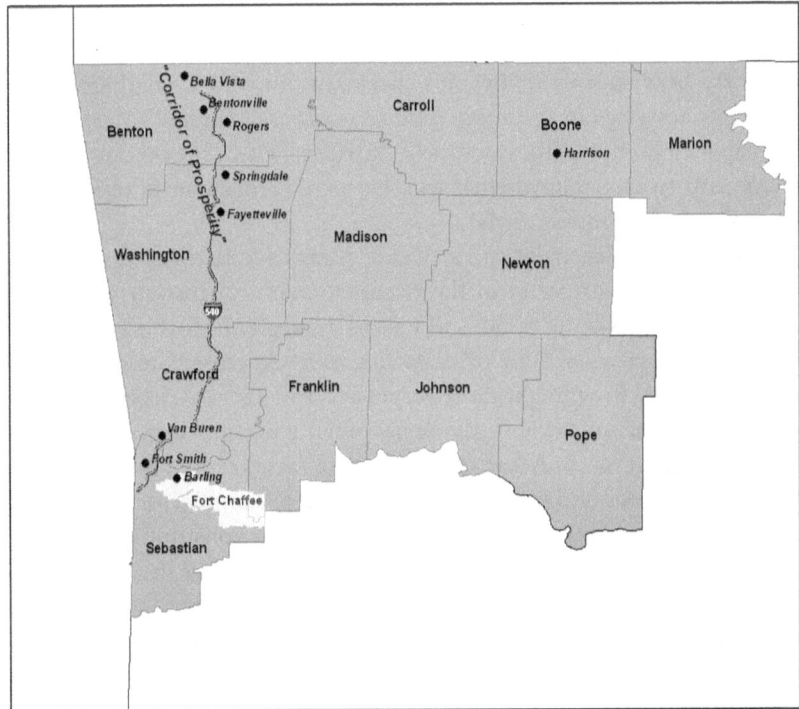

Figure 0.1. Map of northwest Arkansas. The term "corridor of prosperity" comes from Brooks Blevins's *Hill Folks: A History of Arkansas Ozarkers and Their Image.*

While Latina/o high school students were grappling with animosity and tension at school, the larger Latina/o community was being spotlighted in the statewide press. "Rich in Jobs, Northwest Arkansas Becomes Mecca for Illegal Aliens" is how the *Arkansas Democrat-Gazette*, the state's newspaper of record, described and introduced the Latina/o community to other Arkansans.[10] The article was one of the first to mention Latinas/os in the state and to place them in northwest Arkansas. According to Jessee F. Tabor, the chief patrol agent of the New Orleans office of the US Border Patrol who was responsible for overseeing Arkansas, "illegal aliens" were increasingly a "very significant" part of the poultry industry due to the area's low unemployment rate and the industry's high turnover rate. Tabor, however, was quick to point out that poultry companies were following the rules: "Employers (in northwest Arkansas) are complying with the law. To them, the documents appear to be genuine. We cannot expect them to be experts in counterfeit documents."[11] With these words, Tabor, a federal employee and authority figure, depicted "illegal aliens" solely as a readily available workforce who conned their law-abiding employers into hiring them. However, as opposed to Tabor's description of Latinas/os as con artists, individuals reported to their social networks how spottily companies checked employment eligibility, with some businesses gaining a reputation of *"no checan papeles"* ("not checking papers" [literally, "they don't check papers"]; i.e., they did not verify documents to ascertain whether workers were permanent US residents or had work authorization cards).

How did the placement and arrival of Asians and Latinas/os in Arkansas during the last quarter of the twentieth century renovate and make critical already existing notions of race in the region? How do we understand the responses of state officials and white Arkansans to Asians and Latinas/os, and how might those responses demonstrate larger historical processes of race-making in the area? What can the reception of refugees and immigrants in Arkansas tell us about racialization, the process by which institutions and individuals form, invoke, adapt, reformulate, and strengthen racial meanings? How is racialization constitutive of place-specific racial histories? How is racialization multiscalar? In other words, how do racialization processes draw from and contribute to common-sense understandings at local, regional, and national scales? Drawing on newspaper articles, state and federal documents, and in-depth interviews with a variety of Arkansans, this book posits that to fully understand the racialization of Asians and Latinas/os, specifically Vietnamese, Cubans, and Mexicans, we must also understand the history of place-specific ideologies that are at the center of more recent instantiations of racialized relationships.

The South has frequently been studied as a racial binary, as if it had only Black and white people, but scholars have been gradually complicating such an understanding.[12] Nevertheless, much painstaking research remains to be done to uncover the region's nuances and the different kinds of places within it. Scholars have discussed the Souths that are rural or urban, those housing both Black and white communities, and, more recently, those places where Latinas/os have now lived for decades. There is much work left to be done, however, to uncover, learn about, and document the other Souths—those that are neither urban nor rural, that are (or were) close to being 100 percent white, and that have undergone tremendous economic changes in creating wealth where little previously existed. Northwest Arkansas is a South at the intersection of these axes. After being overwhelmingly white for most of the twentieth century, it now has more Latinas/os than African Americans, Native Americans, or Asian Americans. In these ways, it differs significantly from other parts of the state, and its social relations reflect those specificities.¹³ The northwest quadrant has been one of the state's major economic drivers since Tyson Foods and Walmart built their corporate headquarters in the area and have expanded their respective processing plants and warehouses.¹⁴

The receptions for and reactions to Vietnamese and Cuban refugees and Latina/o immigrants in Arkansas in the last quarter of the twentieth century have varied. In April 1975, immediately after the fall of Saigon, many Vietnamese left the country, fleeing communism and the consequences of war. The federal government's selection of Fort Chaffee as a processing and relocation center for Vietnamese surprised the state's representatives and politicians.¹⁵ The decision struck a nerve in Arkansas, as many reacted negatively to what they considered a federal imposition on states' rights. At the same time, however, many Arkansans also recognized that people fleeing Vietnam and other Southeast Asian countries were doing so as a direct result of the United States' failed intervention. That understanding, coupled with the area residents' Christian belief in helping those less fortunate than themselves, spurred some Arkansans to mobilize in support of relocation efforts at Fort Chaffee and in Arkansas communities. Those intentions dissipated, however, with the arrival of the second Southeast Asian cohort. The first cohort consisted of many educated, professional, and English-speaking individuals, but the second cohort, composed of people from the countryside, gave rise to fears of "yellow peril," a historically durable idea that Asians are a foreign horde bent on corrupting America through disease, economic competition, and overpopulation.¹⁶ In the end, Arkansans sponsored 2,061 Southeast Asians. The Asian American community then grew slowly but steadily, reaching a population of more than 36,000, slightly more than 1 percent of the state's population, by 2010.

In 1980 more than 125,000 Cubans were allowed to leave for the United States, but their reception contrasted sharply with that given to Southeast Asians. Unlike prior cohorts of Cubans, who were upper or middle class, college educated, and white, this group consisted largely of the working poor, people of African descent, or those young enough to have grown up under communism, as well as a "noticeable" gay population. After a very brief welcome to refugees fleeing communism, the national, regional, and local news media changed their coverage dramatically, casting the new arrivals as the dregs of society—Communist, criminal, and homosexual—in large part because this is how Fidel Castro characterized them. After protests within the camp established at Fort Chaffee led to an uprising in which Cubans broke through the camp perimeter and the Arkansas Na-

Figure 0.2. Tyson Foods world headquarters; author photo.

Figure 0.3. Tyson Foods world headquarters front entrance; author photo.

tional Guard was activated, Arkansans sponsored only 402 Cubans, and some advocated that the camp at Chaffee be closed and the Cubans removed from the state. More than two decades later, fewer than twenty of the Cubans who had been at Fort Chaffee remained in Arkansas.[17]

In the 1990s, Latinas/os (largely ethnic Mexicans) moved to Arkansas and other southern states, drawn by work in meatpacking, carpeting, and other industries. Immigrants and migrants moved to the region through varied processes, including recruitment efforts in border states, such as Texas. However, my research in Arkansas demonstrates that Latinas/os heard about the opportunities to work in *polleras*, as Spanish speakers often call the poultry industry, from sojourners who passed the information through social networks. Subsequently, Latina/o immigrant and social networks served to recruit family members, friends, and neighbors to leave recession-hit California or their Latin American hometowns to pursue the economic stability that had eluded them. When I asked interviewees why they had moved to Arkansas, they usually gave three reasons: job availability; the state's low cost of living; and workplaces where "*no checan papeles*," which was beneficial for undocumented immigrants. With the exception of three nuclear families that moved to northwest Arkansas in the 1970s and a few professionals who moved for career-related reasons in the 1980s, all the Latinas/os I interviewed moved to the state in the 1990s after hearing about employment opportunities.

In the 1990s the Latina/o population in Arkansas more than quadrupled, reaching nearly 90,000. The exponential growth continued at the turn of the twenty-first century; by 2010 there were more than 186,000 Latinas/os, more than 6 percent of the state's population.[18] In the 1990s close to half lived in northwest Arkansas, a dramatic shift for the area. It is difficult to overemphasize how white these places had been for most of the twentieth century, but to fully understand this social context, we must also make sense of the way this racial dynamic took shape over time.

Racial cleansing and sundown towns served to make northwest Arkansas into a particular kind of place—one that was kept overwhelmingly white through the violent slaughter and removal of African Americans and, before them, Native Americans. I argue that reactions to Vietnamese and Cuban refugees and Latina/o immigrants, including efforts to remove or disperse them, draw on the legacy of white supremacist efforts to preserve a racially homogeneous region in which white people maintain spatial control. Local histories came to the forefront when Arkansans reacted with xenophobia, nativism, and fear to Asians and Latinas/os who started establishing roots in the state. The racializations of people of color were ultimately attempts to stabilize whiteness in a place that had established its meaning through violent racial pogroms and racial exclusion.

The addition of Asians and Latinas/os marked a dramatic change for northwest Arkansas, while the reactions to the groups demonstrated the complexities of place and racial difference. White Arkansans drew on national discourses and local events to racialize Vietnamese and Cuban refugees and Latina/o immigrants in regionally significant ways. Asians and Latinas/os were differently racialized in relationship to each other but also within each group. That Vietnamese and Cubans received contrasting reactions nationally, regionally, and locally, even though both groups fled communism, suggests the complicated ways in which white Arkansans responded to racial, ethnic, and class differences. Their responses varied from initial grudging acceptance of Vietnamese refugees to subsequent panic about other Vietnamese to full rejection and then removal of Cubans. The vitriol that Cubans experienced foreshadowed some of the responses that Mexicans—another Latina/o group—would endure at the turn of the twenty-first century. Significantly, Latina/o migrants and immigrants were the first nonwhite group that white Arkansans could not contain or remove. Once it became clear that they could not expunge and wholly exclude Asians and Latinas/os, they reframed their racial ideology toward the idea of assimilation, even as this standard remained ultimately unattainable for nonwhite populations since they are deemed to be outsiders to the national body. The struggle over space and place and their centrality in racial meanings, however, continues into the twenty-first century in the attempts of some Arkansans to contain, police, and discipline other Arkansans in their use of space.

Toward a Framework of the Nuevo South

There is a growing field of study on Latinas/os in the South, sometimes called the "Nuevo New South" or "Nuevo South." But in many instances the term "Nuevo South" is used as if it were self-explanatory, or, in some of the more egregious cases, the word "nuevo" is used simply in an exoticizing manner—Latinas/os are moving to the South and they speak Spanish, so we can now refer to the South as the "Nuevo South." In these cases, the term is vapid because the authors never define it or explain how using it will help reveal how ideas of race, labor, and belonging are reshuffled and rearticulated in the region.

Some of the scholars who write about the "Nuevo South" have missed an opportunity to engage with the field of history, where the term "New South" has been constructed, defined, argued against, and defended—all productive activities that have contributed some level of clarity to understandings of the region and its places. The literature about the New South, historiographically anchored by W. E. B. Du Bois's *Black Reconstruction* and C. Vann Woodward's *Origins of the New South*, demonstrates that the post-Reconstruction South was marketed as having reinvented the area's dominant ideology in order to produce a business-friendly and supposedly less racist region capable of securing northern investment.[19] New South leaders adjusted their regime of accumulation and used new labor forces in a manner most financially beneficial for them, yet they did little to disrupt the socioeconomic and political landscape.

This book works toward a conceptual framework of "Nuevo South" that scrutinizes the legacies of southern history in terms of dealing with racial difference and driving economic development; it takes into account political and social factors, considering how refugees and immigrants negotiate these dynamics in their daily lives and interactions. The book moves beyond "Nuevo South" as a mere catchphrase and begins to provide some of the rigor necessary to explore how and to what extent difference is reformulated to serve business leaders in exploiting the region for material gain. The framework of the Nuevo South is directly linked to the concept of the New South, because although both are used by boosters and businesses to speak about better conditions for communities of color, they are actually premised on the exploitation of those communities, especially in the labor sphere. In short, the Nuevo South is the newest manifestation of the New South—a regime built on white supremacy, the exploitation of racial difference, and, increasingly, legal statuses such as citizen, refugee, or undocumented immigrant that define the experiences of new southerners.

This framework draws on the work of Clyde Woods, who argues that the blues is a theory of social and economic development and change. He critiques plantation social relations and their extension while expressing the desire for communities to be independent of the plantation monopoly. Woods theorizes that the plantation bloc had been in power since the Trail of Tears and continued until the present, constantly adjusting by building new alliances that always work to keep Black people and poor whites at the bottom of economic development. The plantation bloc enacted what he called Mississippi Plans, characterized by economic and social crises, a shift in the form of social exploitation, and a new and stable regime of accumulation. Within the plantation complex, "slavery, sharecropping, mechanization, and prison, wage and migratory labor are just a few of the permutations possible."[20] Conceptualizing the South as a region that has been constructed through plantation blocs allows us to capture the workings of economic, political, and ideological power and how they are reformed and rearticulated in response to ethnic and racial diversification in specific ways in different places in the region.

The Nuevo South framework allows scholars to explore the extent to which political, economic, and social dynamics have changed with the arrival of new groups of people. Moreover, a focus on political economy allows us to see that many Latinas/os in the South were migrants and immigrants who moved to the region to work in meat-processing plants. In 2006 William Kandel found that "rapid Hispanic growth counties correspond[ed] to high-poultry production counties."[21] Consider that Tyson Foods, the world's largest meat producer, is based in northwest Arkansas and that the industry as a whole has undergone enormous growth that coincides with the migration of Latinas/os and Asians. In other words, immigrants provided the inexpensive labor necessary for the poultry industry to grow quickly and profitably as a new plantation regime.

The poultry industry, however, was not alone in drawing on or benefiting from a new labor pool; among others, agriculture, construction, and service industries expanded with the arrival of Latinas/os. Moreover, growth in one area often had repercussions in other areas, and in some places working-class Black and white people were able to get better-paying jobs or ones that were less physically arduous, while Latinas/os and other immigrants and migrants worked in low-skill and low-paying jobs.[22] In Georgia, farmers benefited from a seasonal workforce that had not been available previously. In southeastern Georgia, one of the largest packinghouses increased its onion production twenty-five-fold between 1978 and 1983. According to Julie M. Weise, "Between 1982 and 1987, the value of Georgia's vegetable crop increased by 60 percent, and growers' use of 'contract labor'—as opposed to tenant farmers or permanent employees—tripled. These were the years in which the migrant labor stream turned over almost entirely to become majority Mexicano."[23] At the turn of the twenty-first century, 90 percent of farmworkers in North Carolina were Latina/o—a dramatic change in Dixie.[24]

By focusing on political economy and social relations, the Nuevo South framework also grapples with the multifaceted ways in which Latinas/os and Asians are sometimes granted a modicum of acceptance by established communities, how they locate themselves within a field of social and racial positions, and whether they do so in opposition to other communities of color, especially Black communities. Latinas/os and Asians might be desirable as a workforce that is more vulnerable and exploitable, but their racial and ethnic difference is also a factor in how they are understood and the extent to which they are accepted.

Latinas/os and Asians can be more exploitable than Black people because of legality issues, language barriers, or a dire economic need to send money home. At the same time, African Americans in the region are more aware of injustices at work and less willing to be exploited. The knowledge that Black communities have about whether they will be safe in a particular place or be paid the wages promised makes it difficult to recruit African American laborers, even when there are jobs available. In this way, industries benefit from drawing people from outside of the region or nation, because newcomers are not aware at first of the working and living conditions that await them.

Place, Racialization, and Racial Formation

Centered on the intersection of Asian American and Latina/o studies and southern history, this book examines the racialization of Vietnamese and Cuban refugees and Latina/o immigrants and migrants in Arkansas at the end of the twentieth century and the beginning of the twenty-first. The settlement of Asians and Latinas/os in a southern state added new complexity to the US racial order and its multiple racial projects. This book's framework is informed by a Gramscian understanding of common sense that allows us to see how race and racial difference come to be defined at the local level, what shapes the definition, and how such a definition might not necessarily fit into the racialized understandings established by law or civil society. In other words, commonsense understandings about difference are grounded in local histories even as they intertwine with regional and national narratives. A focus on place is particularly important for the US South because the region has been discussed through a Black and white binary for too long; such a division serves to perpetuate the idea that Chinese, Mexicans, Syrians, and other groups have not lived in Dixie until recently. The binary has more pernicious repercussions, however, as it also obfuscates the permutations of how place defines and shapes a color line. In other words, how local histories shape local culture and norms can vary dramatically within one state.

In order to use race and place as categories of analysis, I draw from economic geographers and ethnic studies scholars. Economic geographers use frameworks and/or methodologies based on historical materialism, which posits that the production and reproduction of life (forms of consciousness, relationships between people, ideologies, etc.) are based on material conditions, that is, on the mode of production.[25] Thus space is a construction that is produced through an inherently political process because it is the outcome of social relations. Place is a particular form of space, and, likewise, also the outcome of social relations. More precisely, economic geographers base their analyses of space and place on the ebbs and flows of capitalist development, which forms part of the material and social conditions that articulate in a particular way to create categories of difference. Capitalism is a process of circulation that creates and functions through uneven development, which is the geographical expression at several spatial scales of the contradictions inherent in capital. As scholar Neil Smith puts it, "What it [capitalism] achieves in fact is the *production of space* in its own image.... For not only does capital produce space in general, it produces the real spatial scales that give uneven development its coherence."[26] According to Smith, scale is a primary means for spatial differentiation, defining identities and representing differences. Identity and difference are central to the definition of scale, but they are most important at the low scale of the body because it provides access to other scales—home, community, city, region, and nation—since it is the receptacle for race, class, gender, sexuality, and other social constructs used to oppress people. Drawing on this scholarship, I understand the region as a unit of analysis in which the economic, political, social, and cultural spheres at the global, national, and local levels intersect to form different kinds of places.

Generally, literature on racialization posits that race-making is complex, multifaceted, and centered on creating categories for groups of people (races) that are often central to the organization of society. The process involves defining people through legal and economic means as well as in social and cultural ways that are hard to legislate but are carried out by society at large.[27] Michael Omi and Howard Winant argue that racial formation (a sociohistorical process) and racial projects (attempts to codify and distribute resources in particular ways) organize and structure US society. They also argue that everyday activities contribute to racial projects because state policies alone cannot guarantee the particular treatment or racialization of people.[28]

Claire Jean Kim attempts to avoid the vertical hierarchy, which she argues is too rigid, in her discussion of Asian Americans, arguing instead for a field of racial positions that allow for more mobility and nuances. She uses the concept of "racial triangulation" that is formed through the axes of relative valorization and civic ostracism. This field accentuates that ethnic groups are racialized in comparison to one another and that they are therefore racialized differently.[29] Natalia Molina posits that "we understand each new 'other' in relation to groups with which we are already familiar," even if groups are not necessarily simultaneously present. Thus groups are connected in that racialized ideas and understandings about one group can help define another. She proposes "racial scripts" as a term that "emphasize[s] the ways in which we think, talk about, and act toward one racialized group based on our experiences with other groups whose race differs from our own."[30] This concept emphasizes the relational dimensions that define groups in different places and times, and offers a more nuanced way to situate race and place.

While Molina provides one avenue through which to understand a multiracial and multiethnic field of racial positions, another scholar, Wendy Cheng, demonstrates that the region is an important unit of analysis, since race is not constructed or experienced uniformly. In her study of Asians and Latinas/os in suburban Los Angeles, Cheng theorized racial formation by sharply focusing on race and place. Drawing on everyday experiences and landscapes, she found that Latinas/os and Asians in the San Gabriel valley altered racial hierarchies and understandings based on their experiences living in a majority-minority area. Cheng proposes "regional racial formation" as "place-specific processes of racial formation, in which locally accepted racial orders and hierarchies complicate and sometimes challenge hegemonic ideologies and facile notions of race."[31] Following Cheng, this book centers place and race within the US South in order to unpack the racialization of Asians and Latinas/os, as well as to understand how their racialization changed over time and as new "others" entered the picture.

Communities of color are sometimes racialized in ways that overlap or are similar; however, there are also specific anxieties that are projected onto each group. Colleen Lye and Lisa Lowe have demonstrated that fear of Asian people within economic and cultural spheres has a history in the United States that dates back to the late nineteenth century, with the racialization of Asians as physically and intellectually different from white people as well as the intersection of anti-Asian fears and nativism predominating during economic downturns.[32] In particular, Asian immigrants have served as "screens" "on which the nation projects a series of condensed, complicated anxieties regarding external and internal threats" to the nation.[33] The United States has a long history of anti-Asian fears, as demonstrated by the Chinese Exclusion Act of 1882; the anti-Japanese

Gentlemen's Agreement of 1907; the "barred Asiatic zone" under the Immigration Act of 1917; the exclusion of Asians in the Immigration Act of 1924; Japanese American internment during World War II; and the Asia-Pacific quotas under the Immigration and Nationality Act of 1952, also called the McCarran-Walter Act.

Anti-Asian sentiments and anxieties loom particularly large during periods of US wars in Asia, when fears of defeat abroad are projected onto Asian workers within the nation.[34] As Lye points out, these anxieties are based on a foundational belief: if "American universality depends upon the possibility of assimilation, there is always also the danger of discovering aliens in our midst, or the wholesale possibility of American takeover by aliens."[35] The American people and the government fight against this in two ways. On the one hand, cultural producers contribute to and create stereotypes to discursively "fix" Asian people within certain parameters; on the other hand, the state racializes Asian identities through legal classifications that exclude and include, such as "citizen" and "noncitizen" or "US-born" and "permanent resident."[36]

Lowe argues that "the American *citizen* has been defined over and against the Asian *immigrant*, legally, economically, and culturally. These definitions have cast Asian immigrants both as persons and populations to be integrated into the national political sphere and as the contradictory, confusing, unintelligible elements to be marginalized and returned to their alien origins."[37] Moreover, as Lye argues, "yellow peril" is the manifestation of a "long-running racial form, a form whose most salient feature, whether it has been made the basis for exclusion or assimilation, is the trope of economic efficiency."[38] This trope works in such a way as to make Asian economic advancement the danger that threatens white native workers, while race, cultures, and languages construct Asians as foreigners and outside of the national body.[39]

Whereas wars abroad provide a context for Asian American racialization, US immigration laws and border control have largely defined Latina/o racialization. As Mae Ngai argues, US immigration law has racialized Mexicans, Filipinos, and Chinese as undesirable aliens. In the case of Mexicans, increased border restriction produced the "illegal alien"—a *"new legal and political subject*, whose inclusion within the nation was simultaneously a social reality and a legal impossibility—a subject barred from citizenship and without rights."[40] Mexicans eventually emerged as the "iconic illegal aliens," as opposed to Europeans and Canadians, who tended to be dissociated from the category and thus able to assimilate as white American citizens. More significantly, however, "illegal status became constitutive of a racialized Mexican identity and of Mexicans' exclusion from the national community and polity."[41]

Nicholas De Genova also argues that one key aspect to the racialization of Latinas/os, particularly Mexicans, is the discursive and legal power of illegality. He argues that the category of "illegal alien" has served as a means to racialize all Mexicans in particular ways. Furthermore, illegality is primarily a political identity, because it is a juridical status that necessitates a social relation to the state. In this way, illegality is similar to citizenship, as both are political identities formed through juridical status. But whereas the latter defines inclusion, the former defines exclusion and the erasure of legal personhood. Categories have been collapsed so that illegality is equated with "Mexican" as opposed to being only one element of racialization.[42]

While it is true that some Latinas/os in Arkansas were undocumented immigrants, many were also legal US residents, naturalized citizens, and, among the younger generation, US-born nationals. The inability of most Arkansans to fathom that many of the new arrivals were legally present demonstrates Ngai's concept of "alien citizens." This category is based on the "legal racialization of these ethnic groups' [Asians and Mexicans] national origin," which is used to "cast them as permanently foreign and unassimilable to the nation."[43] More specifically, alien citizens are "persons who are American citizens by virtue of their birth in the United States but who are presumed to be foreign by the mainstream of American culture and, at times, by the state."[44] The result of such constructions is the denial of "substantive citizenship."[45]

Substantive citizenship is both "the capacity to exercise rights to which one is formally entitled" and the "enforcement or lack of enforcement of formal citizenship rights by the national, state, or local government or by members of the public."[46] Evelyn Nakano Glenn posits that "at the most general level is the notion of citizenship simply as belonging—membership in the community, sometimes defined as the nation," in addition to other "sub-meanings," including "the notion of nationality (being identified as part of a people who constitute the nation)."[47] The issue of belonging includes civil, political, and social citizenship where boundaries are or are not enforced by individual actors at a local level; this then creates local, regional, and temporal variability.[48] Her discussion of citizenship parallels Ngai's concept of "alien citizens," with both arguing that some groups, including Mexican immigrants and Mexican Americans, lack recognition of formal and substantive citizenship through denial of membership in the community and nation.

According to Jonathan Xavier Inda, the construction of "illegal aliens" is rendered in ethical terms.[49] "The clearest indication that 'illegal' immigrants have been constructed as unethical comes from the widespread tendency to cast them as lawbreakers," he writes. "Indeed, the propensity has been to characterize them as criminals. Their criminality is generally attributed to the simple fact that they have no legal right to be in the United States."[50] Ultimately, Inda argues that "'illegal' immigrants—typically imagined as criminals, job takers, and welfare dependents—have essentially been constructed as imprudent, unethical subjects incapable of exercising responsible self-government and thus as threats to the overall well-being of the social body."[51] As we shall see, in Arkansas the threat to the "social body" took place at different scales—community, state, and nation.

Centering the experiences of Asians and Latinas/os in Arkansas allows an analysis of processes of racialization and elucidates the legacies of southern history. In other words, this book focuses on the experiences of Vietnamese, Cubans, and Mexicans in order to delineate racialization processes in a particular kind of southern place and examine how those processes are shaped by a place's histories, including those of racial violence and the removal of Black communities. By grounding this study in local history with long-lasting consequences for understandings of race, we can begin to analyze deeply the regional racial formations in the South. In the following pages, I show that the groups were racialized differently through legal categorizations, political rhetoric, and everyday discourse that reflected the articulation of the national political moment, regional history, local political economy, religious beliefs, and understandings of family. The project contributes to the growing literature on racialization, especially that which privileges relational notions of race and ethnicity to better understand the power dynamics that shape the lives of people of color in different places in the United States.[52]

Moreover, this study helps explain the elasticity of racialization, as a single group can be defined in shifting and competing ways. In the popular imagination, the Vietnamese went from victims needing rescue (as long as they met certain criteria proving that they were not too different from idealized white Arkansans) to the "yellow peril" (feared for being too different and unassimilable, in part due to their multigenerational family units) to "model minorities" (in contrast to other newcomers, such as Cuban refugees and Mexican immigrants). Cuban refugees arrived in 1980 amid national and international accusations that Fidel Castro's government had unleashed criminals, prostitutes, and the mentally ill. Given these discourses, and the fact that this cohort of Cubans was largely working-class and of African descent and had a substantial number of gay people, Arkansans and their politicians constructed them as deviant criminals and mobilized to remove them from the state.[53] In the 1990s, Mexican migrants and other Latin American immigrants arrived during a significant regional economic reorganization that provided many of them with low-wage work, especially in the poultry industry. At the turn of the twenty-first century, Latinas/os were increasingly racialized as "illegal aliens" but were praised by Mike Huckabee, then the governor of Arkansas, for their devotion to God and family.[54]

Much work remains to be done to explore the role of religious beliefs in racialization, especially in places where faith can be central to community formation and where Christianity was used to justify chattel slavery and racial subjugation. Indeed, one of Arkansans' idiosyncrasies was drawing on Christianity to advocate for accepting Vietnamese who would suffer under communism and, later, for Mexican immigrants, while often denying such acceptance to African Americans, as well as to Cuban refugees who also fled communism. Northwest Arkansas can also illustrate how whiteness and Blackness operate in a place that had been racially homogeneous. More important, it can elucidate how anti-Black racism shapes the lives of refugees and immigrants and reveal the anti-Black structures that continue to exist across the United States.

History and Place-Making

The argument of this book rests on a place-based and multiscalar analysis that considers how definitions of race at a higher scale, such as national understandings of Vietnamese and Cuban refugees and Mexican immigrants, helped to inform understandings at a lower level of the local and, finally, how local experiences also helped to shape understandings regionally. I understand race as dialectical processes. Information is often passed down from a higher scale, such as national ideas that help to define one group, such as Mexicans, as "illegal aliens," but there is also a pathway that provides information from a lower level, such as city or town, to a higher scale, such as region. The process can be observed through the discourses of newspapers and other media because a medium is simultaneously passing information to readers but also receiving information from them.

The three groups that were new to northwest Arkansas—Vietnamese,

Cubans, and Mexicans—were introduced to the public largely through the media because they arrived at specific moments and places and in substantial numbers. The groups were newcomers to northwest Arkansas, but substantial numbers of Cubans and Mexicans already lived elsewhere in the United States, so a particular kind of understanding about who they were supposed to be already existed. In 1975, Vietnamese were only the latest Asians to enter the nation and face Americans' anxieties. Although Arkansans' ideas of Christian charity and duty to refugees configured the arrival of Vietnamese in the state, they were racialized through "yellow peril." The process played out in statewide newspapers that reported on the relocation efforts and the reactions of Arkansas politicians but also involved a flurry of letters to the editor "informing" other Arkansans about the looming threat or, alternatively, about America's obligation to the first cohort of Vietnamese, who had been allies in the Vietnam War. Newspapers were also crucially important for defining Cubans from Mariel through powerful tropes. The Cuban cohorts that preceded those from Mariel had been cast as "golden exiles" and were welcomed for fleeing communism. At first, Mariel Cubans received a warm welcome from exiles and other Americans, that attitude was short-lived, for within weeks the media and some individuals came to believe Castro's depiction of these Cubans as criminals, prostitutes, homosexuals, and the dregs of society.

In the 1990s, when Latinas/os started moving to the state in substantial numbers, Arkansans were aware of rhetoric in other parts of the country about "illegal aliens," but they did not immediately transfer that racialized understanding to newcomers in Arkansas. Instead, Arkansans learned at least in part through statewide newspapers that the new people arriving were Mexicans and that this group constituted "illegal aliens." In other words, the racialized link between Latinas/os and illegality had to be established in local contexts in order for that construct to become a commonsense understanding. The first few newspaper articles about Latinas/os focused on migrant workers who would stay only a short time. They could teach Spanish, so Latinas/os were constructed as knowledge sources; they spent time with locals, so they were constructed as companions. Those articles suggest that Arkansans were quite accepting of migrant workers, people who would toil the land when necessary but leave after the season passed. Once Latinas/os started making claims as Arkansans by renting and buying homes and by sending their children to school, they were no longer curiosities, and increasingly came to be constructed as "illegal aliens" and racialized through commonsense understandings of illegality. This study provides an in-depth analysis of how racial difference is constructed, defined, deployed, and contested in one part of the South.

Research and Methodology

Using the framework outlined previously, I conducted archival and ethnographic research. I constructed an archive from various sources, such as state and federal official reports and the documents of governors, representatives, and senators; newspaper articles; and constituents' letters, which provided a window into how various segments of Arkansans understood and constructed Asians and Latinas/os in public and in private. Accessing papers held in various archives allowed me to see beyond public discourse and statements to determine what government officials thought was at stake in accepting or rejecting Vietnamese, Cubans, and Mexicans, while reading letters from constituents provided a window into a segment of public opinion that might otherwise have remained unexamined.

I use discourse analysis to study these sources. Discourse analysis posits that people use language to make things significant, to give them meaning or value, since the meaning of a word is not inherent. Furthermore, it asks what "social goods" the language is communicating; that is, it takes word choice to indicate what the speaker takes to be normal, good, right, valuable, the way things are, or the way things ought to be. Discourse analysis is about making sense of what is written or said and draws on intertextuality that alludes in some way to other "texts," such as themes, debates, or motifs, whether written, spoken, or cultural. This method allows me to see how language changes over time, to analyze the dialectical process of race-making, and to assess how racialized ideas become commonsense understandings.

The archive that I constructed for each group reflects some of the differences in terms of the means by which Vietnamese, Cubans, and Mexicans arrived in the state, as well as obstacles for conducting archival and ethnographic research. I was able to identify special collections with a plethora of materials for Vietnamese and Cubans; however, that abundance of documents is largely "top-down" because the documents are written by, to, and for city, state, or federal officials. There are two exceptions to that trend. The first is constituents' letters, which can provide great insight into how everyday people understood the various situations. It is also likely that the people who wrote such letters felt quite strongly about the situation, since they took the time to correspond with state or federal officials.

The second is an archive with letters written by the first cohort of Vietnamese at Fort Chaffee; they wrote them in an English-language class they attended as they waited to be sponsored out of the camp.

I began building my archival materials by searching the *Arkansas Gazette* and, after its merger with the *Arkansas Democrat* in 1991, the *Arkansas Democrat-Gazette*, statewide newspapers that covered the arrival of Vietnamese, Cubans, and Mexicans. I identified the first time that each group was mentioned in relationship to Arkansas. For Vietnamese and Cubans, I looked at every article that covered their arrival at Fort Chaffee, life at the camp, sponsorship-related issues, and how their processing and presence affected other state issues. For Vietnamese, that coverage lasted until the early 1980s, when follow-up articles described how refugees were adapting to life in Arkansas; the coverage about Cubans largely ended once Fort Chaffee closed. I also identified two gubernatorial collections and three other special collections that had materials on Vietnamese and Cubans at Fort Chaffee. The gubernatorial papers contained a plethora of documents between the governors at the time, different branches of the federal government, and constituents' letters, and discussed a variety of issues. For Latina/o immigration and migration, I identified keywords and searched for them in the *Arkansas Gazette* and later the *Arkansas Democrat-Gazette*.

Newspaper archives also varied in certain ways. Whereas coverage about Vietnamese and Southeast Asian resettlement lasted a few years, the articles about Cubans ended once Fort Chaffee closed. To determine how Vietnamese and Cuban refugees and Latina/o immigrants were constructed in the media, I conducted keyword searches specific to each group and time period. For Vietnamese I searched terms such as "Vietnamese," "Indochinese," "refugees," "resettlement," and "Fort Chaffee"; I conducted a similar search for Cubans. For Latina/o immigrants I searched terms such as "Mexicans," "Hispanic," "immigrants," "migrants," "illegal," "aliens," "illegal aliens," "undocumented," "migrant workers," "poultry workers," "Latino," "raid," "INS," and many other keywords that I identified along the way. I painstakingly looked at every article that mentioned any person who was Latina/o to see how the narrative about Latinas/os changed over time.

For Vietnamese and Cubans there was another kind of newspaper that was important for both groups: camp newspapers, *Tan Dan* and *La Vida Nueva*, which were published and distributed inside Fort Chaffee while the refugees awaited processing. In the special collections that I accessed, I did not find more than one or two issues of *Tan Dan*, and I did not pursue finding the newspaper because I do not read or write Vietnamese and lacked the financial resources to pay a bicultural and bilingual translator. I hope that scholars who are fluent in Vietnamese will take up the task of reading and researching the paper. I was able to obtain most, if not all, of the issues of *La Vida Nueva*. The paper was published in Spanish, and as a fluent speaker, reader, and writer, I translated the news stories quoted in this study.

For Latina/o immigrants in the 1990s, I was unable to identify a special collection that had relevant information and was open to the public. Instead I used ethnographic methods, especially interviews, to add depth to the newspaper coverage. I conducted a total of fifty-one interviews during four research periods in 2004, 2005, 2008, and 2012 with Latinas/os, Asians, African Americans, and white people to ask them about the changes they saw or experienced with racial and ethnic diversification in the state. Given the dearth of African Americans and the language barriers for first-generation Asian refugees or immigrants, the interviews are skewed toward Latina/o immigrants and their children, followed by white Arkansans.

It was difficult for me to get working-class immigrants who worked in the poultry plants to talk with me about those specifics—even though I had a certain kind of insider status, since I lived or had lived in one of the communities that is the focus of this study and because my dad still worked in a poultry line when I started conducting my research. Initially, I tried to interview Latinas/os in the poultry processing plant where my dad worked, and the company even granted me permission to conduct the interviews on site. They let me use a small office but also required a staff member from human resources to be present during the interview. Unsurprisingly, those interviews were extremely awkward and unproductive; I conducted only a couple of them.

However, even after I conducted research outside of poultry plants and met with potential interviewees in locations of their choosing, my subjects were not forthcoming with good or bad experiences. Working-class immigrants in the early period of my research (2004–2008) largely did not want to talk about labor and the specifics of working in the poultry industry. They reiterated, like other scholars have demonstrated, that they were "happy" to work or that they were committed to working in order to make a better life for themselves and their families. I was able to get a few interviews, but the responses were very short, so I decided to use the snowball method. As a result, I have more interviews with middle- and upper-class, college-educated immigrants who moved to Arkansas in the late 1970s and early 1980s or in the early 2000s and serve as "brokers" between working-class, newer immigrants.

Thus my research demonstrates that even though the literature on Latinas/os in the Nuevo South strongly focuses on working-class immigrants and their adaptation to the region, the heterogeneity of the Latina/o community has been understudied, and so has the position of those that serve as "cultural brokers" or mediators between the normative white community and working-class Latinas/os. This is particularly important because, at least in the case of northwest Arkansas, those who served as cultural brokers were usually not members of the two largest Latina/o communities—Mexicans and Salvadorans—and thus understood those communities in ways that often reproduced them as troubled or deficient. These brokers sometimes were more recent arrivals and thus also lacked the longer history and understanding of community building, thereby lacking some important information. Finally, their educational attainment, professional status, middle-class standing, and English-language proficiency also influenced the ways they experienced racial difference or immigration status.

During a second intensive attempt to expand my interview pool (2010–2012), I also used the snowball method, identifying subsequent interviewees who included a few Black professionals and a substantial number of second-generation Latina/o southerners, people who were born in or moved to the region before they started middle school. In the summer of 2012, a few weeks before Barack Obama announced DACA (Deferred Action for Childhood Arrivals), I identified a large number of my interviewees by attending a community meeting organized by a nonprofit organization. I was driving around Springdale, Arkansas, analyzing the built landscape and spatial layout, and decided to listen to local Spanish-language radio. I heard an announcement for a community meeting and information session for issues important to the Latina/o community. At the end of the meeting I introduced myself to one of the organization's "change agents" and told her about my research project. It turned out that she was not from northwest Arkansas, but she was instrumental in putting me in touch with young people who were; many of them were also change agents or individuals invested in providing information to the larger Latina/o and immigrant community. The youths were also able to guide me to a few first-generation, working-class Latinas/os who had been in Arkansas since the 1980s or early 1990s, and who provided important historical information and memories as well as personal reflections about their own arrival in Arkansas. Significantly, although most of them had begun working in poultry processing plants, they had left those jobs for work in other areas, such as education, politics, entertainment, and entrepreneurial endeavors.

In my research experience, second-generation Latina/o southerners were much more willing to talk about their experiences as children of working-class immigrants. However, these young people between the ages of eighteen and twenty-four were active in community organizing, so in this way they were self-selective and were actively working toward making Arkansas a more welcoming place for Latinas/os and other communities of color.

Scholars need to conduct more research to get a fuller picture of the dynamics playing out in various places across the South. In the case of Arkansas, I hope that scholars fluent in Vietnamese, Laotian, and other Southeast Asian languages will interview people who were processed through Fort Chaffee and into Arkansas, as well as those who moved to the state through their links with refugees from the 1970s, because they have a lot to contribute to studies about race and difference in the South. I hope that my research provides a good starting point for scholars interested in exploring and documenting the Nuevo South.

Chapter Breakdown

The following pages, then, reflect an interdisciplinary investigation of the ways in which immigrants and refugees negotiated issues of place, such as race, labor, and community, during the late twentieth and early twenty-first centuries. Chapter 1, "New South to Nuevo South: Region, Labor, and Race," explores how northwest Arkansas became a particular kind of place (mainly white and working class) to explain the reactions, constructions, and racializations of Asian and Latina/o immigrants. I investigate race, racial cleansing, and labor over the twentieth century. In the early 1900s anti-Black racist terror effectively decreased the African American population so that by 1990, a twelve-county area with a population that was once 8 to 15 percent Black had seen a dramatic fall in that figure. In short, this section of Arkansas had a history of racial terror that would be critical in shaping its later responses to racial difference. This chapter analyzes the creation and maintenance of a regional culture that constructed a white area throughout the twentieth century and examines how it responded and adapted to an increasingly diverse workforce of primarily working-class Latinas/os. The labor sphere was a crucial site that constructed the normative subject, an Arkansan who worked intermittently in a poultry plant, but the work became racialized when workers were no longer majority white. Thus, the region's ideas about whiteness and race changed as the poultry industry's workforce became majority Latina/o.

Chapter 2, "Yellow Peril in Arkansas: War, Christianity, and the Regional Racialization of Vietnamese Refugees," is an in-depth examination of how Vietnamese in 1975 were understood as people and as refugees. The chapter analyzes how national and local elements coalesced and shifted in various ways throughout 1975, especially in debates about the repercussions of having Asians in the United States and the region. I argue that ideas of Christian charity and duty to refugees helped contour the arrival of Vietnamese men and women in the state, but that the politics of race—as they undergirded the antipathy of Arkansans to the federal government and boosted rhetoric that drew on "yellow peril" ideas—restricted and channeled the lives and labor of Vietnamese refugees. Northwest Arkansans rarely invoked their whiteness, but it shaped their encounters with refugees, because they frequently referenced racial and ethnic backgrounds as reasons to shun the Vietnamese. Some individuals feared competition during a difficult economic moment, while others saw opportunities for a more willing and exploitable labor force. Class also became an issue, as some Arkansans embraced educated Vietnamese but rejected those from peasant backgrounds. These contradictions and tensions are illustrated best by two cases involving students. One consisted of medical students and doctors—much-needed resources for rural communities—while the other involved college students eligible for state monies to continue their education in Arkansas. In the case of medical personnel, the governor's office facilitated their exit from Chaffee; in the latter instance the same office kept quiet about the financial aid opportunity.

Chapter 3, "Mariel Cubans as an 'Objectionable Burden' and 'Illegal Aliens,'" demonstrates that in 1980, Cubans from Mariel were received with much greater anxiety than were the Vietnamese in 1975. Arkansans resented the federal government, feeling that they were endangered by the placement of Cubans at Fort Chaffee. The national media coverage referring to this wave of Cubans as criminals and homosexuals greatly influenced their reception in the state, where their sexual orientation was objectionable to conservatives who were most often both Protestants and Republicans. Additionally, many of the Cubans were of African descent, and their racial backgrounds, although not explicitly invoked, played an important role in the growing resentments and apprehensions of white Arkansans. The case was also markedly different from that of Vietnamese due to questions about the Cubans' categorization in the US legal landscape and concomitant questions about who had authority to detain them if they left the base. After an uprising in which Cubans broke the camp perimeter and headed to a nearby town, panic ensued, and Governor Clinton seriously considered using the judicial system to determine whether federal legislation created "objectionable burdens" for the state. The ensuing dispute encompassed the legal categories used to define this wave of Cubans, such as detainee, entrant, refugee, and Cuban/Haitian entrant (status pending), as well as how the designations affected their rights and the state's responsibility for them. In some ways, the urgency and reactions to Cubans from Mariel, indeed their designation as "illegal aliens," foreshadowed what would occur with Latina/o immigrants.

Chapter 4, "Latinas/os and *Polleras*: Social Networks, Multisite Migration, Raids, and Upward Mobility," focuses on the movement of Latinas/os, mainly ethnic Mexicans, to Arkansas in the 1990s. For some Latina/o migrants, Arkansas was a second or third site of settlement. They were drawn by the poultry industry, which was searching for more low-wage workers and workers that were more easily exploited. These workers were offered year-round employment and lax enforcement of immigration documents, while the state's low cost of living provided opportunities for upward mobility and homeownership unavailable in traditional states of immigrant reception and settlement. In contrast to the Vietnamese and Cubans, these Latinas/os had the ability to decide when and where they moved, and they chose to concentrate in a few cities and counties where they worked in the industry that had been central to the Arkansas economy for decades. The poultry industry did more to racially and ethnically diversify northwest Arkansas in one decade than the activation of Fort Chaffee had in 1975 and 1980.

Chapter 5, "'Northwest Arkansas's No. 1 Societal Concern': 'Illegal Aliens,' Acts of Spatial Illegality, and Political Mobilizations," analyzes the responses to and racialization of Latinas/os during these years of change in which some of the area's whitest towns and cities ceased to be so homogeneous. The racialization of Latinas/os as "illegal aliens" and as both Mexicans and criminals occurred rapidly and with increasing force as white Arkansans policed their community borders based on who belonged (white folks) and who did not (Latinas/os); consequently, nearly all of Latina/o behaviors were understood as what I call "acts of spatial illegality." In other words, because Latinas/os were racialized as "illegal aliens," law or social norms were not needed to deem their use of spaces a violation. The result was that Latinas/os themselves became illicit within those spaces. The presence of Latinas/os also mobilized anti-Latina/o, anti–Third World immigrant sentiments as grassroots responses from the Arkansas electorate, though there were also some accepting and positive responses to Latinas/os from politicians, white and Black Arkansans, and area businesses.

The conclusion, "Race, Plantation Bloc, and Nuevo South," explores how racialized ideas play out in Arkansas and how interethnic differences create a nuanced ethnic landscape. Additionally, the chapter asks why Arkansas has not enacted punitive anti-immigrant legislation like Alabama and Georgia. I argue that a "good ol' boys" system, or what Clyde Woods might call a "plantation bloc," exists where business leaders who do not want to scare off a particularly vulnerable and exploitable workforce use their power to persuade politicians to refrain from proposing or passing legislation that will affect their endeavors adversely. Contributing to this system are religious leaders and social activists who work to limit oppressive legislation for Arkansas's communities, thus creating a tenuous alliance.

CHAPTER 1

New South to Nuevo South: Region, Labor, and Race

Like other states in the Union, Arkansas was founded on the displacement, dispossession, and removal of Native peoples. Three to five indigenous peoples lived in the land that eventually became the state of Arkansas: the Osage, Caddo, Quapaw, Tunica, and Chickasaw. In 1686, on Quapaw lands twenty miles west of the Mississippi River, French Canadians established a post on the Arkansas River. More than a century later, in 1804, the United States acquired the land through the Louisiana Purchase. As early as 1808 the US government displaced other tribes to the newly acquired lands. In 1819, Arkansas became a territory, and a year later much of it was either settled by displaced Indians such as the Cherokees and Choctaws or promised to them. Nevertheless, Natives were displaced once again when the designated Indian Territory was created farther west in what is now Oklahoma. Indian removal in Arkansas began with the Caddo in 1824, followed by the federal Indian Removal Act of 1830. The federal government finalized Native displacement, dispossession, and removal in 1834; two years later Arkansas became a state. As of 2017 the US federal government has not recognized any Indian tribes in the state of Arkansas.

During the 1820s and 1830s the slave and plantation systems grew in Arkansas, especially in the southeastern area on former Quapaw lands. Many of the slaveholders in southeast Arkansas were sons and nephews of planters in Kentucky, North Carolina, and Virginia and led the westward expansion of slavery and the plantation system. After the Civil War and emancipation and into the twentieth century, Arkansas's economic development diverged into roughly three patterns: the cotton-growing Delta region in the east and southeast relied on African American sharecroppers and was highly segregated; the prairies became a rice-growing area with mostly white workers; and the hills in the northwest became overwhelmingly white and a center for poultry production. The contrast between the northwest and the southeast are particularly strong. Arkansas's approximately four hundred thousand African Americans are spread throughout the state, but they are largely absent from the northwest quadrant. In the meantime, the Arkansas Delta, especially the state's southeast region, remains heavily agricultural and is one of the US areas in which Blacks are the most disenfranchised, their lives at great risk for premature death.

Northwest Arkansas became overwhelmingly white through racial cleansing. One bloody episode occurred in the town of Harrison in Boone County in 1905. A Black man, identified as Dan, from outside of the community was arrested after he entered a white man's house to seek shelter from the cold. Two days after he was arrested, an angry mob pulled him and another Black man, identified as Rabbit, from the jail. The crowd then rounded up other Black people and took them out into the country, whipped them, and ordered them to leave. The white mob terrorized the Black neighborhood by tying other men and women to trees and whipping them, attempting to drown still others, and burning several houses while demanding that the Black occupants leave town.[1] Some Black families returned to Harrison after a prudent period, but in 1909, after a local young Black man was accused of rape and rumors spread that the alleged victim was near death, the white townspeople once again erupted in mob violence. This time all but one of the Black Harrisonians left for good; Alecta Caledonia Melvina Smith remained with the family that employed her.[2] The impact of these events spread beyond the town, as the African American populations of two adjoining counties dropped dramatically between 1900 and 1910.[3]

Anti-Black racial terror was not contained within one county or state — there were other lynchings and murders in nearby areas. Tulsa, Oklahoma, a few hours to the east, was home to "Black Wall Street" until 1921, when white people exploded in violence after a rumor spread of a Black man touching a white woman. The white rioters burned buildings and killed an estimated three hundred Black men, women, and children, effectively eliminating the Black community and its wealthy business district.[4] Several hours to the northeast, East St. Louis, Illinois, was home to another immensely bloody episode of anti-Black terror that ended with the killing of hundreds of women, children, and men who were burned to death in their homes, shot if they fled the fires, or lynched.[5] There were similarly terrifying ordeals in Pierce City, Joplin, and Springfield, Missouri. In 1901, in the wake of lynchings that culminated in a white mob rioting against the local African American community in Pierce City, the *St. Louis Post-*

Dispatch concluded, "Southwest Missouri is gradually growing into a colorless community. Down here they call it white man's heaven."[6]

In northwest Arkansas, like in many places across the United States, the expulsion of African Americans was maintained through racist practices such as "sundown towns," where Black people could not be present after daylight hours for fear of being beaten, murdered, or lynched. The town of Rogers, Arkansas, had signs at the city limits as well as its bus and rail stations warning, "Nigger, You Better Not Let the Sun Set on You in Rogers."[7] Neighboring Springdale was also a sundown town. The repercussions of white supremacist ideals via racial cleansing and sundown towns resonated through the decades, as evinced by the lack of Black communities in northwest Arkansas throughout the twentieth century.[8]

In the early twentieth century there was also an escalation of racial radicalism facilitated by a strongly racist governor, Jeff Davis, who added to a long tradition of "public displays of punitive aggression" that targeted Black people but at times was also directed toward the white community.[9] The impact of these events, especially those in Harrison, spread beyond the town as the African American populations of two adjoining counties dropped dramatically between 1900 and 1910.[10] By 1930 there were fewer than a thousand Black people in the Arkansas Ozarks; 80 percent lived in Izard, Van Buren, or Washington Counties, and seven counties had no black farm families. By 1969 there were only three Black farm families in a fifteen-county region.[11] In short, the racial terror directed at African Americans in this section of Arkansas would be critical in the future, creating a homogeneous "white man's heaven" and setting a precedent for dealing with racial difference.[12]

This chapter begins by outlining the national and regional factors that helped to make Arkansas into a particular kind of place. It does so by focusing on political economy in the twentieth century. The focus then shifts to northwest Arkansas and its place in history in order to outline the economic and social factors that have defined this subregion and its emergence as an economic powerhouse. The penultimate section addresses states' rights in Arkansas, as well as the impact of states' rights supporters on the desegregation of public schools. The last section assesses the field of study regarding Latinas/os in the South in order to locate this book alongside other, similar works.

The New South, the Sunbelt, and the Twentieth Century

Northwest Arkansas's immigrant, demographic, and class issues at the turn of the twenty-first century reflect ongoing changes in the South's economic, political, and racial landscapes that extend back to the nineteenth century. The South has been reinventing itself since the end of Reconstruction with the aid of the North, the federal government, and business leaders and entrepreneurs from both regions. Post-Reconstruction advocates argued that the Old South was gone, as exemplified by the elimination of racial slavery, and in its place had emerged a region and people ready to embrace industrialization. Since that era, the push to modernize the region has led to a multitude of efforts to "develop" capital and labor in its cities, counties, and states. The federal government has been an extensive investor through social and work programs—many born during the New Deal—and the rise of the military-industrial complex that began during World War II. Bruce Schulman argues with perspicacity that "from the administration of Franklin D. Roosevelt to the presidency of Bill Clinton, federal intervention channeled the South's transformation, catalyzing growth and reform and defining the limits of Sunbelt prosperity."[13]

The antebellum South was based on two central organizing principles—the plantation system and racial slavery—that mutually reinforced each other and shaped the region from its inception to the present. Indeed, Robin D. G. Kelley argues that the way we understand race in the United States—through categories of white, Black, and Other—is based upon ideas that are intimately articulated with racial slavery.[14] When slavery was legal, unpaid labor was associated with Black people and paid labor with free but poor white people. After emancipation, the two were competitors in the same labor market. As David Roediger argues, this competition in the marketplace created a sense of whiteness for working-class people. Whiteness provided a status, privilege, or "wage" for workers being exploited in the labor market, and they defined themselves as "not slaves" and as "not Blacks."[15]

The plantation system also meant that men who got rich through slave labor translated their wealth into power, mainly through the political system. According to Clyde Woods, the plantation bloc has been in power since the Trail of Tears and constantly adjusts by building new alliances that work to keep Black people and poor white people at the bottom of economic development. Beginning with "the ideological and territorial consolidation of the Deep South plantation regime," this bloc has mobilized "Mississippi Delta Plans" to restructure the region's political economy. The causes of these mobilizations have been economic and social crises that resulted in a "shift in the form of social explanation; [and] the establishment of a new stable regime of accumulation."[16] Kelley argues that "slavery provided one of the essential legs upon which modern capitalism was built." Woods similarly asserts, "Slavery and the plantation are not an anathema to capitalism but are pillars of it."[17] As foundational institutions to capitalism, they pervade every aspect of the nation-state.

Some of these mobilizations have been supported by the relationships of the federal government and northern businessmen with southern politicians and industrialists who helped create the "New South." In his groundbreaking work *Origins of the New South*, C. Vann Woodward demonstrated that after the fall of Radical Republicans and the end of Reconstruction, southern Democrats allied with northern Republicans with the goal of industrialization and consequently established foundations in politics, economics, law, and race for a modern South.[18] Woodward argued that though Democrats were associated with the planter class, they were in actuality middle-class capitalists and merchants with little interest in poor white people. Woods makes a similar point and argues that the latter groups allied with the former as opposed to overthrowing them.[19] The changes that occurred after Reconstruction formed the groundwork for a systematic exploitation of the labor power of poor workers, both Black and white. The planter bloc mobilized, shifted "the form of social exploitation," and launched "a new stable regime of accumulation" mainly through southern congressmen and businessmen. The former secured monies from the New Deal through World War II with limited or nonexistent federal oversight so that expenditures on infrastructures such as schools or social services were largely absent while a repressive system of agricultural labor continued. Administrators of New Deal programs often compromised with southern congressmen. For example, the agricultural program was dominated by southern business leaders who facilitated the matters of implementation. The economic policies enacted rarely helped poor areas or poor people; even the minimum wage caused hardships for Black workers, who were replaced by white people or machinery. Efforts aimed at creating economic gains for the region hardly addressed ongoing poverty, racism, and poorly funded education. On the contrary, they often contributed to disparities between urban and rural places, white and Black people, and middle-class and poor people.[20]

As James Cobb argues, the South has been sold to a variety of business interests since the mid-1930s, while its industrial development reflects local, state, national, and global forces that have exacerbated the region's problems. Prospective investors found the South attractive because it was friendly to business, offering low wages, low taxes, and an antiunion climate. However, this led to slow growth and labor-intensive companies that did little to boost the region's economy. Consequently, many local and state developers aligned and allied with lawmakers, public officials, and private citizens to maintain stable labor conditions; as long as there was the promise of growth, government officials and community members maintained a close relationship to industry.[21] Like Schulman, Cobb argues that investments in infrastructure like schools and roads were limited despite the increasing role of the federal government in shaping the region through economic enterprises. John Egerton avers that southern Democrats prevented the New Deal from taking its intended shape because it showed some sympathy for African Americans and supported labor unions.[22] In a piercing analysis of the influence and power of southern representatives who pushed for the marginalization of African Americans or their exclusion from work, war, and welfare policy decisions in the 1930s and 1940s, Ira Katznelson argues that while white war veterans used the GI Bill to increase their education, buy farms, or start businesses, African Americans and other men of color were barred from taking advantage of the bill's various facets. Consequently, inequalities between white and Black people increased as the white US middle class emerged.[23]

By the mid-1950s, industrial recruiters had become reluctant advocates of integration as reports suggested that businesses would not go South due to the racial turmoil.[24] Nevertheless, their advocacy was superficial, aimed at improving the region's appalling image rather than investing in the area's poor Black and white people. The continued exploitation of people and resources created a vicious cycle as "proponents justified the use of subsidies to attract new industries by arguing that areas that lacked investment capital, consumer demand, or skilled workers needed some special feature to make them more alluring to potential investors."[25] The enticements certainly contributed to the region's industrial growth, but they came at the cost of reinforcing exploitative conditions and led to an increase in low-wage manufacturers who depended on an economic environment that suppressed wages. As Cobb writes, "Shackled with poorly paying, slowly growing industries, the region had little opportunity to experience the rapid, self-sustaining expansion that might have generated the capital and demand needed to attract more desirable firms."[26] Though liberals and some moderates hoped that a modernized economy would be incompatible with racial discrimination, they ignored the similarities to the late 1800s, when "New South" leaders promoted industrial growth without disrupting socioeconomic and political landscapes.[27]

By the 1970s the North's economy was in decline, and local boosters were pushing the South's virtues—cheap, nonunion labor; low taxes; low cost of living; and a relaxed lifestyle. The Sunbelt South was built on these conditions.[28] Cobb argues that the boom was the result of seemingly contradictory influences: an influx of relatively affluent consumers, high birth rates, increased federal spending, and traditional development policies (cost advantages and tax breaks). He concludes, however, that "reduced to its essentials, the so-called good business climate of which southern politicians remained so protective in the 1990s still bore a striking resemblance to the planter-industrial policy rapprochement of the 1880s."[29] David Goldfield astutely notes, "The South has absorbed black political power, the growth of a two-party system of government, and a civil rights movement yet policy priorities, tax structure, attitudes toward organized labor, and racial and geographic disparities persist."[30] The plantation bloc was alive and well at the end of the twentieth century, pushing for the exploitation of the South and its people for the benefit of a few at the cost of many.

Northwest Arkansas: "Homogeneity . . . West of the Mississippi"

As slaveholders from states such as Kentucky, North Carolina, and Virginia expanded the slave and plantation system into Arkansas in the 1820s and 1830s, one consequence was the creation and maintenance of the one-party political system that allowed the plantation bloc to dictate social and economic policies to suit their needs and desires.[31] This was especially true in the profitable Black Belt counties—the rich agricultural lands at the center of plantation production where Black people outnumbered white people. In this region, the movements of African Americans were limited through social, legal, and extralegal controls.[32] Through the one-party system, Democratic senators and representatives from Black Belt counties were continually reelected, thereby ensuring their seniority in Congress and ability to block integration and voting rights efforts for African Americans.[33] As a result, the Arkansas Delta still stands in contrast to the "corridor of prosperity" in the northwest in a variety of ways.[34]

The demographics of Arkansas's southeast and northwest regions, for example, remain very different. There are still many African Americans in the Delta, where they form majorities in some counties. In contrast, the northwest is overwhelmingly white. White people from Tennessee, Missouri, Kentucky, North Carolina, South Carolina, and even New York moved into the Arkansas Ozarks shortly after the War of 1812. They found topographic conditions ranging from fertile plains to rocky hillsides and rugged mountains, the latter making farming particularly difficult. Much of the land in northwest Arkansas was in the possession of Cherokees until 1828, when the US government once again displaced them westward. With the Native Americans out of the way, white people flooded into the area. By 1840, eight counties in the northwest had more than 20,000 people. Washington County was the most populous, with 6,000 inhabitants. Its significant slave population of 1,515 accounted for more than half of the total slave population in the area.[35] The heterogeneity of early Ozarkers, however, was limited; by 1850 almost half came from Tennessee, another 20 percent were from Missouri, and many of them came from professional or planter families. This meant that the region's pioneer settlers "possessed a homogeneity rarely witnessed west of the Mississippi," with most of British or Scotch-Irish origin.[36] By the mid-nineteenth century, less than twenty years after statehood, the area's white population had reached 40,000, with 90 percent of them US-born. From 1850 to 1860 a "massive wave of yeoman immigrants" joined their more affluent predecessors from the East, but these newcomers had to settle in less fertile hillsides and rocky uplands that provided few opportunities for cultivation. This led most of them to live off of subsistence farming.[37] By the 1890s, 56 percent of the Ozarks' 200,000 people were in the western counties, with more than 32,000 in Washington County alone.[38]

Most of the yeomen were Baptists, Methodists, Cumberland Presbyterians, or Disciples of Christ.[39] These religions thrived in an area whose people were suspicious of urban and educated ministers. Eventually, northwest Arkansas became part of the so-called Bible Belt—an area with "individualist, provincial, conversion-oriented, and pietistic" attitudes.[40] Of the two largest denominations, Baptists were more successful than Methodists, because the nonhierarchical system of associations and the ordaining of uneducated preachers appealed to Ozarkers' frontier egalitarianism.[41] The Cumberland Presbyterians were prominent in certain areas and reflected the Scotch-Irish heritage of many Ozarkers.[42] Evangelical Protestantism provided a religious homogeneity that extended to the end of the twentieth century. As late as 1936 there were only 723 Roman Catholics, and by 1971 the denomination's numbers had increased to only 3,000.[43]

Ozarkers survived largely on the basis of trapping and hunting animals, subsistence farming, and raising some livestock, but early settlers had claimed the best lands. Many of Washington County's settlers were slaveholding farmers who inhabited fertile bottomlands along the area's rivers. Large-scale plantations, however, were absent: by 1850 there were only three white men who owned more than twenty slaves. Cotton culture did not saturate northwest Arkansas as it did the Delta largely because of the difficulty of transporting the product to major markets. Tobacco was far more important for the region, and by 1859 ten Ozark counties produced more than 450,000 pounds.[44]

The product that would eventually rule northwest Arkansas, however, was poultry. The growth of the industry was largely facilitated by federal monies for infrastructure such as roads and rails used to connect the remote area to surrounding cities. Another vital development was the establishment of the University of Arkansas in Fayetteville in 1871 and the Arkansas Agricultural Experiment Station in 1887. The station was established through federal funds provided by the Hatch Act, which was aimed at creating such centers at state universities. The remote location of the station made this federally subsidized venture a regional and not a state institution, because the farmers in the area were the primary beneficiaries of its research. Likewise, its scientists were influenced by the concerns of local farmers and agriculturalists.[45]

Raising chickens in northwest Arkansas grew as an industry when a representative from a Kansas company opened a small processing and shipping plant in the area in 1914. That year the Experiment Station established a poultry division. In 1931, Missourian John Tyson arrived in Springdale and began hauling chickens to Kansas City and St. Louis. In 1936, after reading that broilers were selling for better prices in Chicago, he made the seven-hundred-mile trek to that city. His success there led him to invest in various aspects of production, from feed to incubators. World War II proved to be a turning point for entrepreneurs such as Tyson, as the US Army contracted the entire production of the Delmarva region (the leading production area on the East Coast) and thus allowed small businesses to compete for domestic consumers. At the same time, the rationing of red meat helped increase chicken consumption. During the war, Tyson expanded his business by building his own mill and establishing company-owned broiler houses on his Springdale farm. In 1957, Tyson Foods became the "first fully integrated broiler" in the area, and in 1986 it became the nation's top poultry processing company after acquiring Lane Processing, Inc. The growth of the poultry industry in northwest Arkansas was swift. By the end of WWII, the region accounted for 90 percent of the poultry produced in the state, with sales in Benton and Washington Counties more than doubling to over $7 million. In 1954 the industry generated more than $11 million in Benton and Washington Counties alone.

By 1974 the region's sales were $250 million, with $100 million emanating from the latter county.[46]

The federal government's farm subsidies and rail, road, and highway construction were especially significant to the rise of the area's most successful companies—Tyson Foods (the world's largest meat producer), Walmart (the world's largest retailer), and J. B. Hunt (the nation's largest trucking company). John Tyson began selling broilers in the early 1930s and benefited from a 1925 law that provided tax exemption to poultry producers, a benefit that Tyson Foods enjoyed until 1988, when it earned close to $1 billion and could anticipate a tax deferment of over $135 million for 1987 alone.[47] The success of Tyson Foods—formerly Tyson's Foods—quickly spawned growth in farms and farmers to meet its increasing demands. The influx in cash flow throughout the area contributed to Sam Walton's successes with discount chains in small towns. Walton, like Tyson, depended on improved roads to move his merchandise and to facilitate a rural Arkansan's trips to his stores. But perhaps the entrepreneur most dependent on improved roads was Johnnie Bryan Hunt, whose rise to the top of the US trucking industry was intimately connected to the poultry industry. After ten years as a truck driver, he invented a machine that converted rice hulls to chicken litter for covering the floors of chicken houses and began selling his product throughout the state, with most of it going to the Arkansas Ozarks. After the Federal Motor Carrier Act deregulated the trucking industry in 1980, the company quickly expanded.[48]

Arkansas's "Corridor of Prosperity"

In the last quarter of the twentieth century, northwest Arkansans were white, Republican, and Protestant like their ancestors. But this did not mean that the area remained unchanged; several national trends, including the evangelical movement and the rise of conservative politics, were at work in reshaping the region. Northwest Arkansas Protestantism was augmented by the midcentury Christian movement that provided a counterculture to the liberal secularism of the postwar period. The evangelical movement made several substantial strides in Arkansas. In the 1970s, Springdale's First Baptist Church launched a "lifestyle evangelism" program that tripled its membership. In 2004 its pastor urged his congregation to "vote God" and elect George W. Bush. By the end of the twentieth century a conservative Christian voting bloc had formed that was largely female, southern, and staunchly opposed to abortion and gay marriage.⁴⁹ To paraphrase Bethany Moreton, these people were devoted to God and Walmart. Although Christianity had long deemed consumption a vice, Sam Walton convinced evangelicals that in fact it could be a Christian virtue, as long as it meant "procuring humble products 'for the family.'"⁵⁰ Moreover, Walmart's early employees—white southern and midwestern women—taught the future international conglomerate that they were very proud of providing "humble service work" because "consumption for oneself fell outside Protestantism's sacred circle. But helping others consume—especially helping them consume necessities 'for their families'—*that* could be a sacred calling."⁵¹

The area's conservatism is also connected to its Republican roots, which go back to the Civil War, when independent yeoman farmers opposed secession and fought for the Union.⁵² After the fall of Republicans in the 1870s, the South's businessmen and politicians strengthened the Democratic Party in opposition to the "Party of Lincoln" and stood for segregation. The alliance of southern states created "the Solid South," a bloc that always voted Democratic and segregationist. For decades after the end of the Civil War, Republicans struggled to be the Democrats' competitors, often to no avail. In his influential work, V. O. Key identified Arkansas as a state with "pure one-party politics"; its people always voted for a Democratic president. In spite of this, Key found that Republicans controlled some local governments and occasionally elected congressmen, as happened in the Ozarks.⁵³ Those traditional Republicans laid the foundations for the development of the GOP in Tennessee, Virginia, and North Carolina and had strong showings in northwest Arkansas.⁵⁴

In the late nineteenth century, Arkansans were enthralled by populism. The Populist Party, also known as the People's Party, represented poor people regardless of race, fighting against corporations that infringed on their rights.⁵⁵ The party's Jeff Davis was elected in 1900 and served three terms. Davis, however, did not subscribe to the Arkansas Populist Party's stance about race. Instead, as Froelich and Zimmermann observe, "Davis freely spewed racist epithets during election campaigns and stump speeches and justified the lynching of blacks as a southern tradition."⁵⁶ This was a populism firmly rooted in racist beliefs and actions, and its legacy would remain strong long after the demise of the Populist Party. By the early 1900s the Republican Party mobilized an effective campaign and ended the Populist Party's run in Arkansas.⁵⁷

The South was a stronghold for the segregationist Democratic Party until the mid-twentieth century. In preparing for the 1948 election, President Harry Truman perceived that Black voters could be the swing votes in some states with numerous electoral votes, so he created the President's Commission on Civil Rights. He pushed a moderate plank, but the Democratic National Convention voted for a stronger civil rights proposal. The Mississippi delegation and half of Alabama's walked out in protest. Later, many southern legislators reconvened and formed the Dixiecrats, or States' Rights Democratic Party.[58] With the expanding civil rights movement, the South's revolt continued. The Republican Dwight D. Eisenhower won in 1952 and 1956 but failed to carry states in the Deep South, though he made inroads in the 1956 election with mountain Republicans. However, these moderates lost control in the South, and after Barry Goldwater voted against the 1964 Civil Rights Act, he became the first Republican to sweep the Deep South.[59]

More recently, the Republican base in northwest Arkansas has been strengthened by thousands of retirees from the Midwest.[60] After the Second World War, white midwesterners began moving to the Ozarks as businessmen mined the scenic landscape for its beauty and built retirement communities.[61] In 1967 John Paul Hammerschmidt became the first post-Reconstruction Republican sent to Congress from the northwest area's Third District. It quickly became common for Republicans to garner more than 40 percent of the vote. In 1996, Tim Hutchinson became the state's first post-Reconstruction Republican senator. Blevins notes that "by the turn of the twenty-first century, the combination of northern Republican immigrants, traditional Ozark Republicans, and middle-class Christian conservatives made northwest Arkansas a stronghold of Republicanism."[62]

The anti-Black racist terror that transpired in the 1900s in the Arkansas Ozarks left a legacy that extends into the twenty-first century, as evidenced by the continued dearth of Black people in that part of the state. In 1990 the Arkansas Ozarks had approximately 2,000 people of color, but 80 percent of them lived in the city of Fayetteville or Washington County, home to the University of Arkansas's flagship campus.[63] In 2005, Shannon Ammons, a Black middle-class professional woman who lived in Rogers, said, "The reputation within the state is that the [northwest] area is racist.... We [she and her husband] knew Harrison was the headquarters for the Ku Klux Klan. No one wanted to come here for college, because this area of the state always had bad connotations."[64] She moved from Atlanta with her husband, Dana, when she became a sales manager at Colgate-Palmolive's northwest Arkansas office, which deals primarily with Walmart (formerly Wal-Mart). According to the 2000 Census, Benton County's Black population was 639, or 0.4 percent of the total (Latinas/os, with a population of 13,469, made up 8.8 percent).[65] The Ammonses observed that the few Black people who live in the area typically moved there for their careers, staying for only two to three years, and that they are mostly college educated and middle-class professionals.[66]

The area shows no signs that its growth will slow down, but it remains to be seen whether Black people from Arkansas will move to the area. It is uncertain as well whether transplants from other parts of the nation will contribute to the northwest's racial diversification. As of now, Arkansas's international corporations seem to be the main entities driving demographic growth. For example, as the Ammonses' move demonstrates, many Walmart vendors have established offices near the conglomerate's Benton County headquarters, which draw thousands of professionals. Marjorie Rosen argues that white, Christian Arkansans are adjusting well to the educated professional people of color of varying non-Christian religious backgrounds, including African Americans, Jews, Hindus, and Muslims, but that there is a lot of tension with the working-class, low-skilled Latina/o community.[67] However, Rosen also writes that the KKK organized a rally at the same time that Coleman Peterson, a Black man, and his wife and children moved into Bentonville. Peterson and his family moved to northwest Arkansas from St. Louis in 1994 after Walmart hired him to be its head of human resources. If Tyson Foods diversified northwest Arkansas by drawing working-class Latinas/os, then Walmart also diversified the area by hiring more people of color.

The professionals of color and of various faiths differ in two important ways from many Latina/o newcomers: they are middle or upper class, and they constitute only a small percentage of the area's population. As we shall see in the following chapters, the outcries from community members against Vietnamese, Cubans, and ethnic Mexicans are racialized fears about an invasion that they see as a threat to the "American way of life." Professionals of color uphold the "American way of life," while their relatively low numbers allow Arkansans to maintain a sense of ownership within their communities. These professionals are also contributing to a construction boom in the area for middle- and upper-class housing developments, while Latinas/os spur the development of working-class apartments and houses. Yet working-class Latinas/os and young professionals have a similar trajectory in that they tend to be outsiders who are drawn to the area by international conglomerates.

By the late twentieth century, the northwest Arkansas economy was booming, but in contrast to much of the rest of the state, the area was overwhelmingly white and Republican. Like the rest of the state, it was heavily evangelical. This homogeneity in terms of race, politics, and religion created a conservative and insular culture that looked warily upon "foreigners," whether from the US North or abroad. The work to keep an area close to 100 percent white throughout a century cannot be undervalued and dismissed as accidental, but must be seen as the maintenance of a regional culture developed over decades. Ann Markusen argues that regions are highly resistant "units of societal structure" built upon economic foundations, political systems, and cultural practices.[68] Some factors that contribute to "internal unity around a regional disruption" are economic, ethnic, and religious conditions "and other cultural traits fashioned over the generations."[69] Northwest Arkansans fashioned an identity for themselves based on a common past, a history they shared because people from outside of the area rarely moved there between the 1850s and early 1990s. Its inhabitants at the end of the twentieth century were descendants of British and Scotch-Irish immigrants who still practiced their ancestors' Protestant faith, though they had adopted the evangelicalism that had become increasingly influential since the midcentury.

The economic and infrastructural changes that occurred throughout the twentieth century were often directly or indirectly subsidized by the federal government through railroads, highway construction, state universities, agricultural subsidies, or tax breaks. Businessmen like Sam Walton, John Tyson, and Johnnie Hunt had the acumen to draw on such benefits in order to build remarkably successful companies. But the federal state played a more direct role in racially diversifying northwest Arkansas when it established Fort Chaffee close to Fort Smith. The fort was built in September 1941 at the beginning of the rise of the military industrial-complex, and during World War II it was used as a prisoner of war camp for Germans. It was not until 1975, when Fort Chaffee was used as a detention and processing center for Southeast Asian refugees, that the area had "new southerners," mainly Vietnamese refugees who were sponsored out of the camp and into communities in the northwest, mainly Fort Smith. The process, however, would be difficult, and the area's homogeneity in terms of race, religion, and politics would play a central role in how the region responded to the group.

States' Rights, the Federal State, and Desegregation of Public Schools

Federal intervention had been a long-standing feature of the southern economy and thus of the local one, but southerners always wanted to control its impact. In this they were largely successful. Their efforts were not limited to the economic and labor sphere, but extended to the social realm as well as they sought to maintain a particular kind of society—one premised on the subjugation of African Americans. This is clearly seen in the Jim Crow laws that arose slowly in the post–Civil War period after Black and white people intermingled.[70] When it became evident that Black and white people interacted with each other, state governments began to institutionalize segregation as they sought to keep members of society in their respective places. Public schools were a primary site for the endeavor. When the Supreme Court announced the *Brown* decision in 1954 and the second *Brown* decision in 1955, state governments could no longer continue to have legally segregated education facilities. Nevertheless, several states, including Arkansas, attempted to halt impending integration through various means. What occurred in Arkansas around the desegregation of its public schools revealed the nature of social relations between Black and white Arkansans as well as the state's hostility toward the federal government.

Arkansas gained international attention on September 2, 1957, when Governor Orval Faubus used the Arkansas National Guard to prevent the integration of Central High School in Little Rock. In doing so, John A. Kirk notes, "Faubus directly challenged the authority of the federal government as no other elected southern official had since the Civil War."[71] After weeks of negotiations with President Eisenhower, Faubus removed the National Guard, but on September 23, when nine Black students attempted to enter the high school, an unruly white mob created an environment that led school officials to remove the students for their own safety. This finally led Eisenhower to send federal troops from the 101st Airborne to secure a safe passage for the students.

But this was not the end of the fight over desegregation in Little Rock. In February 1958 the school board requested a two-and-a-half-year delay in implementing the *Brown* decisions. The case eventually reached the Supreme Court, which ordered integration to continue. On September 12, the same day of the court decision, Faubus closed all of the city's schools. He had recently convened a special session of the Arkansas General Assembly and pushed through six new laws that gave him "sweeping powers to uphold segregation."[72] One law gave him the authority to close any school integrated by federal order; voters in the school district could then decide if they wanted it to be reopened on an integrated basis. In a referendum held on September 27, 72 percent of 27,031 voters decided to keep the schools closed.[73] The schools reopened the following fall only after it became evident that it was impossible to perpetually fund private high schools. The reopening of the schools was the beginning of a decades-long battle to maintain segregated facilities. The school board proposed a series of initiatives, including "freedom of choice," whose implicit aim was minimum compliance with the two *Brown* decisions.[74]

The measures often ended up back in the courts as African American leaders continued to fight for equality. In July 1971 a federal court largely overturned the Little Rock School District's latest plan and instead ordered the busing of high school students for the 1971–1972 school year in order to achieve integration. In response, William F. Rector, a suburban real estate developer, "revealed to a meeting of 600 cheering whites he was building a private school [Pulaski Academy] near the golf course in his western subdivision development." By 2003 only half of white students were in public schools, while Pulaski Academy's graduating class of 102 had only one Black student. The Little Rock School District was finally released from court oversight in February 2007, but by then most of its schools had a "substantial" Black student body.[75]

The continuous court battles and oversight over the Little Rock School District demonstrated that local officials and residents were willing to "risk that [local] authority over their schools rather than support the efforts" to end segregated facilities.[76] This went against a long-standing tradition of fierce state independence. Indeed, leading up to the crisis at Central High School, the state's eligible voters (mainly white) in 1956 passed Amendment 44, which sought to nullify the *Brown* decision by using a logic of states' rights: "The General Assembly of the state of Arkansas shall take appropriate action and pass laws opposing in every constitutional manner the unconstitutional desegregation actions of the United States Supreme Court, including interposing the sovereignty of the state of Arkansas."[77] The idea was that a state could prevent the enforcement of *Brown* until "the states passed an amendment to the United States Constitution giving Congress the power to implement or to deny implementation of integration. The idea of interposition had had no legal credence in American constitutional jurisprudence since at least the time of the Civil War."[78]

The law remained on the books until 1990, when state representatives sought to have it removed in response to a $130 million settlement in a desegregation lawsuit involving the Pulaski County Public Schools (the county is home to Little Rock). The federal court ruled that the government of Arkansas shared responsibility for the desegregation of that county's schools because Amendment 44 defied the US Supreme Court's decisions on school integration.[79] Amendment 3, which repealed Amendment 44, passed by a narrow margin of 11,000 votes, 272,198 to 261,463; fifty-seven of seventy-five counties voted against it, including sixteen of seventeen counties with the state's highest percentage of Black voters.[80] Many political commentators quickly attributed Amendment 3's near defeat to voter confusion or ignorance about the issue, but editorial writer Max Brantley argued that while this theory had some support, especially when the amendment failed to pass in some heavily African American counties, there was another, more nefarious side, since the media had done a good job of explaining what voting "yes" meant. Brantley posits that the other explanation for the vote was most evident in Pulaski County, where white working-class neighborhoods strongly opposed Amendment 3.[81] In other words, its near defeat was due to a backlash by people who had been at the center of battles over integration.

In Little Rock the desegregation of public schools had broken along class lines since the 1950s. John Kirk argues that in Arkansas, as opposed to many other southern states, the most active segregationists were not respected people but white people who were marginalized socially, economically, or politically.[82] Their mobilizations were responses to local forces greater than themselves. Working-class whites had been pushed to the front of the line in the name of racial progress, while the wealthy white elites, often the civic leaders doing the pushing, remained at the back of the line and continued to send their children to all-white schools. This is conspicuous when we consider that Little Rock's first desegregation plan as laid out by the school superintendent, Virgil T. Blossom, was premised on the opening of the new Hall High School in the western part of the city, home to Pulaski Heights, where many of the city's most influential people lived. Central would be desegregated, and the working and middle classes would send their children to the integrated high school.[83] Affluent homeowners, by virtue of their addresses, could postpone integration until a later date, and if they desired they could simply move away from the core of the city, bask in their personal choices, and refuse to acknowledge how they benefited from residential segregation. In fact, many of the mid-1950s integrationists became "Education First" partisans in the late 1950s and 1960s, arguing for neighborhood unity and individual freedom as they moved into expanding white subdivisions in the suburbs.[84]

In northwest Arkansas the desegregation of public schools took a slightly different path, because school boards acted in a different manner than the one in Little Rock. In 1954, Charleston in Franklin County kept its plans quiet, and desegregation occurred peacefully when eleven Black high school students attended classes with their white peers. In contrast to Charleston's secrecy, Fayetteville in Washington County publicly prepared for desegregation and announced its aim on May 22, 1954, five days after the *Brown* decision. That fall, five African American sophomores and two juniors attended the integrated high school. Andrew Brill argues that "Fayetteville was no racial utopia," but that it possessed "important ingredients of successful school integration—namely a lack of excessive pre-existing racial tension coupled with firm local leadership." According to him, Fayetteville's location, racial history, and culture of education were helpful and contributing factors for the smooth processes of initial desegregation. Brill posits that Fayetteville's closeness to Missouri and Oklahoma makes its racial history more like theirs than that of the "volatile Deep South," and that "when the time came to desegregate its schools, Fayetteville was free of much of the weighty racial baggage many other southern communities labored with." That the town was the home for the University of Arkansas influenced the community's culture, since many faculty members were local leaders who came from outside of the South and thus brought "less rigid attitudes about race." The institution also led by example—it integrated its law school in 1948.[85] However, it should be noted that it chose to do so to avert a lawsuit, and that in practice Black students that enrolled were taught in separate classrooms so that "as much as possible the rituals of segregation would apply."[86] In a similar vein, its elementary schools were desegregated more than ten years after the high school, which gestures toward the resistance of integration. Moreover, the desegregation of public schools remained a contentious issue, as exemplified by the graffiti scrawled on a wall in a local high school in 1994. That same year, Rana Peterson, Coleman Peterson's daughter, was one of two Black students in Bentonville High School. In essence, the struggle to desegregate northwest Arkansas's public schools would continue until the turn of the twenty-first century.

The desegregation of Little Rock's public schools demonstrates how far the state of Arkansas was willing to go to resist the federal government's power to effect social change. The battles over integrated educational facilities were conflicts over identity, culture, and ultimately community. Faubus knew how potent these issues were, and he often "painted the federal government in the same color as blacks—that is as a contaminating and intrusive force that threatened the political, economic, social, and sexual privileges of southern white males."[87] The outsiders threatened the very identity of the South as conceptualized by white people, and as Phoebe Godfrey succinctly argues, "like the one-drop rule that defined social status, even one or two or nine black students could, through 'penetrating' a school of over 2,000 whites, transform its color, its identity, and more importantly, its value."[88] Faubus, the state legislature, and many white Arkansas voters could not allow such an attack on their community and way of life. Instead, they invested time and effort in attempts to regain control by implementing plans that in effect maintained segregation. Ironically, in Little Rock this meant that they eventually gave up that which was so dear to them—local authority—as the school district ended up under court supervision for thirty years after 1957. At the same time, their efforts to maintain majority-white schools succeeded, as many white Little Rock residents moved away from the urban center into the suburbs. Once there, they continued to fight desegregation at the county level until the 1990s. Among other issues, the Central High School desegregation crisis left many white Arkansans with bitter and oppositional feelings toward the federal government. In northwest Arkansas, desegregation occurred in what was arguably a "smoother" process, but we have to keep in mind that many communities did not actually have to integrate their schools because the student body was entirely white. For many, integrating public schools would come much later, as would anxiety over their changing communities and local and regional identities. Their brush with a more direct intrusion of the federal state and its consequences would involve the US military and the use of Fort Chaffee as a refugee and processing center, as well as the consequences of sponsoring refugees into the overwhelmingly white community.

The Field of *Nuevo* South

The field of interdisciplinary studies assesses the growth of Latinas/os in the South within a broader "geographic diversification of American immigration," explores "the structure and dynamics of Mexican migration to new destinations in the United States," and views the migration within the national trend of moving out of metropolitan areas.[89] Scholars have also studied the crucial role of social networks in the migration; "pull" factors such as the restructuring of the poultry, beef, and construction industries; and the trend to locate production plants in areas like the South with lower wage rates.[90] There has also been much documentation of the responses of local school districts to the arrival of Latinas/os. With respect to dealing with the sheer growth of school-age children and accommodating Spanish-speaking students, districts have typically been unprepared, overwhelmed, and underfunded.[91]

The historian Raymond Mohl was one of the first scholars to publish articles about "Latinization in the Heart of Dixie" and what he called the "*Nuevo* New South." He connected the migration of Latinas/os to new global trends of deindustrialization and free trade.[92] One of the shortcomings of that early work, however, was that he suggested Latinas/os were adapting and thriving despite describing resentments held by white people and to a lesser extent by African Americans. In part, Mohl argued that whites were moving out of jobs they had held for years, Black people were moving up in employment, and Latinas/os were moving into the state for those less desirable jobs. More than a decade later, however, the notion that everyone benefited, and especially that Latinas/os did not face a severe backlash, has not panned out. By 2011 Alabama had passed one of the most stringent anti-immigrant and anti-Latina/o laws in the country.[93] Nevertheless, the strength of Mohl's work lies in its focus on Alabama's political economy in relationship to regional, national, and global trends. In a similar vein, another early work on Latinas/os in the South, Leon Fink's study of Guatemalan Maya immigrants in Morganton, North Carolina, was particularly strong due to its focus on the local, regional, and hemispheric labor and social issues that were driving factors in establishing a new migration stream and ultimately a new community in the state. Fink focuses on the specificities of Morganton as they relate to labor, union organizing efforts, and issues of community for longtime residents and newcomers alike.[94]

The historians James C. Cobb and William Stueck contributed an edited collection about globalization and the American South. Their book was one of the first that had a regional political economic focus. Its chapters deal with specific places (the Sun Belt South, Atlanta, and Spartanburg, South Carolina), the immigrant groups that were reshaping the region (Latinas/os and Asians), and the role of various industries in the ongoing changes (economic globalization in general and foreign corporations in particular).[95] The authors, however, did not believe that globalization had negative effects nationally or that it exacerbated inequality, because some evidence suggested that "a nation's global economic involvement correlates positively with a rise from day-to-day subsistence to a more stable and secure existence for many of its people."[96]

A few years later, Fran Ansley and Jon Shefner, respectively professors of law and sociology, edited a book that also focused on the relationship between the global and the local. But they and the contributing authors reached a different conclusion than Cobb and Stueck. They argued that despite aggregate economic growth in some Latin American countries, inequality was increasing; they also argued that while US worker salaries stagnated, workers lost jobs only to replace them with lower-paying ones.[97] Ansley and Shefner's book demonstrates that scholars can focus on global forces yet remain grounded in the specificities of place. Their book is an important contribution to the literature about the Nuevo South because it showcases how the same factors played out differently across the region for various Latina/o communities.

Jamie Winders, a geographer, has more recently published a book focused on Nashville and the ways in which recent immigrants, often Latinas/os but also Asians, have changed the city.[98] Her engagement with place is superbly focused and nuanced. Indeed, she has been one of the few scholars in any discipline who has had a sustained engagement with Latinas/os, the US South, and place.[99] Her work, however, would be improved by engaging with Latina/o history and Latina/o studies, because many of the issues occurring in the South in the twenty-first century have historical parallels in the Southwest of the nineteenth and twentieth centuries.

The research has provided vital demographic information on Latinas/os in some parts of the US South, mainly in rural areas, but has until now lacked a keen focus on issues of race or place. Winders has pointed out that most studies note Latinas/os are moving to an area that historically has been defined by its Black and white racial divisions, yet researchers have had an "overall failure to engage two topics: the geographic and place specificity of arguments about Latino migration to the South and the impacts of Latino migration on racial formations and politics in southern communities."[100] Moreover, despite describing simultaneous economic integration and social isolation, scholars have not "analyzed the practices that place Latinos outside the boundaries of community."[101]

The studies published about Latinas/os in the South that have a serious engagement with place and race demonstrate the extent to which every place is unique, with different racial histories and experiences with work and labor. Angela C. Stuesse and Laura E. Helton have written about how the poultry processing industry in central Mississippi recruited workers from south Texas in direct response to the labor organizing efforts of Black workers. Consequently, ethnic Mexicans moved to an area with a majority African American population undergoing a fight about exploitation and fair pay that extends back to the post–Civil War period.[102] In contrast, my research demonstrates that it was a sojourner working in a northwest Arkansas poultry processing plant who told his social network in California and Mexico about the opportunities available. In this case, ethnic Mexican workers moved to an overwhelmingly white area where there was no battle over fair pay and labor rights. What these two studies demonstrate is that place (race, political economy, and history) is of the utmost importance for a nuanced study of the processes that drive migration and the changes that occur when a community begins to grow in a different direction.

The importance of place for racialized definitions is supported by other studies that focus on Arkansas. Julie Weise's book on Mexicans in the US South also demonstrates the importance of "where" and "when" for defining race. Her book reveals that Mexican immigrants have moved to and lived in the region since 1910. In her study, she writes about the experiences of Mexicans in Louisiana, Mississippi, Arkansas, Georgia, and North Carolina and the ways in which they fought against second-class treatment and Jim Crow segregation. Weise's book is one of the first to historicize the presence of Latinas/os in the region. She focuses on documenting how Mexican immigrants, braceros, and workers challenged established racial notions in places across the region, thereby demonstrating the importance of locality as well as time period. In the mid-twentieth century braceros were sent to the Arkansas Delta in the northeast part of the state, where they encountered Jim Crow laws and often had to stay in empty sharecropping cabins.[103] Mexicans frequently received lower wages than what their bracero contracts stipulated, were treated as second-class citizens, and were forced to use the segregated facilities reserved for African Americans; they fought back, however, and successfully petitioned the Mexican government to act on their behalf. Workers and consulates were able to get local authorities to "ensure Mexicans' nominal access to white public spaces" but were unable to secure the entirety of the wages they were due.[104]

More recently, Miranda Cady Hallet demonstrated the importance of the local in studies of racial difference and social positioning, arguing that Salvadorans in Danville, Arkansas, ninety minutes southeast of Fort Smith, locate themselves as "better than White trash."[105] There are several relevant points when thinking about issues of place in this part of greater northwest Arkansas. First, Salvadorans could position themselves as "better than White trash" because Danville had also been overwhelmingly white and became much more ethnically diverse due to Latina/o immigrants and migrants, especially Salvadorans and Mexicans, who moved to the area to work in poultry plants.[106] Second, Salvadorans swiftly learned the commonsense racial hierarchy relevant to Danville that cast "white trash," or poor white people, as inferior human beings and thus positioned themselves as superior to them due to their work ethic. Third, Salvadorans strove to distinguish themselves from Mexicans and the association with illegality. The everyday experiences of Latinas/os in Danville thus vary significantly from those of their counterparts a short distance away.

CHAPTER 2

Yellow Peril in Arkansas: War, Christianity, and the Regional Racialization of Vietnamese Refugees

As Governor David Pryor welcomed Vietnamese to Arkansas and the United States, there was some chaos.[1] Genial signs greeted the newcomers in English and Vietnamese. Unfriendly signs were largely absent, except for one, with a Star of David and a swastika in the background, that read: "RESCUE USA from REDS FIRST!!! WHiTE MAN UNiTE!!! AND FigHT!!"[2] As the governor gave his speech, the man with the racist sign repeatedly yelled that the refugee presence was a Zionist conspiracy. In turn, others in attendance attempted to drown him out by shouting, "Welcome, welcome!" At one point a woman tried to tear down the Nazi sign, but a minister intervened. A scuffle ensued as members of the welcoming group struggled to prevent national news photographers from taking the man's picture and capturing his response to the Vietnamese refugees.[3] Despite attempting to paint the situation in a good light, Pryor could not ignore those dissenters who objected—sometimes vehemently—to the arrival of Vietnamese refugees on US shores and particularly to their placement in Arkansas.

Unlike Little Rock, in the state's central region, or counties in its southeast, northwest Arkansas was overwhelmingly white—a consequence, at least in part, of anti-Black terror at the turn of the twentieth century. In this context, the arrival of twenty-six thousand nonwhite people constituted a huge demographic shift, even if most Vietnamese refugees would be there only temporarily. The scarcity of African Americans in the region made the backgrounds of Southeast Asians that much more important as Arkansans dealt with racial difference.

Situated at the intersection of Asian American studies and southern history, this chapter examines the racialization of Vietnamese refugees in Arkansas in 1975, when the federal government selected Fort Chaffee as a refugee processing center. The settlement of Vietnamese refugees in a southern state added new complexity to the US racial order and its multiple racial projects. This complexity has been explored productively in research by Jana Lipman about the ways in which the presence of the Vietnamese in Fort Chaffee highlights the central role of the US military in guiding relocation efforts and the significance of having refugee camps within the United States.[4] Similarly, Eric Tang has produced a valuable study of the Vietnamese community in New Orleans East, showing how the city's political economy and social relations generated a nuanced racial position for the Vietnamese and mandated interactions with white racial dominance.[5] These studies are important because they contribute to an understanding of larger US processes such as military endeavors and racial formation.

In a similar way, I center on the experiences of the Vietnamese in Arkansas to analyze processes of racialization as well as to elucidate the legacies of southern history. In other words, this chapter focuses on the experiences of Vietnamese refugees in order to delineate racialization processes in a particular kind of southern place and examine how those processes are shaped by a place's histories, including those of racial violence and the removal of Black communities. By grounding this study in local history with long-lasting consequences for understandings of race, we can begin to analyze deeply the regional racial formations of the South.

As Wendy Cheng has demonstrated, the region is an important unit of analysis, since race is not constructed or experienced uniformly. Cheng defines "regional racial formation" as "place-specific processes of racial formation, in which locally accepted racial orders and hierarchies complicate and sometimes challenge hegemonic ideologies and facile notions of race."[6] In her study of Asians and Latinas/os in suburban Los Angeles, Cheng theorized racial formation by sharply focusing on race and place. Drawing on people's everyday experiences as well as everyday landscapes, she found that Latinas/os and Asians in the San Gabriel Valley altered racial hierarchies and understandings based on their experiences living in a majority-minority area. Following Cheng, this chapter centers place and race in order to unpack the racialization of Vietnamese refugees in 1975 and to understand how their racialization changed over a period of months.

This study helps explain the elasticity of racialization, as a single group can be defined in shifting and competing ways. In the popular imagination, the Vietnamese went from victims needing rescue (as long as they met certain criteria proving that they were not too different from idealized white Arkansans) to the "yellow peril" (feared for being too different and unassimilable, in part due to their multigenerational family units) to "model minorities" (in contrast to other newcomers such as Cuban refugees and Mexican immigrants).[7] Cuban refugees arrived in 1980 amid national and international accusations that Fidel Castro's government had unleashed criminals, prostitutes, and the mentally ill. Given these discourses, and the fact that this cohort of Cubans was largely working-class and of African descent and had a substantial number of gay people, Arkansans and their politicians constructed them as deviant criminals and mobilized to remove them from the state.[8] In the 1990s, Mexican migrants and other Latin American immigrants arrived during a significant regional economic reorganization that provided many of them with low-wage work, especially in the poultry industry. At the turn of the twenty-first century, Latinas/os were increasingly racialized as "illegal aliens" but were praised by the governor at that time, Mike Huckabee, for their devotion to God and family.[9]

Much work remains to be done to explore the role of religious beliefs in racialization, especially in places where faith can be central to community formation and where Christianity was used to justify chattel slavery and racial subjugation. Indeed, one of Arkansans' idiosyncrasies was drawing on Christianity to advocate for accepting Vietnamese who would suffer if sent back to live under communism and, later, Mexican immigrants, while often denying such acceptance to African Americans in the state as well as to Cuban refugees, who also fled communism. Northwest Arkansas can also illustrate how whiteness and Blackness operate in a place that had been racially homogenous. More importantly, studying the region can elucidate how anti-Black racism shapes the lives of refugees and immigrants and reveal the anti-Black structures that continue to exist across the United States.

This chapter asks how northwest Arkansas's history shaped the reactions of government agencies and Arkansans to the Vietnamese presence. The responses of the state of Arkansas and Arkansans to the presence of unprecedented numbers of Vietnamese people reflected national factors such as controversy over the Vietnam War, fear of competition in the labor market, and long-standing nationalist, anti-Asian sentiments. These dynamics intersected with Christian beliefs, including the rise of the Moral Majority, with its racial overtones; states' rights; and racial mores grounded in local history. Particularly significant for social relations was the history of anti-Black racial terror, which resulted in the removal and displacement of Black communities from the area in the early 1900s. Consequently, northwest Arkansas was nearly 99 percent white for most of the twentieth century, making Vietnamese and other Southeast Asian refugees a significant and startling demographic presence.

The ideas of Christian charity and duty to refugees helped Arkansans frame the arrival of Vietnamese men and women in the state, but the politics of race—as they undergirded antipathy to the federal government and deployed rhetoric that drew on "yellow peril" ideas—restricted and channeled the lives and labor of Vietnamese refugees. Northwest Arkansans' whiteness shaped their encounters with refugees; they frequently referenced the racial and ethnic backgrounds of Vietnamese people as reasons to shun them. Some individuals feared competition during a difficult economic moment, yet others saw opportunities for a more willing and exploitable labor force.

This is not to suggest that Blackness and Black people were not important to Arkansans' racial mores, but rather to show that tens of thousands of Vietnamese arrivals presented a dramatic shift in a place that had maintained a white regional identity for nearly a century. In short, this history of terror had repercussions for dealing with racial and ethnic difference that would affect Asians and Latinas/os into the late twentieth century. This study offers an entry point to think about how a field of racial positions or a racial hierarchy works, is reified, or is altered by showing how white Arkansans offered a modicum of conditional acceptance to (some) Vietnamese refugees while denying the same to communities already present, such as African Americans.[10]

Arkansas Camps and World War II: Japanese American Internees and European POWs

Camp Chaffee was established at the beginning of the rise of the military-industrial complex, as part of the US effort to increase its military capacity in advance of the Second World War. The federal government paid $1.35 million to acquire 15,163 acres from 712 Arkansas property owners ranging from schools and churches, to families, businesses, and other government agencies.[11] The base, built in only sixteen months, was activated in March 1942, and the Sixth, Fourteenth, and Sixteenth Armored Divisions were stationed there from 1942 until 1946.[12] As a camp, it was supposed to be a temporary facility, and the "frame barracks" reflect that temporary nature. They were two-story structures, approximately thirty by ninety feet with a normal capacity for sixty-three people; stacking of steel cots could increase the maximum occupancy to ninety.[13] Though its main purpose during this time was to train soldiers for combat and prepare units for deployment, it was also used as a prisoner of war (POW) camp for four thousand Germans.[14]

Figure 2.1. Aerial photograph of Fort Chaffee, from the SE Asia Relocation Collection, Artwork/Photographs. Courtesy of the Pebley Center, Boreham Library, University of Arkansas–Fort Smith.

In the 1940s the federal government chose to place two groups of people—Japanese American internees and European prisoners of war—in Arkansas. About seventeen thousand Japanese Americans were relocated to Arkansas, where they lived from September 1942 through June 1944. The camps in Arkansas—Rohwer and Jerome—were the easternmost US locations and the only ones in the South. Land for both camps, each slightly bigger than ten thousand acres, was purchased by the War Relocation Authority (WRA) from the Farm Security Administration, which bought it in the 1930s to resettle and rehabilitate poor farm families; however, the land was never used for this purpose.

Governor Homer Martin Adkins, a rabid racist and former Ku Klux Klan member who began his political career as a KKK candidate in 1924, did not want internment camps in his state. Writing to J. H. Tolan, chairman of the House Committee Investigating National Defense Migration, he said, "The only way I can visualize where we can use them at all would be to fence them in concentration camps under wire fence and the guard of white soldiers." When it was clear to Adkins that despite his disapproval, the federal government was going to place two internment camps in the

Arkansas Delta, he requested guard towers, barbed wire, searchlights, and armed guards.

When Japanese Americans arrived at the camps, they were forced to complete many structures that were unfinished and unfurnished. They also had to clear the land and finish other work, such as digging wells, laying water and sewage pipes, and building roads. Finding enough wood during winter to stave off the cold was a monumental task, as was finding enough material to build furniture or partitions, since the barracks had only old cots for sleeping. Life in the camps was hard and made harder by the local landscape and environment. There were water moccasins, copperheads, rattlesnakes, and mosquitoes. One internee remembers, "When the rains came ... we could not leave our quarters. The water stagnated at the front steps. . . . The mosquitoes that festered there were horrible, and the authorities never had enough quinine for sickness. . . . Rohwer was a living nightmare."[15]

Most Arkansans were unhappy having ethnic Japanese in their midst, but they understood it as a war necessity. They were also very concerned with what was happening inside the camps—they wanted to make sure that internees were not being coddled by camp staff or overfed. Before Japanese Americans had even arrived, rumors flew that that there was not going to be any food rationing, which created a great frenzy until the War Relocation Authority assured residents that food at the camps would be equivalent to Army "B" rations.

The Arkansas legislature introduced several anti-Japanese bills, some of which were passed during this time period. One banned Japanese and Japanese Americans from owning land in the state to ensure that "no Japs can stay in the state," because according to Frank Williams, a state senator who spearheaded the legislation, it was common knowledge that "a white person cannot profitably compete with the Japanese." They also passed legislation prohibiting Japanese and Japanese American children from attending white schools. Japanese American internees in Arkansas who sought to pursue higher education had to take courses via mail from schools outside of the state. During the internment period there were some instances of shootings—a guard shot at three boys, injuring one, while in another case a farmer shot at a guard and three boys who were returning from a deer hunt because he thought the guard was helping the boys to escape. No deaths due to shootings are recorded. Unfortunately, C. B. Ragsdale, a state senator who introduced legislature similar to the ban on Japanese and Japanese Americans owning land, might have been speaking for a large number of Arkansans when he said, "I don't believe anybody wants a Japanese person in Arkansas. If I had my way, we'd put them all on a ship and have the ship torpedoed."[16]

During the same time period, there were also German and Italian prisoners of war in the United States. More than four hundred thousand POWs were held in the country between 1942 and 1945. About twenty-three thousand of them were placed in Arkansas during these years. Fort Chaffee was the first POW camp in the state and held about four thousand Germans. Camp Robinson, near Little Rock, was the second site and held about ten thousand Germans; it eventually played a key role as a supply and administrative center for other smaller camps throughout the state. In 1944, Camp Dermott, whose name had been changed from Jerome after the last of the Japanese American internees were transferred to Rohwer, held about seven thousand German POWs and was used for fanatically pro-Nazi soldiers. Monticello, also in southeast Arkansas, was the fourth camp and was used for two thousand Italian POWs.

Contrary to the squalor, disrepair, and disarray that Japanese Americans found in their internment camps, German and Italian prisoners of war were pleasantly surprised by the conditions of their camps. Camp Robinson, for example, was singled out by Swiss representatives as "one of the best" prison camps ever seen, and they were "particularly impressed with the excellent physical appearance of the camp."[17] Such descriptions contrast greatly with those of the Japanese American internee who described life in Rohwer as a living nightmare. Contrary to the great upheaval about rationing food for Japanese Americans, Arkansans did not notice that POWs were well fed to the point of gaining an average of fifteen pounds over a thirty-day period. Moreover, while all Japanese Americans were expected to work inside the camp grounds, German and Italian officers received monetary payments even if they chose not to work. They were also able to enroll in correspondence courses as well as establish college courses inside the camps. Contrary to their response to Japanese Americans, Arkansans were not outraged at these education programs for POWs. They were, however, finally outraged at camp conditions when news started arriving as to the conditions faced by US prisoners of war in Europe.[18]

In 1943 the War Department announced that POWs could work outside of military installations, something which thrilled most Arkansas businessmen, especially planters. Despite petitions from planters to use Japanese Americans for labor, Adkins denied such requests as well as most work outside of the camps.[19] Contrary to his attitude toward Japanese Americans, Adkins petitioned to put European POWs to work on plantations or in any other jobs necessary throughout the state. Twenty-six of the branch camps were in the Delta, reflecting the agricultural dependence of the state and the determination of its planters. More than thirty smaller work camps were established throughout the state, with the overwhelming majority of them in the Delta.[20] Racism won out over any inclination to aid planters in their economic endeavors as long as they wanted to use Asian laborers. Planters sought to use Japanese and Japanese American internees, a more vulnerable group than the area's Black or white people who were leaving the area in search of better opportunities, but Adkins's beliefs did not allow him to acquiesce to their petitions. However, he held a different perspective in the case of European POWs.

In general, German and Italian POWs were praised by Arkansans for their excellent work in saving crops and getting much-needed work done. There was no outcry about having enemies in Arkansas, and instead it appears such negative feelings were reserved for Americans of Japanese ancestry. Neither Adkins nor other Arkansans saw a contradiction in allowing Italian and German men—some of them fanatical Nazis—to labor outside of their camps and go to worksites throughout the state while denying Japanese Americans the same kind of mobility. By World War II, Italians and Germans were considered white within the United States' racial landscape, and the different responses to POWs and interned Japanese Americans indicate that this was the most important factor in accepting, even embracing, POWs in contrast to Asian internees. This was not the last time race was the most important indicator of how Arkansans reacted to varying groups who were placed in or moved to the state.

The last POWs left Arkansas in 1946, the same year Fort Chaffee was deactivated, only to be reopened in 1948 as the home of the Fifth Army Division until 1957, with the exception of a period from February to August 1950, when Chaffee was again deactivated.[21] From 1942 to 1994, except for brief periods at the end of WWII and from 1959 to 1961, Chaffee was "used continuously for ordnance training that ranged from small arms to Honest John rockets."[22] It was finally designated a base in March 1956, reflecting its more permanent status as a military installation.[23]

Fort Chaffee probably did not become central to the economic well-being of neighboring communities such as Barling, Greenwood, or Fort Smith due to the oscillation between activating and deactivating it. For example, in early 1957 it became the "United States Army Training Center, Field Artillery," and was tasked with instructing Reserve Force personnel prior to their entry into the National Guard or Army reserve units, but only two years later it was placed in "caretaker" status. Then Chaffee was reopened during the Berlin Crisis in 1961 as a training center, but this time to train infantrymen in basic and advanced infantry tactics; the US Army Garrison Reserve Unit from Oklahoma and the 100th Infantry Division, a Kentucky Reserve Unit, trained there. Only a year later, the 100th Division was deactivated and Fort Chaffee's new mission was to help the Third Corps Artillery and the XIX Corps. However, it was again deactivated in 1965, though many National Guard and Reserve Units used it for summer training.[24] In November 1974 it was redesignated as the US Army Garrison, Fort Chaffee, which made it "semi-active," and in early 1975 it served as a "Refugee Processing Center for Indochina Refugees," but in December 1975 it was again closed after all the Southeast Asians had left the camp. In the interim period between Vietnamese and Cuban refugees, the post was used as training grounds for the National Guard and Army Reserve Units, with more than fifty thousand military personnel passing through. The Mariel Boatlift served as a catalyst for the federal government to once again activate Fort Chaffee, this time to process Cubans, but once they left, the camp was again deactivated.[25]

Fort Chaffee was built at the beginning of the military-industrial complex, but unlike Fort Bragg, which essentially dictated the economic environment of Fayetteville, North Carolina, it largely lacked that level of connection with surrounding communities.[26] That is not to say that during the times that it operated, especially when it was used as a refugee processing center, it did not boost the local economy. In the 1980s, when the federal government studied the possibility of designating Chaffee as a facility to hold and process refugees whenever necessary, the Fort Smith City Council and Governor Frank White vehemently opposed the idea on the grounds that it was unfair to expect Arkansas to carry what should have been a national burden. An official of the refugee program said, "I'm not sure what Arkansas's burden has been other than bearing an infusion of about $150 million into the economy of this area." In effect, they turned down an estimated $50 million per year.[27]

Regional History, Race, and Racial Anxieties

Northwest Arkansas became overwhelmingly white through racial-cleansing campaigns that included two vicious episodes in Harrison, Arkansas, in 1905 and 1909. These events were part of a larger pattern of state-sanctioned anti-Black violence that perpetrated the murder, displacement, and removal of African Americans from vast expanses of land in Arkansas, Georgia, Mississippi, Oklahoma, Illinois, and Missouri. White people perpetuated the expulsion of Blacks from communities in northwest Arkansas through racist practices such as creating "sundown towns," where African Americans could not be present after daylight hours for fear of being beaten, murdered, or lynched.[28]

When more than twenty-five thousand Vietnamese refugees arrived in Fort Chaffee, they were numerically comparable to the entire population of Crawford County in 1970. Northwest Arkansans had limited exposure to people from other places and virtually none to Asian people, since Japanese American internment camps had been in the state's southeast, but they were privy to and participated in the racialization of Vietnamese people at the national scale. The Vietnam War was well covered by the media, and when veterans returned, they contributed their stories and perspectives to ongoing discourse.

In the 1970s, the Christian fundamentalist movement was becoming deeply involved in national politics, increasingly fighting against what it perceived as government intrusion and the secularizing of public culture. The counterculturalrevolution of the 1960s was often motivated by patriotism and opposition to the consequences of the Vietnam War, but it launched social changes—second-wave feminism, gay activism, and other challenges to conventional family structures—that were threatening to fundamentalists. To them, the 1963 Supreme Court ruling against reading the Bible in public schools exemplified the demise of their society and the overreaching power of the federal government. Across the nation, with the exception of Southern Baptists, fundamentalists were more concerned with "opposition to the expansion of the powers of civil government" and "its intrusion on people's lives" than with doctrinal erosion. Early on, some Religious Right leaders were drawn from separatist fundamentalists. According to George Marsden, it was only after white southerners no longer voted solidly Democratic that "the Religious Right emerged as a national movement with conspicuous southern leadership, best exemplified by Jerry Falwell, Pat Robertson, and James Robison." The early Moral Majority emerged from the upper South and took over the Southern Baptist Convention, the United States' largest Protestant denomination.[29] In Arkansas, as in the rest of the region, the expanding evangelical movement had a strong base given the area's overwhelmingly Protestant communities.[30]

Religious Right followers were outraged with the federal government for altering their way of life. They opposed school busing, the Equal Rights Amendment, and the ban on prayer in schools. Marsden concludes that "the Christian School movement had gained immensely in popularity as a practical sort of cultural separatism and as an alternative to government controlled secular education. Especially in the South, one motive was to avoid racial integration."[31] The evangelical movement made several substantial strides in Arkansas. In the 1970s, Springdale's First Baptist Church launched a "lifestyle evangelism" program that tripled its membership, while Family, Life, America, and God (FLAG) represented the resurgence of an ultraconservatism that decried the Equal Rights Amendment and supported prayer in school.[32]

These decades were a period of great change, most of which was indeed imposed by the federal government. The so-called Second Reconstruction during the long civil rights era embodied federal intervention in US southern society as it attempted to get the region to accept national changes around issues of equality for African Americans.[33] Many of the transformations were the result of legal challenges taken to courts or mandated through federal legislation, including the *Brown* decisions, the Civil Rights Act, and the Voting Rights Act. Despite massive resistance and episodes of brutal violence, change once again came to the region.[34] Many of the white people who could afford to do so moved from the urban centers to the suburbs in order to maintain their way of life, their segregated social spheres, and their all-white schools.[35]

Vietnamese refugees were only the latest Asians to enter the nation and face US Americans' anxieties about them as allegedly forever foreign and unassimilable. In the case of Arkansas, this confrontation occurred in an area that had been maintained by both custom and coercion as a majority-white region. Although Arkansans' ideas of Christian charity and duty to refugees helped bring about the Vietnamese arrival in the state, their "yellow peril" racialization ideas drew on anti-Asian sentiments. Religion, the received understanding of the war, and regional historical legacies also restricted the kind of welcome the refugees were offered.

States' Rights, the War, and Christianity

When Fort Chaffee opened as a refugee processing center, state officials and Arkansans expressed resentment toward the federal government for imposing on the state and its people. The underlying tension was centered on questions of autonomy and states' rights. During World War II, this tension arose with regard to Japanese American internment in southeast Arkansas. The question had also come up in the state during the integration of Central High School in 1957, as the world watched Governor Faubus deny entry to nine Black students. Although the arrival of Vietnamese refugees in 1975 took place under different circumstances than the establishment of World War II camps and the desegregation of Central High School, at the center of each situation was the issue of states' rights and the presence or containment of nonwhite people.

On April 25, 1975, the *Arkansas Gazette* reported that Fort Chaffee was going to be used as a refugee center, yet among many people in the state the news was treated as a preposterous rumor. The story was likely not given much weight for three reasons: the news came through "unnamed" sources, state officials and congressmen who were contacted did not know of any such move, and army officers at the fort had heard nothing. Senator John L. McClellan, a Democrat, told the newspaper that Chaffee was not being immediately considered because he was "assured by the State Department that no such decision ha[d] been made concerning Fort Chaffee and that it w[ould] not be made without further consultation" with him.[36] The next day, Pentagon officials declared that Fort Chaffee was being considered as a site; state officials were not quoted about the matter.[37] On April 28 the Pentagon announced that it had chosen Fort Chaffee as well as Eglin Air Force Base in Florida, Fort Indiantown Gap in Pennsylvania, and Camp Pendleton in California as processing centers. The centers were chosen to disperse the refugee population, an attempt to preemptively halt the formation of ethnic enclaves. The camps would house up to twenty thousand refugees indefinitely, though the Pentagon hoped to relocate their populations within two weeks.[38] Despite not having been consulted, Arkansas government officials publicly encouraged Arkansans to support the relocation effort. Arkansans' responses, however, varied as they drew on myriad concepts, from moral duty to respect for former loyal allies to good Christian behavior.

Some Arkansans drew on their Christian beliefs to welcome the Vietnamese newcomers and wrote Governor Pryor to commend him for his actions. Caroline L. Brendel's letter is representative of many the governor received: "Please permit me to express my commendation of your Christian charity and kindness in personally welcoming refugees. God will richly bless you and your family for what you have done for 'the least of these etc.'" [sic].[39] To the letter writers who supported his actions, Pryor often replied with a form letter that read in part: "It pleases me to learn of your support of federal and state efforts to assist in providing humanitarian aid to Vietnamese evacuees. Arkansas is a community of people whose spirit and heart offer friendship and aid to all persons who seek our help."[40] Since Arkansas is part of the Bible Belt, it is hardly surprising that many people's comments to the governor reflected Christian beliefs. These sentiments were expressed in editorials written throughout the state.

Other Arkansans believed the United States had a moral duty to the Vietnamese people. According to the *Dumas Clarion* in southeast Arkansas, "The United States ought to find room for the new refugees, to whom this nation owes an obligation" because many of them were relatives of US citizens or worked for the US government.[41] The *Yell County Record* from Danville in the lower northwest put it to readers in the following manner: "What it really gets down to is strictly humane—is it morally right or not for America to bring back the Vietnamese who helped us during the past 10 years? . . . Maybe it's not the right time to bring a 100,000 [sic] refugees and over, to America because of our unemployment and our slow economy, but it's hard to say that it is not our 'moral' obligation." The editors of the *Yell County Record* believed, much like those of the *Dumas Clarion*, that leaving the Vietnamese in their own country would have likely resulted in a massacre. They argued that the United States and its people were morally compelled to offer shelter and relief. The *Yell County Record* editors invoked the United States' moral obligation as emblematic of the country: "Hopefully, we as Americans can retain this value as a people and nation."[42]

Arkansans' Christian values, even if they did not explicitly mention religion, shaped the framework of morality and duty through which they understood their responsibilities as Americans. The Moral Majority was on the upswing and on its way to becoming the Christian Right with a focus on "traditional values" and fighting against the "moral breakdown of America."[43] Because the decision to use the camp was made without any input from local and state officials, Arkansans saw it as an infringement of their rights and as an imposition on the state. But when the decision was made and the people were already there, the situation put many of their beliefs to the test. The moral obligation—the Christian course of action—was to sponsor a refugee or family because it was the right thing to do.

The editors from the *Northwest Arkansas Times* in Fayetteville took it one step further, arguing that turning refugees away would eradicate the moral core of the United States and its people. But their reasons were not solely based on a moral argument; they also relied on the logic of quid pro quo. They endorsed the acceptance of Vietnamese refugees because the United States had a kind of national duty to them: "They suffered dearly, so we should return the favor." The Vietnamese had to deal with

US intervention, and now people in the United States would have to deal with Southeast Asian refugees in their backyards. Moreover, the editors argued, there was no reason to "assume automatically that they will be a plague on our society," and they pointed out that many of the refugees were college educated.[44]

Indeed, many of the groups that fled Vietnam immediately after the fall of Saigon were professionals: doctors, lawyers, and teachers. Three weeks after Fort Chaffee opened, the camp's population of about 26,500 represented a relatively narrow range of Vietnamese society. Whereas Vietnam as a whole was 80 percent Buddhist and 10 percent Catholic, the camp's residents were 47 percent Buddhist, 38 percent Catholic, 6 percent Protestant, and 5 percent Confucian or Cao-Dai, with 4 percent who did not express a religious preference. The majority of the refugees had some mastery of English. Thirty percent rated their English as excellent, while 40 percent claimed that they spoke the language "fairly well." The refugees arrived from Guam, where 28 percent already had secured US sponsors. This was remarkable, because the first cohort of refugees to arrive in Fort Chaffee recounted that they were in Guam for only twenty-four hours, suggesting they fled Vietnam with a strong idea of who might sponsor them. Thirty-four percent had relatives in the states; only 10 percent had no ties to their new country of arrival.[45] The overrepresentation of Catholics, the English-language abilities of the refugees, and their connections to the United States through sponsors and family members strongly indicate that this cohort belonged to the middle and upper classes in their native country. Pointing out the desirable qualifications of these new arrivals served to alleviate anxieties that refugees were going to be a burden on the United States. Notably, this argument was not based on humanitarianism or moral obligation; rather, it was a much more pragmatic approach that acknowledged there was a price to pay for the United States' (failed) intervention in Vietnam.

The editors, however, could not resist invoking the Statue of Liberty and, by extension, its meaning for so many: freedom. They asked, "Or would the opponents, in the final analysis, have us dismantle the statue and send it back to France with a brief note of thanks?" The question was meant to disquiet readers, forcing them to consider the ramifications of their actions. If the US populace, Arkansans in particular, turned their back on Vietnamese refugees, the paper suggested, they might as well put a tombstone on everything the United States purportedly represented.[46]

At the end of the year, Arkansans sponsored a total of 2,061 Vietnamese newcomers in various communities, with 1,840 of them coming from Fort

Chaffee.⁴⁷ The 1980 census shows that between 1975 and 1980, 1,577 Vietnamese people arrived in the state along with 863 "other Asia[ns]." The latter likely represented other Southeast Asians, such as Laotians, who arrived during the refugee resettlement.⁴⁸ The more than two thousand Vietnamese residents in Arkansas were sponsored by citizens in cities throughout the state. The largest concentrations were in Fort Smith with 416, Little Rock with 200, and Grannis with 221.⁴⁹ In the meantime, however, many Arkansans panicked over fears that Fort Chaffee's use as a refugee processing center could hurt them and that having this number of Vietnamese neighbors in their midst would damage their lives.

Yellow Peril: Racialized Fears and Economic Opportunities

Some Arkansans drew on the yellow peril trope to racialize Vietnamese refugees as threatening and unassimilable. As a group, the refugees were seen as menacing outsiders who would at best change the culture and at worst corrupt it. Vietnamese people in Arkansas were thought to be incompatible with US norms in their language, dress, and hygiene, or were viewed as competitors in the labor sphere. Arkansans believed that changes in racial makeup and culture were detrimental to the nation and more immediately to their community, and that competition from foreigners for jobs and benefits was unfair because jobs should be reserved solely for native-born workers, Black and white.⁵⁰ These different reactions were also based on class hierarchies. While Vietnamese professionals and military personnel, who had the English-language proficiency and grooming habits desired by Arkansans, were welcomed to a degree, their rural and poor compatriots were not.

To some Arkansans, the Vietnamese had appeal as a more willing and exploitable workforce than poor whites or Blacks. In April 1975 the unemployment rate in Arkansas was 9.6 percent, higher than the national rate of 8.8 percent.⁵¹ Nevertheless, business owners throughout the state quickly asked for Vietnamese laborers. A manufacturer from the northeast town of Jonesboro asked for fifty workers to begin immediately; two car dealers needed mechanics; others asked for shoemakers and tailors.⁵² Officials in some cities requested doctors and dentists: Winslow, Arkansas, asked for a doctor and his wife as well as for a nurse and her husband. Phil Matthews of the Arkansas Hospital Association sought to find workers with medical training or who were in health-related fields.⁵³ Frolic Footwear requested two hundred workers because the company had not been able to recruit Arkansans to the plant. Leland Harland, the director of personnel, said, "We feel the main reason is that people are making more on unemployment compensation than they would if they were working."[54] According to Harland, many unemployed workers received $84 per week tax free, plus $150 per month in food stamps. "There's no way to get people off unemployment with that kind of money," he said. Since Frolic Footwear's wages averaged $2.75 per hour, a forty-hour workweek would yield $110 minus taxes.[55] The offers for work were not necessarily benevolent, however. A man with a 164-acre farm wanted a boy or girl, or possibly a woman and child, to help him full-time with a "salary to be paid at some future date if arrangement is working out." He was also willing to split up a family because he knew of a farm ten miles away that also needed help.[56] One man was direct when he wrote that the Vietnamese workers he was seeking "must be agile and willing to please."[57]

Other Arkansans had xenophobic fears about Vietnamese refugees ruining the state and the national culture. Gim Shek, a NASA engineer, made the following assessment:

> Our involvement and loss in Vietnam to shame us; the influx of thousands of foreigners to smother our economic growth; [the refugee situation] is making a sucker out of us. Those foreigners coming here are not bringing their hearts. They will eventually bring over more of their kind, and won't be satisfied until they have brought over part of the "Country." . . . We think poor management [in Washington] is going to put us out of business as a nation of might.[58]

Shek's concern was that Vietnamese refugees would eventually take over the country by bringing more relatives. His xenophobia was such that he feared they could even bring down the "mighty" United States. Shek saw the Vietnamese not as refugees fleeing a country wrecked by a US-backed war and all the concomitant terrors, such as hunger, displacement, homelessness, and death, but rather as invaders seeking to transfer part of Vietnam to the United States. In short, he understood Vietnamese identity through the trope of yellow peril.

The arguments Shek and other Arkansans presented contain two crucial components. On the one hand, their fears were personal, as they worried for themselves and their children's economic and educational well-being. They saw the government's investment in refugees as unfair given the harsh circumstances they lived with every day. On the other hand, they were concerned about the nation and its culture, viewing the refugees as a horde that would inevitably destroy everything they loved about their towns and their country.

The cultural arguments against Vietnamese refugees were premised on the group being a blight on society because of their supposedly high birth rates and levels of disease along with their presumed refusal to assimilate. All of these tropes have a long history in the United States. They have been serially and strategically deployed against many communities of color, including people seen as Black, Brown, Yellow, and Red—whether native, immigrant, or refugee. In response, the federal government has made efforts to control the various racial and ethnic communities at different historical moments of crisis. The primary aim of prohibiting Asians from entering the United States was to curtail or halt the growth of those communities altogether. Americans with nativist sentiments have historically advocated for those kinds of restrictions; such attitudes have loomed particularly large during economic downturns and during US wars with Asia. During the Vietnam era, nativism and economic anxiety coalesced as the nation was in the midst of a severe recession. US workers wanted to have jobs and saw Vietnamese people as competitors. Nevertheless, many of the objections were not expressed as fear of competition; instead, they revolved around cultural and racial arguments. Vietnamese people were racialized through negative ascriptions about disease and prostitution, yet they also suffered from positive ascriptions that saw them as potentially successful competitors for resources. Both positive and negative ascriptions were deployed to predict the wholesale destruction of the United States and its identity.

The First Cohort of Vietnamese Refugees at Fort Chaffee

Many of the fears expressed by Arkansans had little basis in fact. Many of the people brought to Fort Chaffee were highly educated professionals: doctors, lawyers, and former military personnel who were anti-Communists. The following section draws directly from the testimony of Vietnamese people who were in Fort Chaffee in the summer of 1975. These are the voices of the first Vietnamese refugees who were able to leave their native country. They represent people with resources—economic, political, social, or military—who therefore had the information, connections, and means to escape a few days before or after the fall of Saigon. A handful of the refugees recounted how they got to Fort Chaffee; taking their timeline as a basis for this cohort, it took them three stops and three months to reach Arkansas. They were first picked up in April by an aircraft carrier, where they spent the night before being sent to a civilian ship. They reached Guam on May 10 and were sent to Wake Island the following day. Finally, after nearly three months, they arrived at Fort Chaffee at the end of July.[59]

This archive of testimonials about life at Fort Chaffee is inherently uneven for a few reasons. It is based on what one camp teacher kept and subsequently donated to the University of Arkansas–Fort Smith. Thus, the materials were defined through the power imbalance of the "student-teacher" relationship in the refugee process that produced them. The record is also shaped by the larger dynamic of US foreign policy and Cold War politics that created the conditions that ultimately made Vietnamese people into refugees. It presents testimony only from advanced students: those who had the resources in Vietnam to study English and other languages, such as French, for several years. Since the archive does not have the work of other students, it is impossible to know how representative this group was of the entire Vietnamese population in Fort Chaffee. Nevertheless, their English-language skills align with other sources that reported that nearly 70 percent of the camp refugees spoke English excellently or fairly well.[60] There are eight "sign-in sheets" that served as a record of attendance. Most had only individuals' names, but three sheets offered additional information such as age, number of family members at Chaffee, and assigned building number. According to those sheets, the youngest student in those English classes was fifteen and the oldest was forty-eight, while family size ranged from one to fourteen. Only three women identified their gender explicitly, so I cannot reach any conclusions about the number of women in Fort Chaffee during that time period. This archive is an important source because it holds refugee voices—their thoughts, feelings, fears, hopes, and prayers written at a camp as they awaited sponsors.[61] However, it has only Vietnamese voices and lacks the perspectives of other Southeast Asians, such as Cambodians, who were also at Fort Chaffee in 1975.[62]

Hoa Thi Kim Tran, a twenty-two-year-old who fled Vietnam with eight family members, shared her story with Jerry Turner, her advanced English teacher.

> When I was in Saigon, I never imagined the day I would stop my studies and should leave my country for ever.... Like most Vietnamese refugees, the reason why I left Viet Nam is that I love Freedom. I wept bitterly the day I left my country. But I must choose the best way: the Liberty....

Figure 2.2. Picture #6 (group photo), Sondra Lamar Collection. Courtesy of the Pebley Center, Boreham Library, University of Arkansas–Fort Smith.

> I dare say that the days of evacuation we spent were the most terrible days. We escaped from Viet Nam in an awful panic. But, arriving at United States, we were consoled by the American volunteers who helped all the refugees with an unceasing smile. On behalf of all Vietnamese, I want to say "many thanks for your help" to the staff, nurses, doctors and especially to the teachers (who always hope us to improve our English) who are working in this camp.[63]

Not all Vietnamese students wrote about their escape or their feelings, but those who did shared Tran's sentiments and gratitude. She also knew that difficulties awaited her family:

> The problem for us is we are afraid that we cannot adapt ourselves to the american life. According to me, one of many differences between american and Vietnamese people is that Vietnamese like to live together in the same house with grand parents, parents, children, relatives while most americans live alone, think themselves when they become major and when they begin to earn their living. In Viet Nam, although sons and

daughters are married, the Father (even who is very old) behaves like the leader of the family until his death.[64]

Even within the confines of Fort Chaffee, she was aware that Vietnamese family units were out of the norm in the United States and might appear odd.

About two weeks later, on Friday, September 5, Tran and her family left Fort Chaffee at 5 a.m. to join her sponsor in Provo, Utah. On Saturday, the sponsor took them to see the Rocky Mountains. On Sunday they went to the Mormon church. On Tuesday, Tran joined her sponsor at his office in Salt Lake City, where she worked as a "clerk typist" for a computer corporation. "I'm so busy in my office and when I come home I'm tired but I have to help my sponsor's wife to cook and take a bath and have a supper," she wrote.[65] Her responsibilities as a refugee with a sponsor, then, consisted of doing triple work—her employment, her tasks for her sponsor, and her duties to her family.

Shortly after arriving in Provo, the Tran family encountered the first challenge posed by their multigenerational household—they were unable to rent a trailer because the owner did not want so many people living in the unit. Instead, they had to rent an unfurnished two-bedroom house, even though they did not have any furniture. Tran immediately came up with a plan to alleviate the financial strain of renting the house—they would move to Salt Lake City, where rents were cheaper and she had been told it would be easy for other family members to find jobs. Plus, that city had bus services that would allow them to get around. She closed her letter to the Turners by asking about Fort Chaffee ("Do you hear anything about Vietnamese refugees? We can't hear from them. We only meet 2 Vietnamese in this city") and apologizing for her "weak" English.[66]

Tran's language abilities aligned with those of her peers, at least those whose letters exist in the archive; contrary to her own perceptions, her English was strong enough to allow her to work in a clerical position as soon as she arrived. Tran's compatriots in the classroom in August 1975 included former soldiers, one of whom enlisted in the "Vietnamese army to fight against the communist force and also was a student in law college of University of Saigon," and who had studied "English as a foreign language during [his] seven years in French high school many years ago."[67] Thuan Van Do and his wife were also present; he wrote, "I was in V.N. Armed Forces and I'd twenty years in that. I'd working in the Airborne training center for the Airborn Division. . . . I'd leaving my country in April 29th, 1975 under a rainy bomb by the V.C. Army." This was his third time in the United States; his previous trips were related to parachute training and competitions. He closed his essay by writing, "I hope in the future sweet day, I'll become a good citizen in the U.S. community."[68] Mrs. Thuan Van Do wrote that she "had been in English classes for 2 years I had finished VI course and my school was VAA. I was employed of the U.S. Army since 1967 till 1973."[69] A month after their arrival they had yet to be matched by the volunteer agencies, but she wrote that "day after I prayed for a perfect sponsor we would have in the future. . . . I hope for couples of year later I could written better in English and spoke little better than now." Indeed, nearly all of the Vietnamese refugees expressed their desire to learn English well and to do so quickly, and several of them thanked Turner for his work in the classroom.

Hong Thi Cam Trinh, twenty-four, left Saigon on April 27 with her sixty-year-old parents, who left properties behind. Their departure interrupted her medical studies, and in Fort Chaffee she worked in the dispensary until a doctor introduced her to the obstetrics/gynecology ward, where she volunteered as an interpreter because it reminded her of her time in Vietnamese hospitals.

> Where will be resettled? I don't know. How is our future? I don't know. How is about my education, my medical training? I don't have any sure answer. "It is very difficult to get in a medical school in the U.S." They always repeat when I ask to. But I think "Aide-toi, le ciel t'aidera," then I will try and try more and more and try to keep my hope, my mind.

In her essay she described the phrase as a French proverb and translated it as "Help yourself, God will help you after."[70]

Trinh was the kind of person that nativist and xenophobic Arkansans could not imagine. But she and others like her—medical personnel—quickly came to Governor Pryor's attention. He appointed a special committee to determine the possibility of licensing them along with some advanced medical students as certified physicians under Arkansas law due to a "critical need for trained medical personnel in many of Arkansas's rural counties."[71] By early August the governor's office estimated that 130 doctors remained in Fort Chaffee; however, they were being sponsored at a rate of four per day, making it "imperative that [a] training program should be initiated as soon as practicable." The special committee determined that there were approximately five senior medical students and fifteen physicians interested in becoming certified to practice medicine in Arkansas. To be licensed, however, the individuals had to pass the Educational Council for Foreign Medical Graduates (ECFMG) exam and serve a one-year internship in an approved medical facility. The University of Arkansas Medical Center (UAMS) would prepare the candidates for the exam, which was scheduled for July 1976 at a cost of approximately $10,000 per person. The committee felt that the costs of the program should be borne by local communities through loans to the individuals, "who, by contractual obligation, agreed to practice in that community for a specified period of time after completion of [their] internship[s]. The loan would be repaid through actual service in the community by the physician."[72] The Legislative Council voted to support the program at its August 8 meeting.[73] On August 15, Pryor released a statement authorizing the expenditure of $165,000 from the state's emergency fund—$100,000 for stipends and direct expenses, $42,000 for housing and maintenance, and $23,000 for education expenses incurred by UAMS.[74] I was unable to find documents that reported the result of this endeavor, but it is nonetheless indicative that despite racial fears, the governor was quite willing to place professionals in rural areas where they were desperately needed.

Several constituents wrote to Pryor to warn him about the dangers of the Vietnamese presence in Arkansas, citing the threat of yellow peril. Their letters argued that Vietnamese refugees were not entitled to valuable resources offered by the state and federal governments—and the governor and his office agreed.[75] On July 30, 1975, Rick Osborne, a staff member in Pryor's office, reported that Colonel Morris, director of both the Arkansas Student Loan Program and the Guaranteed Student Loan Foundation, called to inquire whether any Vietnamese refugees would be interested in a loan. Osborne told Morris "to discreetly check and not alert them of existence of the funds more than necessary in keeping with the Governor's policy of not encouraging the refugees to stay any longer than necessary. State loans—federal funds, but Arkansans *need* the money too."[76] Thus the governor and his office agreed with the logic and goals of many Arkansas residents in wishing the Vietnamese refugees' stay in Arkansas to be as short as possible. Pryor's efforts to facilitate the stay of twenty doctors and advanced medical students were in sharp contrast to this stance. That program, however, provided benefits to the state and to Arkansans as well as to the Vietnamese. It was in the state's best interests to send qualified medical personnel to rural areas, while participating in the program provided the sponsorship refugees needed to leave the camp. This situation, however, was an exception, because for the most part neither Arkansans nor the state government wanted Vietnamese refugees to stay in the state. These sentiments fell in line with research demonstrating that although many US citizens said they did not object to Vietnamese refugees in the

United States, they greatly disapproved of intermarriage with their own families and said they would refuse to have refugees as guests in their homes.[77] In short, most people in the United States did not want them to be too close by.

Conclusion

The approaches to the two groups of students demonstrate some of the contradictions in the response to Vietnamese refugees. In the case of medical students and doctors, Governor Pryor ignored constituents' objections and secured funds for their training for the ECFMG. In the other case, he impeded students from finding out that they might be eligible for state monies. Arguably, both groups of students would contribute to the state, though advanced medical students and doctors would presumably do so more quickly. But the note from the governor's office shows that the objection was not solely to the use of state or federal funds: Governor Pryor did not want to encourage Vietnamese refugees to stay in the state, even if they were pursuing higher education. The governor's efforts to keep racial "others" from settling in Arkansas mirror the legacy of anti-Black racism. That history helped construct regional identity around the rewards and presumptions of whiteness, and it also meant that Vietnamese refugees could count on fewer potential allies in communities of color, which, while hardly immune to anti-Asian racism, might at least have been open to a more diverse demography.

In the case of the doctors, Pryor went against his policy of not encouraging Vietnamese refugees to live in Arkansas because he saw them as a valuable resource that filled a critical gap in his constituents' needs. Like their less educated compatriots, the Vietnamese doctors were potentially a more willing and exploitable labor force than native Arkansans. Their legal situation necessitated a remedy that could be resolved only through finding a sponsor. By facilitating the links that let Vietnamese doctors leave Chaffee, Arkansas secured a more controllable workforce: medical personnel were dependent on the resources the state provided in order to pass the ECFMG exam and presumably to receive their first jobs in the country. More importantly, the group of medical practitioners consisted of a handful of individuals as opposed to hundreds or thousands of people. The refusal to advertise available funds to other students reveals the governor's intention of limiting the Vietnamese stay in Arkansas, perhaps from the fear of an Asian horde that would destroy the United States.

However, Vietnamese refugees also benefited from anti-Black structural forces. Although some Arkansans did not want them to be processed at Fort Chaffee, they begrudgingly accepted them. Even when the racializing discourse shifted to that of yellow peril, Arkansans and state government officials did not mobilize to remove the Vietnamese completely or to shut down Fort Chaffee. In contrast, Arkansans did not offer this grudging acceptance to Cubans in 1980. The case of the Cubans, who were largely of African descent, demonstrates how quickly the state and its people would mobilize against a Black community. The rumors that the Cubans were gay and Communist also fed negative feelings.

The Cuban refugees were primarily single males, a factor that also shaped processes of racialization and affected the welcome that was offered. More work is necessary to further study the role of family in immigration discourses, especially the power of the trope of the traditional nuclear family, which can serve to make some immigrants more legible and desirable to communities. For example, in 1975, yellow peril notions represented Vietnamese and other Southeast Asian refugees as having too many children, while their multigenerational family units—grandparents, parents, siblings, and children—were considered nonnormative and too odd for Arkansas. In contrast, Mexican immigrants in the 1990s benefited from having families who mirrored the idealized nuclear family unit—mom, dad, and children. At the beginning of a substantial Latina/o migration, largely Mexican, to Arkansas, the supposed Latina/o family unit served to cast these migrants in a positive light. Their nuclear families were emblematic of the so-called traditional family values that many southerners embraced. Such an understanding even facilitated the interpretation of Latina/o teen pregnancies as positive:

> It seemed that the Hispanic family unit was very sound, that [they had a] respect and love of children, and they had a family cohesiveness which was admirable.... Of course we were very aware that [with] the wave of Hispanic[s] coming in, that the girls were getting pregnant very early, having lots of babies, but it did not seem to be, um, as in the Black population, where there are a lot of out-of-wedlock births, it seemed that in the Hispanic population that the girls were married, these pregnancies were welcomed and planned.[78]

In those instances, Latinas/os benefited from anti-Black racism that understood Black teenage pregnancies as emblematic of a larger racialized notion—the Black broken family.

Yet in the twenty-first century, white Arkansans often compare Mexicans unfavorably to the Vietnamese. Some Arkansans, in passing or as an indictment, have lamented, "We never had to put signs up in Vietnamese for Asians; they just learned English. I don't know why Mexicans can't do the same."[79] Such a statement draws from a sanitized version of past experiences with the Vietnamese to mark Latinas/os as inferior in a racialized hierarchy or field of racial positions for their supposed inability or unwillingness to learn English. It also conceals the fact that multiple agencies and organizations funded and coordinated efforts to process Southeast Asian refugees, providing English interpreters and translators when necessary. It completely ignores the English-language abilities already present in at least the first cohort of refugees that was sent to Fort Chaffee.

CHAPTER 3

Mariel Cubans as an "Objectionable Burden" and "Illegal Aliens"

On Sunday, June 1, 1980, at midmorning, about one hundred Cubans gathered on Fourth Avenue inside of Fort Chaffee and approached one of the gates. A Cuban refugee talked to the group, and they dispersed. At noon they "returned with rocks and empty bottles," which they threw at military police and state troopers stationed at the gate—three were injured.[1] At 1:30 p.m. about two hundred Cubans broke through the entrance on Highway 22. "They encountered no resistance, other than verbal commands from Army guards to retreat. Upon reaching the highway, the refugees appeared puzzled and confused until one, shouting '*Libertad!*' struck out toward Barling." The crowd followed him toward a bridge a few hundred yards west of the gate while continuing the recitation of "liberty!" Two state police cars stopped in front of them, then "two troopers, wielding nightsticks, attempted to confront the Cubans until an unidentified Army major, jumping between the troopers and refugees, shouted, 'Don't hit them!'" More state police vehicles blocked the road, but the Cubans ran around the barricade. State troopers and local policemen then formed a "human barricade and managed to turn back about half of the crowd. Officers chased retreating refugees to the front gates, kicking and clubbing the Cubans on the heads, backs and arms. The seventy-five or more refugees who slipped through this barricade were finally halted about fifty yards from the Barling city limit by a line of local police and deputies."[2] By the following week, Fort Chaffee was fortified with "barbed concertina wire and guarded by more than 2,000 federal troops."[3]

From April to October of that year, about 125,000 Cubans left the island after Fidel Castro initiated his "Back Door Policy," which allowed many people wishing to leave the island to do so. The majority arrived in the United States, where they were temporarily detained in Florida, but the US government was unprepared to deal with so many people reaching the shores. Thus, they were sent to processing centers throughout the country. Fort McCoy, Wisconsin, as well as two of the three military camps used in the 1970s to process and hold Vietnamese refugees—Fort Indiantown Gap, Pennsylvania, and Fort Chaffee, Arkansas—were once again utilized for this task, in part because of their prior experience.[4] Arkansans resented the federal government's placement of Cubans in their state more deeply than they had resented the Vietnamese. At first glance it seems that the reactions to the two groups should have mirrored each other, if for no other reason than that in both cases, refugees were fleeing Communist countries at a time when anti-Communist feelings were still prevalent in the United States. Yet negative reaction to the reactivation of the camp and to the Cubans themselves was swift.

To Arkansas and Arkansans, the use of Fort Chaffee as a refugee holding and processing center for the second time in a five-year period was an "objectionable burden," and one which added to the acrimony that had developed between the state and the federal government. The matter was further complicated by negative media coverage of the Cubans that constructed them as murderers, prostitutes, and homosexuals—that is, as criminals and deviants—as well as by protests at each of the camps. The resentment of Arkansans toward Cubans was also influenced by two national trends: economic anxiety and evangelical fundamentalism. The 1970s had been rocked by high unemployment rates and inflation, and the latter peaked in 1980. At such a time, aid to foreigners, even those fleeing a Communist country, stirred bitterness that outsiders were being "taken care of" while Americans were struggling to survive. Some Americans, white men in particular, increasingly saw themselves as victimized by compatriots seeking "special" treatment. For them, the end of de jure segregation and disenfranchisement at the ballot box provided equality. They objected to women, people of color, and gays who sought "special" treatment because it resulted in an encroachment of their rights. At the same time, evangelicals sought to impede what they saw as the slackening of morality and the deterioration of (heteronormative) gender and sexual roles, which they thought was threatening familial structures and the nation's Judeo-Christian values. Their solution was to go back to fundamentalist doctrines and fight against secular culture, and to do so through the political arena, where they could influence policies to secure their vision.

The processing of the Mariel Cubans in Arkansas was a fractious issue due to the protests staged by Cubans as well as questions about their legal status, with concomitant concerns about which authorities could detain them and how much force could be used to prevent them from leaving Fort Chaffee. As the opening description demonstrates, policing of the refugees was shared by the US military, the Military Police, the Arkansas State Police, the Arkansas National Guard, county police departments, and local police departments. While local and state law enforcement officers were more than willing to use extreme force to prevent Cubans from reaching Barling, military officials used only verbal commands to attempt to prevent them from leaving the base. The ensuing dispute encompassed more than simply the orders the US military at Chaffee had or had not received. It ventured into the legal categories used to define this wave of Cubans—detainee, entrant, refugee, or Cuban/Haitian entrant (status pending)—and how the designations affected their rights in the country and the State of Arkansas's responsibility for them.

Whereas Christian virtues and morality were often used by Arkansans to support the resettlement effort and sponsor Vietnamese into communities across the state, this outlook was largely absent with Mariel Cubans. Arkansans had reached the limits of their Christian brotherhood. Again, media representation of the cohort as criminals and homosexuals colored their reception. Arkansas evangelicals, especially Southern Baptists, objected strongly to their sexual orientation and that they were basking in it as opposed to attempting to curtail it. The Moral Majority had been founded the previous year, and the Religious Right was on the rise. These fundamentalists also objected to the expanding role of the federal government and its placement of what they thought were gay men, Communists, and criminals in their communities. In their minds, it demonstrated that the Democratic Party–led federal state embraced low values and was willing to place its native white people in danger. Their Christian rectitude would not have allowed them to aid Arkansas's latest refugees.

In this chapter I begin by analyzing the national mood in more detail and then discuss a letter written by the National Governors' Association to President Jimmy Carter reminding him of the responsibilities of the federal government once it accepted Cubans (and Haitians) into the United States. I then address media representations of the cohort and their role in shaping how Cubans were perceived by the public. From there I focus on the events that led to the June 1 uprising. I close with Governor Clinton's apprehension about whether "federal legislation impose[d] objectionable burdens" on Arkansas as well as subsequent concerns, particularly the Arkansas attorney general's opinions about the legal status of Cubans, assessing the implications for state and local law enforcement officers.

The New Right, Fundamentalist Evangelicals, and Ongoing Recession

The so-called Second Reconstruction, a period in the mid-twentieth century during the long civil rights era, emerged from the federal government's intervention in US southern society as Washington attempted to get the region to accept national changes around issues of equality for African Americans.[5] Many of the transformations resulted from legal challenges taken to courts or mandated through federal legislation, including the *Brown* decisions, the Civil Rights Act, and the Voting Rights Act. Despite violent and brutal episodes and massive resistance, change once again came to the region.[6] Many of the white people who could afford it moved away from the urban centers to the suburbs to maintain their way of life, their segregated lifestyle.[7]

To white people, especially in the working class, the change came at the cost of their standing, because during slavery and segregation, whiteness was a kind of "wage," a benefit that provided certain kinds of privileges and entitlements.[8] In the ensuing decades various politicians tapped into white rage and resentment. Dan Carter points to George Wallace as the first politician to exploit "white backlash" as a means to further his political career.[9] In doing so, Wallace set the precedent for a "politics of rage" that has been central to the rise of the Republican Party. Carter posits that by 1972 the GOP was solidly identified with conservative American values. Subsequent politicians like Nixon and Reagan used such a values system to mobilize a base of supporters against the liberal Democratic Party, which they argued was out of touch with traditional values as it supported African Americans, gay people, and (lazy) welfare recipients.[10]

Much of the conservative push, the rise of the New Right, came from the suburbs, though mobilization occurred at the city, state, regional, and national levels.[11] According to Clive Webb, modern conservatism "utilizes racially encoded concepts to legitimize attacks on minorities. There is a distinct echo of segregationist rhetoric in the New Right defense of states' rights from the tyranny of centralized government."[12] However, the rise of conservative politics was in response not solely to the civil rights movement but also to other struggles for equality, such as the gay rights movement and the feminist movement. Many Americans thought that these and other groups were asking for "special" rights, resented them for the illegitimate claims, and saw themselves as "defenders of the core American values and ideals."[13] According to Jeffrey Dudas, "scholars agree that the resentment that accompanied the rights revolutions of the twentieth century was motivated by self-interested concerns that egalitarian social change threatened existing patterns of privilege," though the arguments were couched within discussions about a "way of life."[14] Dudas argued that "resentful Americans have made sense of, and condemned, redistributive social change by appealing to such ingrained values as states' rights, anti-communism, color blindness, traditional racial and gender stereotypes, evangelical Christianity, free market ideology, and nostalgia for allegedly harmonious communities."[15] The rancor arose from a sense of victimization over groups claiming "special" rights in violation of the legitimate rights of the rest of society.

In Arkansas, as in the region, issues of states' rights were particularly salient, while the expanding evangelical movement also had a strong base within the area's overwhelmingly Protestant communities.[16] By the 1970s fundamentalism was growing, especially in the South, and its proponents were expounding "core concerns for proclaiming the Gospel, its fundamentalist doctrines, its concern for personal piety, and its militant opposition to liberal theology and to secularizing culture" while becoming deeply involved in national politics.[17] Some of the early leadership of the Religious Right was drawn from separatist fundamentalists. According to George Marsden, it was only after white southerners were no longer solidly voting Democratic that "the Religious Right emerged as a national movement with conspicuous southern leadership, best exemplified by Jerry Falwell, Pat Robertson, and James Robison." Marsden also argues that "fundamentalist militancy typically arises when proponents of a once-dominant religious culture feel threatened by trends in the larger surrounding culture." Thus, it is unsurprising that the early Moral Majority emerged from the upper South and took over the Southern Baptist Convention, the United States' largest Protestant denomination.[18]

Marsden also posits that the countercultural revolution of the 1960s was motivated by patriotism and the Vietnam War, but that the transformation of the family and sexuality had a greater impact in shaping 1970s fundamentalism. "Dramatic changes in standards of public decency, aggressive second-wave feminism, gay activism, and challenges to conventional family structures all generated alarm.... This revolution in standards for sexuality and gender coincided with aggressive efforts to secularize public culture," with the 1963 Supreme Court ruling against reading the Bible in public schools a primary symbol.[19] With the exception of Southern Baptists, fundamentalists were more influenced by "opposition to the expansion of the powers of civil government" and "its intrusion on people's lives" than by concern about doctrinal erosion. There was strong opposition to affirmative action, school busing, the Equal Rights

Amendment, and the ban on prayer in schools, which all fueled antigovernment resentment. Marsden concludes that "the Christian School movement had gained immensely in popularity as a practical sort of cultural separatism and as an alternative to government controlled secular education. Especially in the South, one motive was to avoid racial integration but resistance to other cultural trends soon became more basic to the national movement."[20] In Arkansas, Family, Life, America, and God (FLAG) represented the resurgence of an ultraconservatism that decried the Equal Rights Amendment and supported prayer in school.[21]

Along with these issues, the US economy suffered in the 1970s. At that time, James T. Patterson argues, Americans were "conditioned to expect progress[;] they were impatient, and they resisted leaders who asked them to sacrifice. Suspicious of authority figures, they were quick to direct their wrath at Ford, congressional leaders, big businessmen, lawyers—anyone in position of power."[22] After Jimmy Carter took office in 1977, the per capita income improved by an average of 1.8 percent a year while overall per capita income in the South rose from 60 percent of the national average in 1960 to 80 percent in 1980.[23] But inflation soared, and the index of consumer prices rose from 4.9 percent in 1976 to 12.5 percent in 1980; in that year the economy went into another recession. Anthony Campagna summed up the nation's ailments in the following way: "The economy was floundering, and the political atmosphere was contentious. The nation was in the grip of stagflation, and the mood of the public was gloomy. Having just emerged from a sharp recession, the economy did not appear to be growing strongly enough, and unemployment was still hovering around 7.5%."[24] In response, Carter supported fiscal restraint, which often meant cutting expansive spending programs and attempting to persuade unions to reduce their demands for raises.[25] Although the South objected to federal oversight, the region was more than willing to receive federal largesse. In 1979, for example, it received more in federal aid than it contributed to tax revenues ($1.24 received per every $1 sent).[26] Arkansas, however, remained one of the poorest states, and many of its people depended on federally subsidized programs for subsistence.

Communists, Criminals, and Homosexuals: Mariel Cubans as a Dangerous Triumvirate

It was during this period of economic instability and cultural upheaval that Castro announced he would allow an unrestricted number of Cubans to leave the island. When he made the announcement, on April 20, the US press reacted positively, seeing these Cubans as only the latest cohort fleeing the Communist regime. Anticommunism was still a potent point of mobilization.[27] These Cubans, raised under Castro's leadership, were "children of the revolution," and yet they wanted to leave the island; many in the United States viewed the prospect of people "voting with their feet" as a clear rebuke of communism.

The two prior "waves" of exiles from Cuba had consisted of upper-class and middle-class people: professionals, business owners, managers, and skilled workers who were overwhelmingly white. The first to leave the island did so soon after Castro took power or immediately after he nationalized industry (1960–1964). Many of them were able to transfer their savings to the United States, while others were rehired by the US companies that had employed them in Cuba. When the second cohort (1965–1974) arrived, many of its small merchants and skilled or semi-skilled workers were hired by Cuban-born business owners. However, social class distinctions from the island were transferred to the United States; for example, those who had belonged to the five most exclusive yacht and country clubs in Havana founded a club in Miami and nicknamed it "The Big Five."[28] Cuban exiles in the United States initially embraced those leaving from Mariel with enthusiasm, but when the press began reporting that they were social deviants, many Cuban Americans distanced themselves, fearing that the new cohort would tarnish the reputation of Cubans in the United States as "golden exiles." Unlike their predecessors, this group of Cubans was working-class and less white; close to 71 percent were blue-collar workers, and Blacks or Mulattos made up more than 20 percent of the new arrivals.[29]

The media coverage of the Mariel Cubans changed quickly after Castro cast them as criminals, delinquents, and parasites in an effort to discredit the group.[30] Brian Hufker and Gray Cavender argue that the positive April news stories were followed in May by negative ones as the press began to focus on criminality, mental illness, and homosexuality as the three primary deviant themes.[31] Susana Peña concluded that, consequently, "racialization, class stigma, and sexual deviance were thus embedded in coverage of the Mariel migration, reinforcing the notion that these migrants were no loss to Cuba and posed a potential problem for the United States."[32] In the end, however, fewer than 2 percent of the Cubans from Mariel were judged serious criminals and denied asylum.[33] John Borneman argues that "what is most perverse about the classification of the Marielitos is that we have an odd actual convergence 'in practice' of three major American demons—'communists,' 'criminals,' and 'homosexuals'—which usually converge only in the mind."[34] He further argues: "A seemingly political threat is actually perceived as if it were a sexual one, where political boundaries are perceived as if—i.e., felt like—they are boundaries of the body."[35] This is more the case in a country such as the United States, where immigration laws are structured in terms of kinship—where family reunification is generally of the utmost importance and the law is aimed at facilitating the replication of heteronormative families. Communities are often conceived as a body that needs to be taken care of and protected, especially from certain outsiders. Protection of "a way of life" often takes on these tones, as was the case during the integration of Central High School, when the community was in danger of being "contaminated" by the federal government and African Americans. In 1980 the threat came from gay Communist criminals, many of whom were also Black or of mixed race.

In the past the United States has used sexual, gender, and moral norms to exclude certain groups from entering the country, including prostitutes and homosexuals.[36] However, the authorities never invoked the Immigration and Nationality Act of 1952 (the McCarran-Walter Act), which excluded homosexuals based on a framework of "psychopathic personality or a mental defect," against the Mariel Cubans.[37] According to Lourdes Arguelles and Rudy Rich, "the Cuban gay immigration posed a difficult contradiction for the US government, pitting its strong desire for a real advantage in the Cold War against its equally strong homophobia. Then, as now, anticommunism won out. Those fleeing the socialist revolution were welcomed despite their frequently open homosexuality."[38] Less than a year prior to the Mariel boatlift, the Public Health Service had ceased to use homosexuality as a "Class A medical exclusion," and in September 1980 David Crosland, the acting Immigration and Naturalization Service (INS) commissioner, sent a memorandum that "the Department of Justice [DOJ] and INS were to exclude homosexuals entering the United States, but 'solely upon the voluntary admission by the alien that he or she is homosexual.' Aliens making an 'unsolicited, unambiguous admission of homosexuality' and those so identified by a third party or parties would undergo secondary inspection."[39] At the secondary screening they were only to be asked if they were gay. If they answered in the negative, they were released; if they answered in the positive, they were to sign an admission, and exclusion procedures would be initiated.[40] It is unclear how closely these rules were followed during the processing of Mariel Cubans. One man, for example, could not recall whether federal officials asked him about his sexual orientation, but Peña posits that local state and federal officials "demonstrated a strong yet inconsistently focused interest in the sexuality of Mariel immigrants."[41]

Obtaining an accurate number of how many gay men and women left Cuba during the Mariel boatlift is difficult. At that time Judy Weiss, Federal Emergency Management Agency (FEMA) spokesperson, said, "I don't think there are any accurate statistics at all on this issue. A refugee's sexual preference is not one of those questions that is part of our system of interrogation here." Dorothy Riccio, a police officer from Albuquerque who volunteered for thirty days at Fort Chaffee, estimated that only four hundred refugees were gay, but that is on the lower end of estimates. A military corporal on guard duty at Chaffee said the government did not try to sort people, but as everyone rearranged themselves, some barracks ended up with more gay men.[42] The *Chaffee—Resettlement, Consolidation* report notes that many gay men self-segregated, giving them a high level of visibility which in turn fueled media estimates that up to 20,000 of the refugees were gay. For example, a *Washington Post* article in July claimed US and private agency sources declared that up to 50 percent of the 40,000 Cubans in the centers were gay.[43] The report notes that the Cuban-Haitian Task Force (CHTF) estimated 1,000 self-identified as gay and takes care to state that it is "a figure well within the expected distribution of homosexuals in any large population."[44] A later report from the CHTF stated that 2,500 gay men had arrived.[45] Bill Traugh, director of FEMA at Chaffee, said, "All we know is that we have a lot of gay people here among our 10,179 remaining refugees."[46] In the same article, however, he is also quoted as saying that those who were openly gay self-segregated into two barracks, each holding up to 125 people. If that was the case, then Fort Chaffee's gay population was 250, making them about 2.5 percent of the camp's population. The caveat was that those were the people who "acknowledged" their homosexuality; the suggestion was that many disavowed it.[47] Cubans might also have been confused as to whether they needed to avow or disavow their sexual orientation; because many used their homosexuality to get out of Cuba and perceived the United States to be more liberal, they were unaware that sexual orientation could be used to deny their entry.[48]

Cubans hoping to pick up their relatives had other theories as to why there were so many gay men in this cohort of refugees. Francisco Vasquez Ruiz explained, "In Cuba, a homosexual is classified as '*peligrosidad.*' When Castro began to let *peligrosidad* prisoners leave for America, I knew heterosexual men who went so far as to shave their eyebrows and put on dresses, pretending to be homosexuals in their attempt to be declared *peligrosidad*.[49] Even "obviously" gay men in Cuba played up their homosexuality in order to be granted an exit permit by the government. For example, one man who had been told he was too "obviously" gay to be a teacher made sure to wear "the gayest outfit he could find," which included a flowery shirt and a snugly fitting chain, for his interview with the Cuban police.[50] Attempting to figure out accurate numbers for queer migrants is a formidable task because, as Eithne Luibhéid argues, this group "in many ways comprise[s] 'impossible subjects' with unrepresentable histories that exceed existing categories."[51] Because sexual orientation or nonnormative gender identity is used to exclude immigrants from entering the United States, it is a category that cannot be accurately represented. It is impossible to determine how many gay men and lesbians lived in Chaffee, though as I noted before, at least two barracks housed gay people.

When Mariel Cubans arrived in Fort Chaffee on May 9, "the oblong white exteriors were barely visible in the dusk, giving these first 128 refugees a glimpse of what would become their first home in the United States. The men, mostly ranging from 20 to 40 years of age, would be joined in coming days by more than 19,000 of their countrymen, including several thousand women and 220 minors, temporarily forming the 11th largest city in Arkansas."[52] This reflected the trend in May in which 74 percent of arrivals were men and 26 percent women; 18 percent of the total were children (younger than eighteen years old).[53] These demographics added to the difficulty of finding sponsors, as Americans were more likely to sponsor families than single men.[54] For Arkansans, Mariel men constituted a threatening triumvirate—criminal/homosexual/communist—like they did for many other Americans across the nation. Race also played a significant role in how Arkansas constructed and received the refugees. Gastón Fernandez estimated that Fort Chaffee's nonwhite population was nearly double the cohort average at nearly 40 percent, with almost 30 percent Black and 7 percent Mulatto.[55] This meant that "Arkansas's 11th largest city" was also almost half nonwhite, a significant demographic change in northwest Arkansas's overwhelmingly white landscape, while the possibility that so many gay men were in their community also alarmed area residents.[56] Before Arkansans had a chance to panic about the backgrounds of the group, however, the primary concern was the federal government's responsibility to the state.

Arkansas's Assistance to the Federal Government

Federal authorities informed Governor Clinton that Fort Chaffee had been selected as a refugee processing center on May 7, 1980—only two days before Cubans arrived in the state and just a few days past the five-year anniversary of the arrival date of Vietnamese.[57] Upon receipt of the news, he released a statement to the press asserting that he knew all Arkansans understood the Cubans' desire for freedom, especially as they fled from a Communist dictatorship. In many ways, this statement was similar to the one Governor Pryor had made when Vietnamese refugees arrived; Pryor said that Arkansans understood their experience and that there was a long tradition in the state and the nation of sharing with others.[58] Yet the messages were different in tone. Most notably, Pryor's address was infused with Christian feeling through his reference that Arkansans tried to live by the biblical admonition to treat others the way they want to be treated.[59] Unlike Pryor, who focused greatly on the refugees and their transition, Clinton centered on the role of the federal government, talking about how it "imposed" the burden and "responsibilities" on Arkansas, its officials, and its people:

> The Cuban refugees who are now temporarily housed in Florida came to this country in flight from a Communist dictatorship. I know that everyone in this state sympathizes and identifies with them in their desire for freedom. I will do all I can to fulfill whatever responsibilities the President imposes upon Arkansas to facilitate the refugees' resettlement in this country. I have ordered all appropriate state agencies to co-operate with Federal officials in working out details of the resettlement at Fort Chaffee.[60]

The authority the federal government exercised in accepting Cubans and placing them at their discretion in various states of the Union is a role that Clinton and other governors did not forget.

By the end of the month John P. Lagomarcino, general counsel and legislative director of the National Governors' Association, had written a letter to Gene Eidenberg, deputy assistant to the president for intergovernmental affairs, reminding the federal government of its responsibilities in providing funds for all the expenses associated with Cubans and Haitians. During this time hundreds of Haitians were arriving on US shores, being detained, and getting sent back to their country despite its repressive dictatorship, while Cubans were automatically allowed to stay. The immigration policy toward Haitians had been unfair since Lyndon Johnson's administration, and by 1980 Haitians had "acquired the dubious distinction of having the highest rejection rate of political asylum applicants" because the INS constructed them as economic migrants and deported them despite testimony of political persecution.[61] The Haitian Refugee Center worked tirelessly to attempt to get them equal treatment, and federal courts often ordered INS to respect Haitians' rights and give them a fair hearing. Despite ongoing legal challenges, the INS kept its track record of denying Haitians applications for asylum. In 1980 Jesse Jackson, the Congressional Black Caucus, and Senator Edward Kennedy, among others, fought to ensure that Haitians received the same treatment as Cubans.[62] A new US District Court decision validated their struggles; Judge James King found that the INS continually committed "a wholesale violation of due process" in their concerted efforts to deny entrance to Haitians and ordered that the facts be considered in each application.[63] Finally, President Carter formed the CHTF, which "promised equal treatment" for both groups. However, the victory was short-lived with the election of Ronald Reagan, who quickly implemented an effort to keep Haitians out by interdicting boats.[64]

The ongoing arrival of Cubans and Haitians provided the context in which Lagomarcino wrote to the Carter administration. The letter opens in a tone similar to a parental admonition to children about taking responsibility for their actions: "The decision to admit Cubans and Haitians to the United States—when, where, and how many, under what conditions, and with what status—or a decision to allow them to remain once they have arrived, are unquestionably federal decisions. But decisions made fully by the federal government carry with them responsibilities which must be borne by the federal government."[65] Lagomarcino further noted that the National Governors' Association "recognize[d] that the federal government is determining the formal status of the newly arrived Cubans and Haitians. Regardless of the decision made in this matter, the obligation of the federal government to fully cover the costs of services and assistance to the Cubans and Haitians during their first years in the United States remains unchanged."[66]

Lagomarcino's reference to "the formal status" of Cubans and Haitians gestured to the ongoing processes of defining the legal status these national groups would hold within the US legal landscape. The designation the groups received would be important, because each status allowed certain federal benefits and limitations and told state governments the programs and funds for which the groups were eligible. Lagomarcino listed five areas in which "virtually all Cubans and Haitians will need some services or assistance from government": "income security," "health," "social services," "employment and training," and "education."⁶⁷ Under "income security" the association noted that while many Cubans and Haitians would be eligible for "federal, state-federal, and state assistance programs," nearly 40 percent were young, single males who would be ineligible under federal guidelines. They proposed that "categorical limitations" should be waived for "Cubans and Haitians so that assistance costs for these persons are fully federally covered." In other words, they advocated for granting these arrivals permission to obtain services from assistance programs, but as a means of ensuring that the federal government paid for such expenses. Under "social services" they would be eligible for Title XX, but most states had already exhausted their funds; "consequently, there is not room whatsoever in most states for purchasing or providing additional services under Title XX unless desperately needed services now being provided to other vulnerable populations are halted or severely cut."⁶⁸ A similar scenario awaited "employment and training," since the Comprehensive Employment and Training Act (CETA) Titles II-D and VI had few vacant slots, and severe cuts had been proposed for the following year. Finally, children and many adults would also enroll in local public schools, and the National Governors' Association estimated that on average they would require an additional $1,000 per person.

The purpose of the letter was at least twofold: (1) to remind the federal government of their decisions and responsibilities and (2) to remind them that state budgets were already strained. Lagomarcino affirmed:

> State governments recognize that, in the long run, there will be increased costs to state and local governments attributable to the Cubans and Haitians approximately equivalent to the costs of services to similar numbers of their general population. We accept this responsibility and are fully prepared to do our part to assist these Cubans and Haitians in becoming productive citizens. But the acute and disproportionate needs of the vast majority of these people for intensive assistance in the areas noted above is something which state governments should not be asked to finance and which they cannot finance now when, simultaneously we are experiencing severe cutbacks in federal aid for many of the programs which would provide assistance. Additionally, the recession is reducing state revenues and increasing the need for services among current residents.⁶⁹

Lagomarcino alluded to Carter's fiscal restraint approach to inflation when he referenced the cutbacks to Social Security's Title XX and job training and explicitly contrasted Cubans' and Haitians' well-being with average and needy Americans who required the same services as these entrants. Both programs would likely be essential in Arkansas, as the state remained at the bottom of national personal income and comparative rates of poverty through the 1990s.[70] The governors' fears, however, were anticipatory, since they did not know how many Cubans and Haitians would end up in each of their states. Arkansans had also feared Vietnamese refugees on economic grounds, arguing that they would either take much-needed jobs or live off of the welfare rolls; however, by 1980 this apprehension had proved unfounded.[71]

Immigration opponents frequently argue that foreign-born workers are the root cause for the denial and elimination of services to US native-born people.[72] This fits within the framework of victimization, because the implication or assumption is that if there were not so many immigrants using the services, the system would not be overburdened and on the brink of collapse. In this way, foreigners deprive natives of their birthright. Frank White, a former Democrat who filed as a Republican to challenge Clinton for the governor's office, said as much in an interview: "The people in Arkansas question severely the wisdom of spending $385 million to have an unlimited refugee program from Cuba and Haiti at a time when we have unemployment. These people have a language barrier and they're going to be on welfare and food stamps and require support of the federal and state government."[73] The issue, however, is also racialized, as African Americans are frequently accused of partaking too much from the system, especially welfare.[74] The "welfare queen" famously portrayed by Ronald Reagan is frequently used as "the public identity of all welfare recipients" according to Ange-Marie Hancock, but it is shorthand for biologically overproductive Black women who then expect the federal government to pay to maintain their children. The letter is also a subtler version of accusations state governors would make in the 1990s about the failure of the federal government to secure the US-Mexico border and how that breakdown impacted their states and the well-being of their constituents. Perhaps the best example of this tactic came from California Governor Pete Wilson, who sued the federal government to pay for expenses his state incurred due to failed federal law enforcement of the border.[75] While Arkansas, Pennsylvania, and Wisconsin governors anticipated their financial concerns, none foresaw the high levels of anxiety that would encompass their states, their constituents, and the refugees.

Mounting Anxieties, Tensions, and Frustrations: "Castro Agents," Protests, and *Libertad!*

On May 19, only ten days after the first refugees arrived, Clinton released a press statement publicizing his distress over the security at Fort Chaffee. That same day Bill Tidball, coordinator for FEMA, reported that the military police (MP) were on stations, that there were foot patrols along the perimeter, and that Cubans were going off base for cigarettes.[76] In order to keep Cubans in, more cigarettes were to be provided and announcements made through a loudspeaker that if they went off base their processing would be delayed. Governor Clinton used state and local law enforcement to secure the perimeter around the camp, but according to the Fort Chaffee Task Force Situation Reports (SITREP), there were only a few "notable incidents" during the days leading up to May 19, none of which included refugees leaving the base or having serious altercations with military personnel.[77] Nevertheless, Clinton talked with local officials regarding "the concern of citizens in the area about problems which could be caused by some of the refugee population at Fort Chaffee."[78] The governor further stated that "this is a Federal problem and the Federal Government must take responsibility for providing more adequate security. Until it does, we will provide whatever assistance is necessary from the state to enable the local officials to do the job."[79] He spoke with Sebastian County Sheriff Bill Cauthron, Arkansas State Police (ASP) Director Colonel Doug Harp, and other local law enforcement officials to "maintain adequate 24-hour-a-day security." Major General Jimmie "Red" Jones, the adjutant general of Arkansas, recommended two courses of action. First, he suggested reinforcing the ASP with noncommissioned officers of the Arkansas National Guard to allow the state police to reassign personnel to the Troop H area near Fort Chaffee. The state military could also provide sedans to patrol the roads and highways surrounding the base. Second, Jones's office had been in contact with Lieutenant Colonel Moye of the ASP, who assigned one additional sergeant and four men to Troop H to aid in patrolling duties.[80] However, the federal government agreed to provide more security personnel only after the June 1 uprising.[81]

By the end of May there were already concerns about the kind of force the military could use to impede Cubans from leaving the base. For example, a notation from the "military" section of a May 27 meeting about security at Fort Chaffee stated that the military had not received orders from the Pentagon giving them additional security. However, the US attorney told Clinton's staff that the DOJ gave the military the order to maintain security.[82] At that point, the city, state, and county law enforcement officials were still patrolling the area. Lieutenant Colonel A. T. Brainerd, a spokesman at Fort Chaffee, said that security was adequate, adding, "Cubans are not actually incarcerated here. After all, we're not running a concentration camp."[83] But area residents were afraid because "for a while a year ago the average Arkansan envisioned the Cubans in Arkansas as nothing more than a pack of criminals."[84] Jack Moseley, the editor of a Fort Smith newspaper, said, "No one was very high on the Cubans. It was a totally different reaction than to the Vietnamese who were out there in the 1970s."[85]

Local nerves were set on edge based in part on the negative media reports. Bill McAda, a spokesman for FEMA, attempted to address these reports when he told reporters that thieves, murderers, and psychopaths did not form the majority of these Cubans. It was true that many had been to jail in Cuba, but only because they had been deemed a threat to the Cuban government.[86] Arkansans were unaware that in order to leave the island Cubans had to apply for an exit permit and obtain a *carta de escoria* ("dreg" letter) in which they publicly confessed to crimes they supposedly committed.[87] Among the so-called criminals were former political prisoners or other Cubans who had been sent to jail for participating in the black market, running an illegal business, or other offenses which were misdemeanors within the United States.[88] McAda implied that if they were a threat to the Cuban government then they were anti-Communist and thus held a political perspective most Americans supported. He also noted that he and other officials had not found drugs in Fort Chaffee and had no knowledge about drugs being present in the camp, despite media reports.[89]

On the night of Monday, May 26, about 350 Cubans protesting their detention broke through the southwest gate and into the neighboring community of Jenny Lind after somebody yelled "Liberty!" According to one report, the military and park police did not attempt to stop them because of "questions about the military police's authority over civilians."[90] The Jenny Lind community is a subsection of the Barling area. Its population in 1980 was 3,761 (unfortunately, the 1980 Census did not list the racial breakdown of the town). In 1990 the population grew to 4,078, with white people constituting 90 percent and African Americans 1.2 percent, or 48 people.[91] Barling and its Jenny Lind area were overwhelmingly white, like the majority of northwest Arkansas, and Cubans in Fort Chaffee quintupled the town's population while its nearly 7,600 Black and Mulatto people were double the size of the town.

To Arkansans, Cubans were dangerous criminals, and their Blackness only added to residents' fears. The racial and ethnic backgrounds of Mariel Cubans were rarely discussed; however, that did not mean they did not play a role in how the group was racialized nationally and locally. For example, although only about 20 percent of the cohort was Black or Mulatto, 75 percent of the 6,547 Cubans left at Fort Chaffee at the end of 1980 fit the category, and 93 percent of them were single men, demonstrating the reluctance of Americans to sponsor single Black men. By March 1981, only 402 Cubans had found sponsors in the state, as opposed to the 500 or so Vietnamese sponsored into the northwest Arkansas area alone.[92] In contrast to the Southeast Asian community that grew after sponsorship, Cubans largely left the area. By 2001 only about 15 refugees from Mariel lived in the area. Billye and Don Carter, a Black couple who sponsored several Cubans, said people were fearful, but racism also played a part. Billye Carter said people reacted differently to the Black Cubans than to the white ones, while Don Carter stated that "after the darker-skinned Cubans came, people started getting leery and the sponsorships stopped."[93]

A local historian recalled that people were "scared to death" and "carrying guns." But McAda compared the Cubans' energy to a college "panty raid," though Arkansans claimed that they ran through the streets shouting threatening slogans such as "Come on, Castro, let's kill some Americans." Locals fired shots into the air as the refugees approached the houses, even though Cauthron said "there seemingly were no overt acts on the part of the refugees to damage any property."[94] McAda reminded Arkansans that the Cubans had come to the United States for freedom and that "no citizen has been threatened or harmed in any way."[95] However, Arkansans in Jenny Lind and other communities were outraged at his response. The situation was fanned by the press on the day of the Arkansas Democratic Primary, and Governor Clinton immediately labeled the security at Fort Chaffee "totally inadequate."[96] He pleaded with the federal government to handle the situation by sending more personnel: "They're going to have to send those soldiers in there, and they're going to have to establish a perimeter of mobility more narrowly restricted than the 72,000 acres of Fort Chaffee."[97] He ordered 64 Army National Guards from the Second Battalion 142nd Artillery Brigade and later another 140 guards to assist local and county law enforcement officials. For the rest of the week, life at Fort Chaffee proceeded without major incidents. On the afternoon of Friday, May 30, about 30 Cubans assembled on Fourth Avenue roughly a thousand yards from the gates. They were threatening a hunger strike to protest their slow processing; however, camp officials were able to calm them down. Their confinement did not make sense to them, because they knew their predecessors had not faced such an experience.[98]

The rate of processing was one of the key and volatile issues at Fort Chaffee during the summer of 1980. All the parties involved—Cubans from the Mariel boatlift and volunteer agencies inside the camp, and Cuban Americans and Arkansans outside of it—were getting anxious about the slow processing rate, but none more so than the refugees themselves. McAda said that when FEMA was given the task of finding sponsors for Cubans, the agency expected them to be cleared by the INS and health officials as the Vietnamese had been, as opposed to arriving unprocessed. Moreover, FEMA had also expected 80 percent of the refugees sent to Fort Chaffee to be families and only 20 percent to be single males, but instead the percentages were reversed, which made finding sponsors more difficult. Dave Lewis, the head of the United States Catholic Conference (USCC), one of the largest volunteer agencies responsible for finding sponsors, said that delays were due to INS processing. By early June the USCC had registered about 9,500 of the Cubans and found sponsors for 4,500, but they had yet to get clearance from immigration officials. Federal officials countered that it was not due to their screening procedures but because of a lack of sponsors.[99]

After the Carter administration formed the CHTF, twelve federal agencies became involved and worked with seven volunteer agencies, most of which had experience with Southeast Asian resettlement efforts in 1975.[100] A report by the Department of Health and Human Services (DHHS), the federal agency in charge at the end of 1980 and which served as the umbrella for the CHTF, stated that nine agencies were involved in resettling Cubans "without direct family ties in the United States, and all those processed through the resettlement camps."[101] In addition to the USCC, the Church World Service, the International Rescue Committee, the World Relief Rescue Service, the Lutheran Immigration Refugee Service, the Southern Baptist Convention, the Hebrew Immigration Aid Society, the American Council for Nationalities Service, and the Tolstoy Foundation helped to process and resettle 116,349 Cubans. Part of the reason that the paperwork took such a long time was that each agency had unique forms a refugee needed to fill out (some were even supposed to be updated daily). Some of the volunteers also had limited Spanish ability, and information was often lost or rearranged in translation.[102] Joe Daly, the assistant operations officer at Fort Chaffee, outlined the procedure as it took place in mid-May: first, a medical screening with hospitalization, if required; an "alien number" assignment; initial personal questionnaire and screening;

placement in barracks; a more detailed screening by INS with information checked in Washington; a more thorough medical screening conducted by federal officials; and finally, possibly a screening by the FBI or the CIA.[103] By the end of May, more than 19,000 Cubans had been at Fort Chaffee since midmonth, but only 767 had actually left the base to join their sponsors. What Cubans did not know was that 15,913 of them had been cleared by the DHHS, the INS had interviewed nearly 8,400, and about 2,500 had been cleared for relocation.[104]

To the Cubans it looked as though nearly nothing was being done to process their departure. One Cuban refugee expressed his frustration with the process as follows:

> They [federal officials] tell me to get on this plane [in Florida] and we will go to Arkansas for one week only. But it took ten days to fill out all government papers, to get myself clear with Immigration, with Health Services. Then they say, "Wait some more time," so I wait. Now, I am here three weeks and the government tells me I must continue to wait. I have family I want to see here in America. I have a job waiting for me in New Jersey. I have a sister at Eglin Air Force Base camp. Why should I wait any longer?[105]

Cuban American relatives waiting outside of the camp were also getting anxious about how long it was taking government officials to process the cohort. At various points throughout May they gathered outside of Fort Chaffee and called in to their relatives, "You've got to get out of there. They can't keep you!" The process that those from the boatlift were subjected to was in sharp contrast to the treatment previous Cuban exiles received during the height of the US "open door" policy, and because of that history, their detention seemed arbitrary.[106] The process reflected the changes in US immigration policies as well as the White House's poor control over the administration of the program. In fact, the administration was cautious about how to classify Cubans and Haitians because they did not want to encourage Mexicans, Salvadorans, Nicaraguans, or other groups from Latin America and the Caribbean to seek shelter in the United States.[107] Part of the reason the relatives of the Cuban refugees were apprehensive was due to rumors that drugs, gambling, and homosexuality were rampant in the camp. Moraisa Martinez declared, "We want our decent people out of there. Did you know there are many, many decent people forced to live in that camp?"[108] With her declaration, Martinez implicitly acknowledged that there were also bad people in Chaffee, but she was concerned about her relatives, who were good people.

The rhetoric that Cuban Americans and Cubans from Mariel used to discuss the cohort drew from and was a response to the negative media coverage portraying the new arrivals as criminals and deviants. While the Cuban American community at first went as far as renting boats and going to Cuba to pick up family members, they began to distance themselves from most of the Mariel Cubans after media coverage became negative.[109] Within Fort Chaffee, Cubans (with the help of the Department of the Army) published a newspaper, *La Vida Nueva*, from May 10 through November 1980 and had more than fifteen reporters who discussed events at the camp and around the world. The issues from May 27 through June 10 had front-page articles and editorials chastising "impatient" Cubans for the various protests and the demonstrations that escalated to breaking the camp perimeter, as well as for forgetting what life was like in Cuba. They reminded readers that such actions served only to mar the group's image nationally and internationally. One writer, Ruben Tormo Bravo, stated, "It appears you have forgotten what we went through in Cuba. Many of us were prisoners and it does not need to be said that we all know the repressive tools used in those 'prisons.'" Bravo continued, "We were never treated in such a respectful way, so kindly. . . . They are treating us like human beings, without distinctions to race or class. Nevertheless, a tiny group of 'strongmen,' politicos without a cause, troublemakers and who knows, invisible agents of Castro, have planted that classification within the Cuban Colony that's sheltered in the Fort."[110] Bravo wrote at length about the great organization of the United States, that Cubans were "immigrants who entered the country illegally" ("nosotros somos Inmigrantes que hemos entrado al Pais de forma illegal"), and that they had to remember the Cold War, which mandated that the "great powers" be careful about whom they let in.

A theme throughout much of the newspaper's run was that of "Castro agents" as the instigators of chaos and destruction on the base. An article published on May 28 acknowledges that there were many impatient people, but that engaging in "truly embarrassing attitudes" ("actitudes realmente vergonzosas") only damaged their cause. Moreover, the "United States has the right to protect its people against the irreparable damages that uncontrolled immigration always brings about." The author says that Castro had let them go in order to be a burden to the United States, and that by acting in ways which violated the simplest standards of civility, they were doing his job for him. Moreover, there were "Castro agents" at Fort Chaffee, but in insignificant numbers. The author concludes the article by writing, "Only a perfect imbecile or Castro agent could be impatient" given all the accommodations provided for them at the base.[111] After the June 1 break, the newspaper reported proudly on the Cuban "vigilantes" who helped to reestablish order and prevent more property damage; they wore white armbands to be easily identified by federal, state, and local officials on the scene. The local and state press also reported on the group.[112] Overall, *La Vida Nueva* encouraged Cubans to demonstrate how "grateful" and "educated" they were and provided civic lessons to teach them how to be good and valuable citizens. The overwhelming majority of people interviewed supported all the raids, inspections, and curfews implemented by the military and law enforcement officers in the months after June 1.

La Vida Nueva's tone provides insight into camp life. Cubans were suspicious of each other, and they accepted there were "criminal elements" and policed each other's behaviors as best they could. There were some people who assaulted men, women, and children, so Cubans also had to protect themselves to the best of their ability. The situation resulted from a lack of centrally organized processing and clearly defined law enforcement order. When Cubans broke camp laws or built some weapons, it served as confirmation to those who believed that they were indeed criminals. There was little to no understanding of how the problems were a reflection of the larger institutions not doing their jobs. Bureaucratic infighting often led to neither state governments nor federal offices taking responsibility for the Cubans' welfare, while law enforcement officials continued to be confused about their jurisdiction or refused to get involved.[113]

The events that occurred during *El Domingo*, as the uprising came to be called by Cubans, came from tensions that had built up for weeks. The governor and other state and local officials were upset about the lack of security, Cubans were suspicious of each other as "Castro agents," and Cuban Americans were becoming exasperated with the wait to be released. On Saturday, May 31, Cubans staged another protest. After the Cubans stood their ground, FEMA authorities asked Victor Valdez, a refugee at Fort Chaffee, to calm the dissenters as he had done on two previous occasions. Valdez spoke with the crowd for fifteen minutes and persuaded them to go back inside their designated area. He told his peers they needed to understand that the US government was attempting to process them quickly, but that it was a chaotic task. Valdez asked one of the men in the crowd how long he had waited for the opportunity to move to the United States. The man replied, "For 21 years—ever since Fidel." Valdez responded, "So you waited 21 years to come here. Surely you can wait 21 more days or so to enter a country that offers you a new life." Valdez diffused the situation, but the next day he told camp authorities that he would no longer be a peacemaker; he also urged the INS to speed up processing before Cubans took action, which he thought would happen "in a few days."[114]

The clash occurred on a Sunday and became a serious point of contention between Arkansas's state government and the federal government, as each understood the event and its causes in different ways. One photo shows the Cubans leaving Fort Chaffee; it appears that they were all men who were unarmed. The picture is of poor quality so that smaller weapons such as rocks would be harder to spot, but the men look as though they are speed walking, perhaps jogging, toward a destination that makes them happy. The crowd does not look enraged. Nevertheless, they had broken through the boundaries established by the military and were headed into Barling until they were stopped by the officers. After the afternoon skirmish another group, "bolstered by the military's ineffective response to gate-crashers," started throwing rocks at MPs across the highway, who shielded themselves with their cars. The situation continued to escalate until 6:20 p.m., "when the troopers, in defense, finally opened fire with pistols and shotguns, wounding three Cubans and clubbing another. In ten minutes, federal authorities and soldiers, armed with tear gas and clubs, finally forced the hostile refugees back inside Chaffee's gates."[115] At 8 p.m. about a thousand Cubans headed toward the front gate, but the MPs responded by forming a line five deep; upon seeing the line, the refugees dispersed into the compound.

At 8:30 p.m. Major Brian McWilliams, Fort Chaffee's information officer, reported that everything was calm as Cubans started building fires to make their coffee. Apparently, the refugees insisted on cooking inside the wooden barracks, despite being told it was dangerous.[116] Nine MPs sent to put out the unauthorized fires had to take cover and called for reinforcements as Cubans assaulted them with bricks and stones:

> In minutes, the assault grew out of control as more than a thousand frustrated Cubans went on a rampage through the compound overturning guard stations and setting fire to four buildings, including three mess halls. As MPs roamed through the area attempting to corral rioters they were joined by large numbers of refugees, each wearing a white arm band for identity as a non-combatant vowing to hunt down "those Communist agitators."[117]

The outbreak subsided by 10:30 p.m. Later that night McAda said he did not know of any law enforcement officials who had been injured (Bob Plunkett, an Arkansas journalist, noted that more than fifty were hurt) and could not explain why four Cubans were sent to a hospital in Fort Smith with gunshots and other wounds. The events at Fort Chaffee greatly outraged the surrounding community, which "all agreed their town would have been overrun with refugees had it not been for the last-ditch stand made by local police and sheriff's deputies."[118]

After the uprising, the military put up concertina wire, and more than two thousand federal troops were stationed at Fort Chaffee to watch over the camp.[119] A map of the camp shows some of the ways in which it was divided between families, youths, protective custody, and the stockade. Unfortunately, it does not indicate where the gay barracks were located or the position of Fourth Avenue, which would provide an understanding of how the Cubans organized themselves, since they often altered the arrangements that were provided to them.

The reasons given for the June 1 uprising depend on who answers the question. Many Cubans in Fort Chaffee attributed it to "Castro agents" and naïve compatriots who were persuaded by demagogues; local residents were certain all the Cubans were criminals who threatened their communities and their lives and immediately needed to be removed from the state; local, state, and federal officials interpreted the events within those extremes, which caused even more tension between the state and the federal government. It had been offensive that Arkansas was chosen without a consultation with Governor Clinton, Senators Pryor and Dale Bumpers, and Representative Hammerschmidt, but the events of *El Domingo* had endangered Arkansan lives. To them it proved how little Washington cared about Arkansas and its people. When Clinton had petitioned that security be increased two weeks prior to no avail, it demonstrated to them that the federal government and particularly the Carter White House were willing to risk American lives for people that were dangerous. Arkansans regarded the Cubans in Fort Chaffee as a traumatic experience; they were the victims of the federal government and a "mob of maniacs" out to kill Americans, and the only reason they survived is because of the valiant efforts of the local and state police.

Does Federal Legislation Impose "Objectionable Burdens on Our State"?

Clinton arrived at Fort Chaffee in the early hours of June 2 and said he was "furious" over the "long disputed" question of whether the military could use force to control the refugees.[120] At a meeting with outraged Barling residents the next day, he defended himself by placing the failure squarely on the shoulders of President Carter and, by extension, the federal government: "In spite of what I was told on election day by the highest authority at the White House, there was still no security on that Fort, and the only thing between you and it were the State Police, who risked themselves to protect you."¹²¹ Clinton's finger-pointing, however, fell short of the accusations made by Senator David Pryor, who said that the White House's attitude was "almost contemptuous" and that President Carter seemed "totally indifferent" to Arkansans.¹²² Senator Bumpers added that his warnings of the dire situation had gone unheeded: "I sent a telegram to the president Thursday and I told them [the Carter administration] it was a powderkeg, but no one at the White House paid much attention."¹²³

The president's assistant Gene Eidenberg, who went to Fort Chaffee at Clinton's insistence, told reporters that he was "appalled" that the order for tougher security measures had not been carried out.¹²⁴ During that visit he and Clinton implemented a policy of "reasonable but not lethal force" to control the refugees, in which "hard-core agitators" were to be removed to federal detention. Clinton eventually understood the situation as a miscommunication, that "somehow in the chain of command of the military the message didn't get down" because the White House and the DOJ told him the order to use "necessary force" had been given.¹²⁵ The army, however, maintained that it could not use force unless it received specific orders from a superior military command.¹²⁶ Moreover, Brigadier General James Drummond, the task force commander at Fort Chaffee, asserted that "there was no breakdown in communications."¹²⁷ He affirmed that they had been authorized to use "reasonable force" but that such an order did not include physical restraint. Drummond also remarked that he had no control over Governor Clinton's interpretation of what constituted "reasonable force." He added that he had received an order on Monday afternoon that provided for an "amplification of powers," which meant the military could physically restrain refugees.¹²⁸

When a reporter asked Drummond if the base "was out of control" he said, "No. I wouldn't say that. I'd say the state police of Arkansas is kind of bad, though." (Reporter Ray Robinson suggested that Drummond was likely referencing the use of clubs to get the refugees back on camp grounds.)¹²⁹ Ten days later, however, the general called the governor's office and told them that he had made an incorrect statement about the actions of the ASP; he had reviewed the tape and now asserted that the officers acted correctly, as they were under attack and in danger.¹³⁰ McAda and Thomas R. Casey, the deputy associate director of FEMA, supported the actions by the state police from the beginning. The former said that the officers had used necessary force, while the latter held that they had acted in that manner because "the military has not done a damn thing."¹³¹

Drummond's lack of response to the events in Fort Chaffee upset many people throughout the state, and lawyer Fines F. Batchelor Jr. offered to help Steve Clark, the Arkansas attorney general, in any possible litigation against Drummond for "his feeble attempt to excuse his inaction":

> For General Drummond to expect anyone familiar with federal military law to believe that 18 U.S.C. 1385, the "Posse Comitatus" statute, ... prevented him from taking any action to prevent the wholesale destruction of military property under his command, or to reasonably exclude from, or retain on the military installation under his command, persons there to be either excluded or retained upon the military facility is complete farce.[132]

Batchelor further argued that Drummond's justification for inaction constituted "a very serious injustice and damage" to "our beloved United States of America," to the majority of Cubans who did not participate in the disturbance, and to the state and local law officials who did his "job for him."[133] After the incident there were some debates over whether state law officials were authorized to detain Cubans heading to town and push them back into camp grounds.[134] In response to this, Batchelor claimed that state and local officers were enforcing not federal law but state law. Clinton accepted the lawyer's offer and told Clark to seek Batchelor's assistance.[135]

Jesse L. Long, a real estate broker who lived in the Jenny Lind community, which borders Fort Chaffee, was also outraged at Drummond's actions on the night of May 26, when 350 Cubans broke through the southwest gate and went into that community. Long indicted the general's actions and argued that the Cubans' penetration of the camp's perimeter was "a breach of law. This is a usurpation of the legal constitutional and civil right each of us has to 'domestic tranquility.'" He condemned Drummond for letting a "raving, hostile, belligerent, rioting mob of maniacs armed with knives, clubs and rocks, weapons with which they did menace our lives here, run screaming and yelling through our community.... we were subjected to the horror and terror of them rampaging by and around our homes and community."[136] The federal government's failure to maintain law and order had subjected the community of Jenny Lind to a dangerous throng who violated their rights, and the US government needed to make amends:

> Let legal and lawful charges in his control and legal command deliberately trample our lawful and legal rights—just as though our rights

didn't exist.... Governor, atone and redress this gross wrong we've had to undergo because of Drummond's inaction and because of the Federal Government's failure to take steps to insure that our constitutional and civil rights were not violated by these Cubans, lawful and legal charges of the Federal Government, we must have redress from the Federal Government.[137]

He demanded "redress for the pain, suffering, humiliation, degradation and contempt wrecked [sic] upon us by the Cubans in Drummond's lawful charge."[138]

Long's elaborate complaint accurately captured the mood as Arkansans felt threatened and neglected by their government because it had decided to protect and take care of outsiders. Long aimed his panic, fear, indignation, and resentment at the federal government and the Cubans, the former for abandoning him, his local community, and his state, and the latter for criminal and violent behaviors that threatened Arkansans' lives. The rage and indignation that Long showcased in his letter fell in line with the feelings of victimization that many white people expressed following the civil rights, gay rights, and feminist movements, though these emotions had special resonance in the South, since the federal government had been deemed a meddling outsider there since the Civil War. The demographics of the area were also significant because whiteness had been protected in the 1900s with anti-Black terror campaigns that kept the area overwhelmingly white, yet the federal government kept imposing nonwhite foreigners on the area.

The resettlement of Vietnamese refugees had been a success, though only about five hundred were sponsored into northwest Arkansas communities. Southeast Asians, however, largely arrived in family units and were college-educated people who spoke English, while the media generally supported the US refugee endeavor and the need for resettlement of people who had been allies of the United States. In contrast, the Cubans were single men of color whom the news media pathologized as criminals and deviants, and the uprising at Fort Chaffee served only to cement such an understanding in Arkansans minds. To Arkansans, the Cubans were a dangerous triumvirate—Communists, criminals, and homosexuals—and having them walk down the street was cause for panic, more so if they were armed with rocks. According to Long, the Cubans violated his rights, and the federal government had allowed them to do so. That Long framed the discussion in terms of civil rights is telling, because he tapped into the simmering resentment to the ongoing "rights revolution."

He made himself and other Arkansans the victims of a Cuban horde of criminals that rampaged through the community, though by all accounts they did little other than walk down a road after they broke through Fort Chaffee's perimeter.

Long spoke of civil rights but ignored those guaranteed to the Cubans despite their special "Cuban/Haitian entrant (status pending)" designation. The Federal Bureau of Investigations (FBI), however, did not ignore the rights of the Cubans. The FBI conducted a "limited inquiry" into the actions of the ASP during the events that took place in and around Fort Chaffee on June 1 at the request of the Civil Rights Division of the DOJ. Clinton soon thereafter sent a letter to William E. Kell, the special agent in charge of the investigation, stating his support of the police officers as well as requesting to include his actions "within the scope of your inquiry." He informed Kell that the ASP had acted under his "direct orders . . . to contain disturbances and rioting that were taking place on the perimeter of the base. I bear full responsibility for their efforts to quell this disturbance." He also informed the FBI that the state government had also conducted its own investigation, and it believed not only that the ASP had acted within the orders Clinton gave but also that "their actions were both reasonable and necessary under the circumstances." Moreover, their actions prevented "tragic violence" to Arkansans and refugees "due to the inability of Federal security personnel to contain the disturbance." Finally, he argued the state police deserved commendation.[139] The DOJ concluded, based on the FBI's investigation, that the ASP did not deprive the Cubans of their civil rights through excessive use of force.[140] On October 31 Clinton sent a memorandum to "all state police personnel involved in the Fort Chaffee incident" informing them that the DOJ investigation was closed, that no offenses had been committed, and that their actions were in "keeping with the highest traditions of law enforcement and public service" which won them "renewed respect" from him and every Arkansas citizen.[141] Ironically, Long suggested that Clinton sue Drummond, FEMA, and other entities through the Civil Rights Division of the DOJ for the incident on May 26 and did not wait for the governor to heed his words; he filed a complaint with the Civil Rights Division as well as a citizen complaint with the inspector general of the US Army.[142] Clinton responded that he preferred to wait for Clark's "inquiry into the failure by the Federal Military Officials to maintain law and order" before considering a lawsuit.[143]

Governor Clinton and Attorney General Clark spoke on June 17 about pursuing an inquiry into the possibility that federal action or inaction at

Fort Chaffee "resulted in objectionable or harmful encroachments upon the normal field of state functions and powers."[144] The governor opined that the legal position taken by the military prevented them from providing adequate security at Fort Chaffee and, "therefore, imposed upon our State the burden of doing so." The military argued that 18 USC section 1385, also known as the Posse Comitatus Act, "prohibited military personnel from using force to keep refugees on the fort grounds and to maintain law and order within the fort."[145] The act prohibits the "social control of civilians."[146] Clinton also argued that he was given an "interpretation" of the law and was led to believe the military received the same explanation by the White House or DOJ; only later did he find about their differing understandings.

Clark investigated the military's inaction based upon Arkansas Statute 5-401, which allowed the attorney general to "determine whether federal legislation imposes objectionable burdens on our State."[147] The question was urgent because Fort Chaffee had already been used as a relocation center in 1975 for Vietnamese and was likely to serve that purpose again in the future.[148] Clark argued that the federal statute in question was 18 USC section 1385 because federal military authorities had cited it as the reason for their lack of action to control the situation and by extension provide "security to the civilian population residing near the main gates to Fort Chaffee."[149] In the context of the summer's events, "the burden ultimately imposed in this instance was the cost associated with the use of State and local personnel, officials and equipment used to control the June 1 riot. The cost would also include the risk of loss of life and risk of injury to which the State and local officials were subjected. The cost would also include the civilian unrest and insecurity that resulted from the federal inaction." Clark concluded that the military position that 18 USC section 1385 prohibited them from controlling Fort Chaffee was erroneous.[150] He noted that federal military authorities were under orders to "exercise the minimum amount of restraint, or physical force necessary" in order to provide safety to persons and property inside the compound and, in cases such as May 26 and June 1, outside the compound as well; "to take a contrary view is to ignore the fact that the federal authorities created the general situation (i.e., the use of Fort Chaffee as a relocation center), and in so doing accepted the simultaneous commensurate responsibility and obligation to confine the refugees to the military installation."[151] He also argued that it was "an inescapable conclusion that federal authorities did not provide for proper security planning and implementation" because procedures were not laid out, nor did military officials have the power to act according to what the situation demanded.[152]

One of Clark's arguments mirrored that made by the National Governors' Association about the federal government's need to take responsibility for its actions; like the association, he also rebuked Washington for shirking its responsibilities. There was a three-month difference, however, between the letters, so that Clark had more support for his stance than was true of the Governors' Association. By August, President Carter had proposed rather insistently that states and local government share the financial cost of resettlement, a position that was in contrast to how other administrations handled refugee processing. The proposal reflected Carter's fiscal conservatism and was politically naïve since he had just cut some federally funded programs due to the country's poor economic situation, yet he thought breaking with precedent and asking local and state governments to share the cost would not be a problem. Arkansas was not alone in rejecting such a proposal; local and state governments affected by influxes of Cubans and Haitians fought against such legislation. For a time, the federal government reimbursed states for 75 percent of what they spent in one year to cover Cubans and Haitians eligible for SSI, Medicaid, and AFDC; because each state had a differing cost for each of those programs, there were severe discrepancies between states and people. Florida government officials were especially incensed because that was the first stop, and often the last one, for both Cubans and Haitians. In response, they put forth the Refugee Education Assistance Act (REAA) as a means of covering their costs and forcing the federal government to pay for resettlement. They also managed to authorize the use of FEMA monies to pay for the resettlement program.[153]

Arkansas was not alone in its confusion over Posse Comitatus; other camps also had "jurisdictional conflicts" between the army and civil agencies that centered on the act, as well as questions about authority, the use of force, and coordination with local authorities that were "never satisfactorily resolved."[154] The military invoked Posse Comitatus because the camp populations were civilians, not soldiers, but state and local law enforcement agents did not understand them solely as that. They were certainly not regarded as having freedom of movement similar to that of US civilians.

In the meantime, Clinton admonished the federal government for the confusion about the orders and made certain that Fort Chaffee's military received clear orders. US military installations "designated to receive 'Cuban aliens'" were sent an order on June 2 telling them what to do if detainees attempted to breach their housing area or the camp perimeter.[155] First, they had to establish a clearly marked perimeter with signs in English and Spanish that notified the Cubans that unauthorized exits were unacceptable.[156] Military personnel at that perimeter were to take "reasonable measures," such as:

> oral warnings and, if those fail, reasonable, but whole non-lethal, measures ... only the minimum measures required to deter detainees is authorized: such measures should not impose a threat of death or serious bodily harm. Military personnel may be authorized to use nightsticks and riot control equipment. Use of the nightstick or baton as a barrier may be sufficient to deter individuals from leaving the enclave; however, individuals should not be struck in the head or otherwise subjected to excessive measures. Firearms without ammunition may be used.[157]

They were to use the same measures to keep Cubans from leaving the camp, but "military personnel shall not leave the installation to pursue and apprehend detainees."[158] Clinton probably did not read the order, because the limits imposed were not what he would have approved; after all, he supported the actions of the ASP, which included the use of batons to hit Cubans on the head as well as the use of loaded firearms. Moreover, he had been incensed that the military had not physically tried to stop refugees from leaving or pursued them after they broke through the gates, yet this order prevented the military from chasing Cubans who left the camp. State officials would thus be responsible for detaining Cubans meandering through Jenny Lind and Barling. The order, however, raised an important concomitant question: did local law enforcement officers in fact have the legal authority to detain Cubans found outside of Fort Chaffee?

Looming Questions about Cubans' Status and the Authority to Detain Them

When Cubans arrived on US shores, the Refugee Act of 1980 established an annual quota of fifty thousand refugees from any part of the world. The number of arrivals from the Mariel boatlift would quickly exhaust the quota. Only the first four thousand Mariel Cubans entered as refugees. Moreover, the act adopted the United Nation's definition of refugees as individuals who fled their country due to persecution, making people who fled from communism more likely to receive asylum. For a while, Cubans were considered applicants for asylum; however, the process was long and cumbersome, with review procedures that were too time-consuming, and this classification was also discarded. In an effort to streamline procedures, the US attorney general created the parolee "Cuban/Haitian entrant (status pending)" category on June 20.[159] Benigno Aguirre argues that "this was a new, anomalous migratory category. There was no provision in the law for 'entrant' aliens."[160] There was political fallout over the administration's actions, and in October the Carter White House supported the Fascell-Stone Amendment to the Refugee Act of 1980 pushed by Florida legislators, which gave Cubans and Haitians "official recognition and levels of social assistance similar to those granted to refugee populations."[161] However, David Engstrom argues that the administration failed to secure the necessary legislation to legally fix their category, so that President Ronald Reagan's attorney general, William French Smith, had to keep extending their parole. Reagan did not treat Cubans and Haitians as equals and quickly implemented a harsh policy toward the latter group. He also carried Cuban Americans in the presidential election, making them a valuable constituency, while his own anti-Communist stance about the "'pariah' of the Western Hemisphere" (Cuba) led him to allow his attorney general to adjust Cubans' status to permanent residents by using provisions in the Cuban Adjustment Act of 1966.[162]

In Arkansas, the question about the Cubans' legal status came to the fore after the White House announced that Fort Chaffee would be used as a consolidation center, with refugees from Fort McCoy, Wisconsin, and Indiantown Gap, Pennsylvania, transferred to Arkansas.[163] Carter's administration had previously promised Clinton that it would not send any more refugees; however, on August 2 they announced that Chaffee would be the only camp to remain open through the winter. Eidenberg told Senator Bumpers that the camp was the only place in the United States they could put refugees. In a fair response, Bumpers said, "It may be the easiest place to put them, it may be the most convenient place to put them, it may even be the most economical place to put them, but this is not the only place they could put the refugees."[164] One theory that explained the decision was that with the upcoming presidential election, the state was chosen over Pennsylvania, Wisconsin, and Florida because it had fewer electoral votes than the other three states and also historically voted Democratic in presidential elections.[165]

Unhappy but acquiescent, Clinton made sure that security would not be an issue again. He negotiated a deal in which he had to concur with the Joint Security Plan outlined by the federal operatives running the camp.[166]

The governor and his staff also sought to make sure that "certain categories of Cubans," such as those with mental and medical problems, minors, and "hardcore troublemakers," were not taken to Fort Chaffee but were sent instead to appropriate facilities.[167] Robert Lyford, an aide to the governor, told Clinton he needed to ask Carter for a document that defined the Cubans' status because the governor's staff had been told previously that "they were applicants for asylum, not detainees[,] refugees, or aliens. Whatever their status it needs to be committed to writing. Also the authority or lack thereof for a local law enforcement officer to return a Cuban to the base needs to be clarified."[168] The attempt to obtain a clear legal definition about the Cubans' status was not an exercise in legal doctrine but instead had important consequences for local and state police officers assigned to duties in and around Fort Chaffee.[169]

As Clinton spoke with local and state authorities about the Joint Security Plan, they wanted to know what authority they had to arrest or detain Cubans when they left Fort Chaffee without permission. Clinton asked Christian R. Holmes, director of the CHTF, who responded that "state and local authorities may arrest and/or detain only for violation of the laws of the State of Arkansas. In the final analysis, however, the actions of state and local enforcement officers would of course be governed by legal guidance provided by the State of Arkansas."[170] In other words, local authorities could not arrest or detain Cubans walking down the road from Fort Chaffee or in Barling, because strolling down the street was a not a crime according to Arkansas ordinances. A few days later Attorney General Clark made the point explicit when he said, "Six thousand Cubans walking on Highway 22 adjacent to Fort Chaffee aren't guilty of anything."[171] At the same time, however, the June 2 order prevented military personnel from leaving federal facilities to pursue Cubans, thus creating a loophole whereby if refugees could penetrate the camp perimeter, they were technically allowed to roam and do as they pleased as long as they did not commit crimes. As a lawyer and former attorney general for Arkansas, Clinton understood the ramifications of Holmes's reply, but sought Clark's opinion nonetheless. The governor asked him, "What authority, if any, do State and local law enforcement officials have to arrest or detain Cuban entrants who leave Fort Chaffee without permission?"[172]

Clark responded with two letters; the first addressed the Cubans' legal status, while the second answered the governor's question. The first had three components. Clark pointed out that "entrants" was not a recognized category in federal immigration law like "immigrants," "refugees," "illegal" immigrants, and parolees, for which there existed processing procedures.[173] Because no regulations were written that defined the status, Clark wrote, "it appears to me that the Cuban 'entrants' are being confined in detention or 'relocation' centers pursuant to insufficiently defined authority." For that reason, the "authority of federal officials to take into custody Cuban 'entrants' who have left Fort Chaffee 'without permission' is suspect and certainly open to question."[174] It appears that Clark's conclusion actually supported the argument the military made about Posse Comitatus, because to them, "entrants" were civilians and fell under the jurisdiction of the act. Clark even remarked that there was no authority which permitted the president of the United States to allow the admission of thousands of people into the country, whether as detainees, parolees, refugees, or entrants.[175] Second, he advised Clinton to attempt to secure a definition of the Cubans' status in the Joint Security Plan, and if he could not achieve that, then he should ask the US attorney general to declare a legal status as well as a designation and character for the Fort Chaffee "military reservation."[176]

Third, if the federal government failed to act, then it was time for state action based on the US Constitution's Tenth Amendment, "which provides that states have the authority to exercise police power except in those areas specifically pre-empted by the federal government."[177] Clark proposed that Clinton might need to file a suit in US District Court for the Western District of Arkansas "seeking declaratory judgment as to the construction of federal immigration laws and actions arising thereunder. This suit should address the issue of legal authority of the federal government to act in the area of law enforcement in contrast to the authority of state and local officials."[178] The Cubans in Fort Chaffee presented a new situation for the state because of their ambiguous categorization; the Vietnamese had been refugees since their arrival, and there was never a question of that status.

Clark also put forth that Clinton might consider seeking "injunctive relief" to prevent the transfer of more Cubans to Chaffee until the questions were resolved. This last point was timely, since the camps were being consolidated and more Cubans were already on their way to Arkansas. Clark reached the conclusion that "the authority of State and local law enforcement is severely circumscribed. Further, the position of the federal military authorities is that their enforcement capabilities are limited to events occurring within the federal facility. Thus, there still remains confusion over who has the responsibility to act."[179] The orders the military received on June 2 stating that they were not to leave the base in pursuit of Cubans made the question Clinton asked Clark urgent as more Cubans were transferred to Chaffee.

The second letter explicitly answered Clinton's question regarding the authority of state and local officials to detain Cubans.[180] Clark told the governor that any person not a citizen or national of the United States was an "alien," with the INS determining whether they could stay, while enforcement of the Immigration and Nationality Act was in the hands of the US attorney general.[181] Arkansas and county police, sheriffs, and deputies were responsible for enforcement of the criminal, highway, and traffic laws of the state; Cubans who violated any of those Arkansas regulations could be arrested by state and local officials. With respect to Cubans who left Fort Chaffee without permission, however, law enforcement personnel could stop and hold a person only if the officer suspected the person had committed or was about to commit a felony or misdemeanor. In this situation, the officer had a maximum of fifteen minutes to charge the person with crimes or else let him or her go.[182] Clark concluded the letter by saying that he was "unaware of any law of this State which prohibits or makes it a crime for an alien person to leave a federal compound or institution without permission. It is my opinion, then, that State and local authorities would have no authority to arrest or detain Cuban entrants for this reason alone."[183]

As the consolidation plan was put into action, Clark still sought a written document from US Attorney General Benjamin R. Civiletti in order not to file a suit in US District Court.[184] The stipulations Clark demanded were (1) that "Cubans are detainees under the exclusive jurisdiction of the Feds and that, as detainees, the local and state law enforcement people can provide assistance under color of law for any escapees or people who walk off" and (2) that Cubans sponsored by Arkansans or living in the state be ineligible for federal or state benefits. While it is understandable that Clark wanted a legal designation for the Cubans so that the state could understand its legal basis for action, the second stipulation had no precedent in the ongoing discussion with Clinton and ran contrary to what state governments were seeking from the Carter administration—that Cubans be declared eligible for federal aid in particular so that they would not be a burden on the state.

Civiletti responded to Clinton by saying that Cubans at Fort Chaffee were "detainees who are in the exclusive custody of the US Government pursuant to the Immigration and Nationality Act, specifically Sections 233(b) and 235(b). Accordingly, these aliens, who have not been admitted to the United States, are not free to depart Fort Chaffee, and may be restrained and be kept on the military installation by Federal Government personnel."[185] Civiletti added:

> Any Cuban entrant, except one who has been placed with a sponsor, paroled by my authority, and released by INS into the community, who departs from Fort Chaffee is in violation of the Immigration and Nationality Act and INS rules and regulations. A contingent of Border Patrol officers is responsible for finding any such "escapees" and returning them to INS custody at Fort Chaffee. I hereby request that, whenever needed, law enforcement officials of the state of Arkansas and local communities therein render assistance to the Border Patrol or other federal personnel regarding the detection, temporary custody, and return to INS detention, of any such Cuban entrants.[186]

The issue was resolved when the Joint Security Plan called for extra Border Patrol agents and deputized US Park Police, who would have the capacity to detain Cubans.[187] Appendix O of the Joint Security Plan, "Guidance for State and Local Law Enforcement Agencies," stipulated that camp authorities would notify state officers if they learned that any Cubans had escaped, but the latter could pick them up only if the Cubans violated local or state laws. Otherwise, the local and state officials had to notify agents with the Border Patrol, "the only agency authorized by law to arrest illegal aliens."[188]

Conclusion

The consolidation occurred smoothly, and no other major incidents occurred. Fort Chaffee finally closed as a refugee holding and processing center for Cubans in February 1982, at which point 395 people were sent to a federal penitentiary in Atlanta and a much smaller group to federal psychiatric facilities.[189] For Clinton it was a political catastrophe during an election year; Frank White won the governor's office with strong support from staunch conservatives and the Arkansas Christian Right.[190] The episode was so negative to Arkansans that they turned down a $50-million-per-year proposal to use Fort Chaffee as a permanent place to process refugees. Jack Freeze, the mayor of Fort Smith, denied that city officials had turned down the proposal due to xenophobia, claiming instead, "Our people are unique in that they don't want to get involved in anything but being happy. Quality of life is more important to our people than making a dollar."[191] However, these words were made in a coded language; instead of saying "way of life," Freeze and other Arkansans talked about their "quality of life," which fits within the framework that conservatives use to defend "core American values" and attempt to maintain the white privilege which is based on the oppression of people of color.

The experiences most northwest Arkansans had with foreign-born people before the Cubans were limited to the Vietnamese refugees five years earlier. There were differences between Cubans and Vietnamese that significantly affected their respective receptions in Arkansas. First, the majority of Vietnamese arrived as families, as opposed to the large numbers of single Cuban men from the boatlift, many of whom were suspected of being gay. Second, the Vietnamese in one way or another were constructed as victims, whether of war or communism, who needed to be helped, particularly given the US involvement in their country. In contrast, Cubans from Mariel were quickly depicted as criminals and deviants and made out to be more threatening than anything that was said about Vietnamese. Arkansans might have feared the Vietnamese were backward, non-Westernized, lazy people who would live off the government, but they did not fear them as murderers or criminals, as mentally ill, or as homosexuals. They might have feared the Vietnamese for being unassimilable Asians, but they also felt a call to support them based on Christian rectitude. By contrast, Cubans did not elicit this response. In my research, I did not find evidence to indicate that Christian churches sponsored Cubans like they had Vietnamese, nor did I encounter letters that advocated for them based on a Christian sense of morality. The rise of fundamentalist evangelicalism would have worked against Cubans, as homosexuality was strongly condemned within the Christian Right.

There was never a question that the Vietnamese were refugees, that they fled a Communist country, and that Americans needed to do their part to aid them by sponsoring them. There was a kind of benevolent acceptance, not always, but often. The Cubans, however, arrived weeks after the US Refugee Act of 1980, and most were denied the categorization "refugee," instead classified eventually as "Cuban/Haitian entrant (status pending)." For Arkansas, this designation was particularly important given the ongoing debate about local and state authority to detain them. Additionally, despite the ongoing battles to define them within immigration law, they were constructed discursively as "economic migrants" by the Carter administration as opposed to people fleeing a Communist government.[192] The convoluted process to find an appropriate category for the Cubans reflected the US government's growing apprehension about Latin American and Caribbean people arriving in the nation despite valid claims of persecution and terror. Haitians, Salvadorans, and Nicaraguans, to name a few, never received the kind of open-door policy granted to the Cubans, even though they had fled a violent dictatorship and civil wars.

In the end the legal title assigned to Cubans in Arkansas mirrored that of undocumented immigrants, as they were "aliens" that had not been admitted to the country. This was made even clearer when the Border Patrol was the only federal agency authorized to detain Cubans found off Fort Chaffee. The agency had exclusive jurisdiction to arrest them, and local law enforcement had to call them in. It might be telling that Cubans—a Latina/o group—preceded Mexican immigrants as "illegal aliens" in Arkansas. The rhetoric about criminality is also something the two groups shared. Mexican immigrants are often presumed to be undocumented, and as lawbreakers they are considered criminals that threaten communities in Arkansas.

In addition to the tens of thousands of Cubans held in Fort Chaffee, a handful of other Latinas/os had made their way to Arkansas around the same time. The families of Genoveva, Gustavo, and Gretel knew each other from a glass factory in Brooklyn, New York, and each family migrated to Arkansas for the same reason—work.[193] All three families moved to Fort Smith between 1978 and 1981 because nearby Van Buren had a glass factory where their parents could continue the work they had done in Brooklyn. Genoveva and Gustavo each had family and friends in the United States and in Mexico in the 1980s, but aside from their immediate family members, other relatives did not move to Fort Smith because despite a low cost of living and steady employment, there were insufficient "push" factors to attract them from other US regions or from abroad.

Their arrival in state at the same time that Arkansas and Arkansans were trying to remove Cubans was coincidence, but they all remembered that the Cubans were strongly disliked. "People wanted to get rid of the Cubans," Gretel said, "because they started acting with malice, stealing, not all."[194] At that time all the Latina/o families knew each other, including those few Cubans who were sponsored out of Fort Chaffee. "We knew some of them who were very good people; they were very happy to be here, but they [Arkansans] removed them [Cubans] for being bad. The few that remained here were able to get ahead, but they went through a lot of things. They had to make a lot of efforts. Only two or three remained here [in Fort Smith]."

In contrast to the Cubans and Vietnamese who were contained within a military installation and eventually dispersed throughout the country, ethnic Mexicans arrived in Arkansas at their will and lived where they chose. Arkansans could not control how many settled in the state, where they were also the largest group of new southerners and quickly surpassed the Asian American and African American communities in historically white northwest Arkansas. The reactionary responses to Latina/o migrants and immigrants were also centered on the protection of Arkansas communities and their way of life, where Latinas/os violated both even when they acted within the norms of society.

CHAPTER 4

Latinas/os and *Polleras*: Social Networks, Multisite Migration, Raids, and Upward Mobility

Polleras, as Latinas/os call poultry processing plants, are central to Arkansas and have been for decades. As home to the headquarters of Tyson Foods, the world's largest meat producer, northwest Arkansas is part of what one scholar called the "Feathered Kingdom," an area where the poultry industry is king.[1] For decades John Tyson and Sam Walton were local heroes as they expanded their companies into upper-echelon multibillion-dollar international corporations. Most Arkansans were proud of what these Ozarkers accomplished, despite, in the case of Tyson, an increasing stench that emanated from the farms that produced the chickens, the feathers and dead birds that littered the area's highways, and the illegal disposal of poultry waste into the area's waterways. When Arkansans realized that Latinas/os were drawn to the area by the poultry industry, they started objecting, sometimes vehemently, to the industry's role in the area's growing racial and ethnic diversification.[2] Poultry has been a powerful agent of change in northwest Arkansas, drawing tens of thousands of migrants and immigrants, especially ethnic Mexicans, from Latin America. This industry did more to diversify northwest Arkansas in one decade than did the activation of Fort Chaffee in 1975 and 1980 to process Vietnamese and Cuban refugees.

For some Latina/o migrants, Arkansas was a second or third site of settlement; they had already spent years or even decades living in more traditional states of immigrant settlement, such as California and Texas. They were working-class people who thought they had found their US homes, only to realize that their livelihoods were threatened or eliminated in the recession of the 1990s.[3] Other factors facilitated the migration and settlement of these new southerners, but as Steve Striffler argues, "the role of chicken [should not] be underestimated."[4] The poultry industry was searching for low-wage, exploitable workers, offering them year-round employment and lax enforcement of immigration documents as enticements; in addition, the state's low cost of living provided Latinas/os with opportunities for upward mobility and homeownership that were unavailable to them in traditional states of immigrant reception and settlement.

Mexicans who had engaged in circular migration for years also discovered these opportunities. Lucia said she stayed behind each time her husband left for the United States because of the living conditions at the migrant camps in California, not because she was unable to do the work. After her husband's first trip to Arkansas, he rented a trailer and asked Lucia to join him. She was quick to note that her family struggled in both California and Arkansas, but that they "advanced" in the latter. In Arkansas they accomplished in a few years what her husband had been unable to do after years of working in California's agricultural fields: they bought a house. And so did her children and the rest of her family members. This upward mobility, however, often had a tremendous cost, as work in the *polleras* is arduous and too often permanently damages the workers' health.[5] Many working-class Latinas/os, especially darker-skinned, monolingual Spanish speakers, also paid another price in experiencing rejection from white people of varying class backgrounds.[6]

The demographic shifts that changed Arkansas and the South, as well as the industry's eventual reliance on an immigrant, mainly Latina/o workforce, were facilitated by globalization and its effects, a trend with roots going back to the 1940s. The industry began in the US Northeast but was effectively moved to the South during World War II, when the federal government contracted all the production from the Delmarva Peninsula (occupied by Delaware, Maryland, and Virginia), then the national center for poultry production. Southern entrepreneurs like John Tyson took the opportunity to expand their businesses to fill the vacuum in domestic markets created by military procurements. Poultry producers received an additional boost from the federal government's efforts to encourage households to eat more chicken so that red meat would be more readily available to soldiers. This dramatically changed domestic poultry consumption patterns, laying the groundwork for the industry to become the nation's number one source of meat. But raising and producing young chickens, also known as broilers, was not a lucrative endeavor, and companies and farmers struggled to increase their profits. The industry's answer to this challenge was to engage in vertical integration and to develop "further-processed" or "value-added" poultry products. Vertical integration resulted in further concentration in the South, where poultry companies located processing plants close to feed mills, chicken farms, and a historically low-wage labor force in an antiunion region. Companies also changed their relationship to farmers as they began to make more demands on the size and shape of the birds they accepted and hired farmers on a contract basis, so that the latter were always on the losing end, working without an economic safety net and in danger of service cancellations that would leave them hundreds of thousands of dollars in debt. Meanwhile, with Tyson often leading the way, the industry began selling parts of the bird as opposed to the whole, creating products such as boneless breasts and tenders that permitted a de-skilling of labor but an increase in line speeds and repetitive motions, which made working conditions even more heinous.[7]

The increased demand for chicken coincided with the regional economic boom in the South and the growth of what is often called the Sunbelt. The boom was founded on industrial growth in a variety of sectors ranging from the military-industrial complex to aeronautics to technology, along with jobs in the service sector, construction, and manufacturing. These endeavors created employment opportunities for some southerners, mainly white men, who often relocated from their rural homes to urban areas, creating a need in the rural areas for laborers willing to do the strenuous jobs at poultry plants. From 1980 to 2000, white workers dropped from being just under 70 percent of the workforce to just over 30 percent, while Black workers increased from 30 to 50 percent and Latina/o laborers from 1 to 17 percent. During the same period, the number of workers in the industry nationwide more than doubled.[8] At some plants there was also a small percentage of other workers, such as Southeast Asians. Migrant Latinas/os sometimes worked in poultry plants, but through the late 1980s they were not a significant percentage of the workforce, entering the industry only when agricultural work slowed down or when there was a poor harvest.[9] By the 1990s, however, Latinas/os had migrated in significant numbers to the South to work in poultry plants, and the industry discovered a variety of benefits in hiring Latinas/os, especially undocumented people, who were eager to work, did not complain about working conditions, and rarely filed worker's compensation claims. In 1995, John Caplinger, district director of the Immigration and Naturalization Service in New Orleans, said in reference to Arkansas, "Obviously, illegal aliens working in the poultry industry is not new, but (in the past) you had a rush before Christmas, a rush before summer, but not this long term employment."[10] By 2005 Latinas/os constituted a major percentage of the industry's workforce, and in some plants in northwest Arkansas their numbers had reached into the seventieth percentile.[11]

I begin this chapter by addressing social relations between Black and white people, because in the wake of the legacies of slavery and segregation, African Americans continued to be denied fair treatment and representation even though they constituted 16 percent of Arkansans. I then present the demographic changes in the last two decades of the twentieth century through a focus on Latina/o growth, particularly in northwest Arkansas. From there I follow the life of a Mexican immigrant couple to briefly trace the factors for Latinas/os who engaged in multisite migration from their home states to California to Arkansas. The last section addresses the difficulties and opportunities they found in their new locations: on the one hand, grueling work in *polleras* and workplace raids, and on the other hand, lax enforcement of immigration documents, *tranquilidad*, and a reasonable possibility of homeownership with working-class earnings.[12]

African American Struggles for Equality in the Late Twentieth Century

In 1988 and 1990 Arkansas's First District (made up of six counties with large African American populations) sent a Black representative and senator to the state legislature for the first time since Reconstruction.[13] White Arkansans in the 1990s were still having difficulties addressing issues of representation, structural racism, and integration in both communities at large and public schools. In this section I examine issues ranging from white flight to redrawing congressional districts, defeating a segregationist law from the era of "massive resistance," and attempting to pass the state's first civil rights law in order to provide some context for ongoing social justice issues.

In the 1980s Pulaski County, home to Little Rock, grew 13 percent in terms of its Black population while its white population decreased slightly, yet all the counties surrounding it except for one grew steadily in white population, suggesting these areas were becoming bedroom communities. In other words, people commuted to Little Rock for work, but lived outside the city.[14] According to the journalist Karen Rafinski, the growth of bedroom communities reflected a desire for the "advantages of the big city without the drawbacks . . . lower housing costs, lower crime rates and—in their own eyes, at least—better schools. They also typically find a less diverse ethnic population."[15] A few miles west, in Garland County, Hot Springs's population decreased more than 10 percent despite its county growing more than 19 percent. According to Melinda Baran, the city's mayor, Hot Springs was "a victim of its school district lines" as white people left for more rural areas in order to send their kids to the county's predominantly white school districts.[16] She even made it clear that several industrial plant closings were not the cause for people's moves. Two weeks later, Baran added that the population shift was "wealth flight" and that both Black and white people left the city in search of "good schools" or to escape from "what is perceived to be the bad schools."[17] Though reporters did not use the term "white flight," the process they described fit that pattern, as white Arkansans moved out of the cities and into more rural areas. It was a pattern that could be seen across the nation, as white people who had the financial resources to leave communities and schools that were becoming integrated searched for neighborhoods and areas that were still predominantly white. In Little Rock, the middle- and upper-class white people who pushed to integrate Central High School and its working-class people increasingly moved west and facilitated the growth of Pulaski Heights, which would become one of the city's wealthier (and white) neighborhoods. However, white flight was only one part of the larger concerns about equality.

In December 1989 a three-judge federal panel found that the 1981 districts designed by state officials diluted the voting power of African Americans and ordered the state to create majority-Black legislative districts in east and south Arkansas.[18] The decision was part of a series of lawsuits filed by Black lawyers aimed at gaining representation on councils at a variety of levels, from school districts to city councils to quorum courts. The goal was often to change from at-large to single-member elections.[19] According to Viney Johnson of the Hope School Board and Mable Mitchell of the North Little Rock School Board, "it's the only way for blacks to get elected." John W. Walker, a Little Rock civil rights lawyer who brought several of the lawsuits, believed that change depended on increasing Black representation, but that it might require "disproportional representation" in order to "be able to make the necessary deals to make this state a decent place."[20] Walker sought to make Arkansas a respectable place to live, where people could make their voices heard by participating in a variety of governing bodies, but many white Arkansans, including government officials, did not share his view. The Board of Apportionment, consisting of Bill Clinton (who had been reelected governor in 1982); Steve Clark, the state attorney general; and Bill McCuen, the secretary of state, unanimously appealed the court-ordered decision, for two interrelated reasons.[21] First, the board objected to the creation of three "supermajority" districts where African Americans made up 60 percent or more of the population.²² They failed to see the longtime existence of white "supermajority" districts throughout the state, even in the Delta, with its historically large numbers of African American constituents. Second, they sought guidance in terms of reapportionment because the court-ordered redistricting had Black majorities of varying sizes. Other government officials also objected to the ruling.

Representative Doug Wood of Sherwood believed race relations would deteriorate in the legislature due to redistricting. According to Wood, whose district was not affected, "a lot of bitter, bitter feelings" were created when African Americans resorted to the federal courts.²³ "Anytime you use the court or judicial system, it really causes inflamed emotions. . . . It's going to take a lot of bridge-building and fence-mending."²⁴ The ruling fit into the trajectory of federal mandates that changed the way society was organized in Arkansas, where many white people did not see anything wrong with the legal and political structures in place. Wood and others who objected to the decision failed to understand why the African American community, faced with an appalling lack of Black representatives even in counties where they were in the majority, would resort to the courts. They also failed to acknowledge that Black Arkansans might have been left with no option but to resort to federal courts after decades of discrimination and opposition to change.

Senator Paul Benham Jr. from Marianna, in Lee County, had harsh sentiments toward redistricting. In fact, he rejected a need for such a move, arguing that "his" Blacks were satisfied with the status quo.²⁵ He had been a state senator since 1973 and was secure in his position, or so he thought. But after the court-mandated changes affected his district, he lost to an African American opponent and angrily told the press that Governor Clinton "took my damn district from me and gave it to the niggers."²⁶ His paternalism came through in the remark where he claimed ownership over the Black people in his district, but his racism was clear when he used that racial slur to refer to some of his constituents. The following day Clinton stated, "I think what Benham said was wrong. . . . Those were the comments of a mindset that dominated the Delta for too long." But Clinton then justified their utterance by saying they were made by a man who was in "great personal pain" because he "lost something he cared a great deal about—his seat in the state senate—because the rules were changed."²⁷ Clinton attempted to make Benham anachronistic for his time by speaking about the mentality that dominated the Delta as if it was in the past, but the power of that mind-set was evident in the lack of African American representatives from counties with populations that were between

30 and 60 percent Black. Clinton also said he "repudiate[d]" Benham's statement but "did not personally feel any pain or anger" over it because Benham was simply lashing out. The governor's attitude supported Benham and other white men in government who blatantly disenfranchised African Americans. Clinton's attitude also obfuscated other instances in which Benham used racial slurs, such as when he referred to then presidential candidate Jesse Jackson as "da coon" and said it was an example of his kind of humor.[28] Moreover, although Clinton might not have been as racist as Benham, he exemplified some of the Delta thinking when he opposed the legislative redistricting.

However, limiting recognition of such a mind-set to the Delta region was misguided, as became clear when an effort to overturn a segregationist law from the age of "massive resistance" and to implement the state's first civil rights law nearly failed. As discussed, in the late 1980s the Pulaski County schools faced a desegregation lawsuit in which the federal judge ruled the state bore responsibility for the county's school problems due to the 1956 law (Amendment 44) passed by Arkansans mandating that the state interpose its sovereignty and prevent school integration. State officials put Amendment 3 on the ballot to overturn Amendment 44 in order to avoid other lawsuits that would hold the state responsible for segregation. Amendment 3 passed, but only by a narrow margin. Afterward, an interdenominational, interracial group called Religious Leaders for Racial Justice said the vote revealed residual and entrenched racism. They released a statement that said in part, "The Amendment 3 vote count is clear and present proof that racism is alive and well in the hearts, minds, and ballots of too many Arkansans."[29] Reverend Wendell Griffen, the pastor of Emmanuel Baptist Church of Little Rock and a member of the organization, put it in the following manner: "Much of the post-vote analysis can be summarized by a collective sigh of relief. . . . That's a terrible, terrible fallacy. That's the same kind of attitude there was in Louisiana when David Duke didn't get elected. Forty percent voted for a Klansman."[30] What Griffen and the organization understood was the significance of more than 260,000 people voting for maintaining an amendment that opposed integration throughout Arkansas. Editorial pieces sometimes argued that the state had to overturn the amendment, because otherwise it would look bad on the national stage. Partially responding to this thrust, Religious Leaders for Racial Justice argued that "to speak of changing the image of Arkansas without changing the character of Arkansans is hypocrisy."[31] Griffen closed by saying the vote fell in line with a pattern established in the country in the past decade, as exemplified by President George Bush's veto of a civil rights legislation earlier in the year.

The topic was close to home as well because the Arkansas legislature attempted to implement the state's first civil rights law in 1991. At that point, the only other states without any such statutes were Alabama, Mississippi, and Louisiana.³² A group of legislators, including Senator John Pagan and Representative Roy C. "Bill" Lewellen, hoped to emulate legislation from the Reconstruction era that gave people the right to sue public officials if they violated people's rights in the name of state business.³³ By March of that year, the House Judiciary Committee had unanimously recommended a proposal for a state civil rights act, despite opposition from the Arkansas Chamber of Commerce, but it added four amendments; one exempted from punitive damages employers found liable "for intimidation, harassment, violence or vandalism against an employee or that employee's property."³⁴ Pagan said it was "a stupid exemption," but that the issues were covered under another section.

Although this legislation was based on a far-reaching law, many legislators and special interests, such as the Arkansas Chamber of Commerce, the Arkansas Poultry Federation, Union National Bank, and the International Paper Company, objected to various versions of it.³⁵ Ron Russell, the executive director of the Arkansas State Chamber of Commerce, said his organization opposed provisions that guaranteed jury trials, provided a three-year statute of limitations, and allowed punitive damages. Moreover, according to Russell, the chamber of commerce felt the bill "would hamper the growth and development of business and industry in the state" and that large punitive damage awards would be a "deterrent against business."³⁶ The chamber of commerce, the Arkansas Poultry Federation, the Arkansas Human Resources Association, and other business interests drafted another version with a three- to six-month statute of limitations. According to the backers of this bill, it was fair to employers and employees but removed the "harsh provisions that would severely impact small business and make Arkansas less attractive to industry moving here."³⁷

Senator Pagan said, "It's a fraud, a trick, a sham," adding, "It's not a civil rights bill. It is a bill written by and for the Chamber of Commerce in order to give its allies in the legislature a political excuse to vote for a bill with civil rights on it when in fact it does not deal with discrimination."³⁸ The *Arkansas Gazette* concurred and wrote an editorial criticizing the chamber's bill because it was "so restrictive that it would have almost no effect on employment discrimination."³⁹ The debates continued until the Senate Judiciary Committee was ready to block a version of the bill backed by the chamber of commerce because they felt it did not adequately address civil rights concerns. At the end of the legislative session, the committee requested a blue-ribbon commission to conduct a study and propose a state civil rights law.[40] The stalemate lasted until 1993, when legislation modeled on Pagan and Lewellen's bill was signed into law. The end product included a comprehensive hate crimes section as well as compensatory and punitive damages, attorney fees, and litigation costs.[41] Despite supporting the bill, Lewellen called it "weak" but thought it provided a beginning that could become productive.

The focus on being friendly to business interests mirrors similar rhetoric in the 1950s, when businessmen feared that the South was losing out on business endeavors from northerners who found segregation unappetizing. In that instance, business interests helped to end de jure segregation and increase more equitable conditions, but in the 1990s, supporting a more just civil rights bill served business no purpose. This was characteristic of the Nuevo South. The focus on business-friendly or antiworker policies was aimed at maintaining the region's long-standing and accurate reputation for having workers who were more easily exploited than their northern brethren. The "selling of the South" to the US North and, increasingly, to the Global North has been based on favorable conditions for companies, from tax breaks to lower wages to nonunion labor.[42] The active role of the Arkansas Poultry Federation in formulating the bill was important, because the industry is a big employer in the state and one with many labor violations and accidents. The 1990s would be a decade of consistency and transition. The poultry industry would continue its reign as a top employer as it drew Latinas/os to Arkansas and eventually came to rely on both documented and undocumented workers.

Arkansas's Demographics: 1980–2000

Latinas/os were not entirely new to Arkansas. Earlier in the twentieth century, Arkansans had some experience with Mexican-origin migrant workers and braceros. Most of these workers were concentrated in the southeastern part of the state, where they picked cotton or tomatoes. Some settled in Arkansas and fought to be recognized as white as they sought to limit the effects of Jim Crow on themselves.[43] But the Latina/o community remained small, and Arkansas did not become a place of settlement for large numbers of migrant workers like Texas or California.[44] Nevertheless, in 1980 there were nearly seventeen thousand "Spanish origin" people in Arkansas, 91 percent of whom were native born. Only 615 were foreign-born Mexicans, and of this group, only 290 had immigrated to the United States between 1970 and 1980.[45] By 1990 the group now defined as "His-

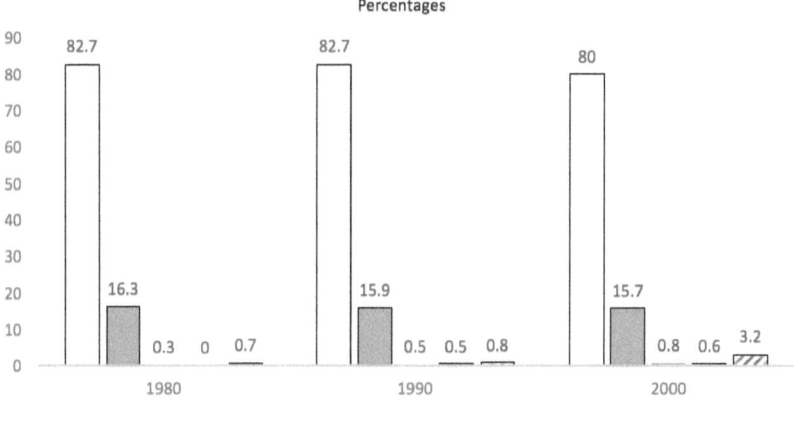

Chart 4.1. Arkansas population, 1980–2000

panic origin (of any race)" had grown by less than three thousand and still constituted less than 1 percent of Arkansans. Within the group, Mexican-origin people made up 63 percent (12,496); "other Hispanic," 29 percent (5,710); Puerto Ricans, nearly 6 percent (1,176); and Cubans, 2.5 percent (494), though there is no way to determine from the census how many of the latter were sponsored from the Mariel boatlift.[46] Meanwhile, the Asian/Pacific Islander population had tripled from 1980 to 2000. Eighty-six percent of Asians in 1980 were foreign born, and of these, Vietnamese accounted for nearly 26 percent (1,623). In 1990, Vietnamese were still the largest group, at 20 percent (2,348), followed closely by Laotians, at 16 percent (1,982). Between 1990 and 2000 the group with the most dynamic growth was Latinas/os, whose population quadrupled to more than eighty-six thousand, though some local agencies and community organizations noted that the official numbers were low.

In the 1990s there were positive Latina/o growth rates in every county, including those with net population losses.[47] More than half of the Latina/o population (44,290) lived in the Third Congressional District in the state's northwest corner, with nearly 80 percent in Benton, Washington, and Sebastian Counties. They were concentrated even within those counties: the Fayetteville-Springdale-Rogers Metropolitan Statistical Area (MSA) in Benton and Washington Counties had the fastest-growing Latina/o population in the United States, with a growth rate of 1,630 percent and a population of 26,401. Benton also led all US counties in Latina/o population growth rate, at 891 percent, an increase from 1,359 to 13,489.[48] In

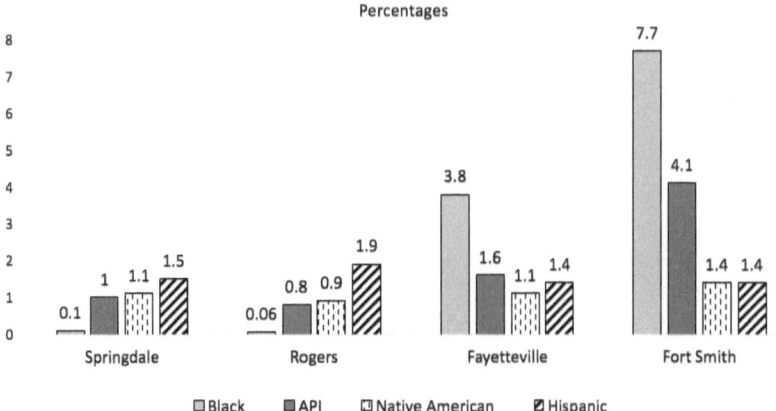

Chart 4.2. Populations of four Arkansas cities, 1990

the northwest, Springdale, Fayetteville, Rogers, and Fort Smith (Sebastian County) were the primary towns and cities of settlement. Springdale and Rogers were overwhelmingly white, with so few African Americans that in 1990 Latinas/os were already the largest group of people of color, despite a population of fewer than five hundred people. Fayetteville and Fort Smith had larger Black populations, with the latter's 5,600 leading the way. By 2000, Latinas/os constituted nearly 20 percent of the population in Springdale and Rogers, far surpassing any other population except for white people. In Fayetteville and Fort Smith, Latinas/os and African Americans were within a percentage point of each other.

Northwest Arkansas's Third Congressional District in 2000 also adequately represented the area's whiteness. The district's 14,015 African Americans constituted less than 2 percent of the population, in contrast to the three remaining districts, in which Black people made up from 18 to 27 percent of the population (and constituted between 112,000 and 163,000 people). Even within District 3, 50 percent of African Americans were in Fort Smith and another 20 percent in Fayetteville. In contrast to the rest of the state, Latinas/os in the northwest were the largest group of people of color, whether native or foreign born. To understand the reasons why many Latin Americans and their US-born children immigrated to Arkansas in the 1990s, I use Javier and Andrea's life as an example to delineate some of the contours of the movement.

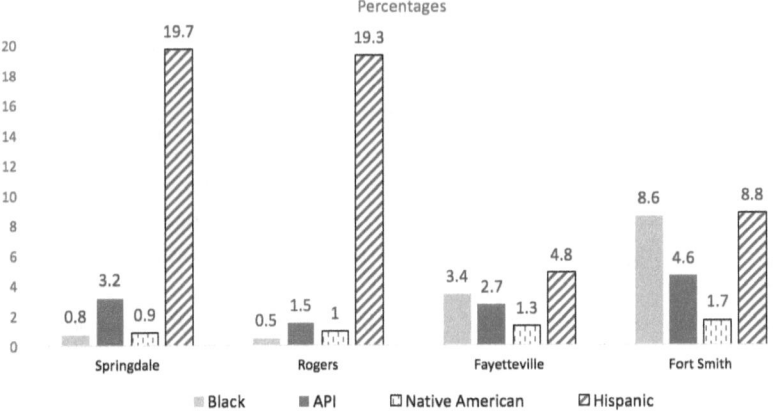

Chart 4.3. Populations of four Arkansas cities, 2000

Social Networks and Multisite Migration: Zacatecas, California, and Arkansas

Javier was born in the small community of La Blanca, Zacatecas, and as a teenager he decided to follow in the footsteps of men who traveled to the United States in search of better employment opportunities. Migrating to the United States also meant periodically returning home for special events, such as weddings, birthdays, and the town's annual fiesta commemorating its founding. It was at one such event that Javier became reacquainted with Andrea—they had gone to elementary school together—and they courted while he was in town; before leaving he asked for Andrea's hand in marriage and promised to return the following year so they could marry. He did, and they left for Pico Rivera, California, in 1985.

La Blanca: A Mythical Place

La Blanca, in the state of Zacatecas, forms part of western Mexico, which has a long tradition of migration to the United States. This community, fifty kilometers from the capital, is located on hilly, arid land that makes agricultural cultivation difficult though not impossible.[49] La Blanca is in the *municipio* (roughly equivalent to a US county) of General Pánfilo Natera and is the county seat. In the past, the area had a reputation for growing *tunas blancas* (white cactus fruit), and people said "Vamos a la blanca" when picking the fruit. The saying evolved to officially become the name of the area, but La Blanca no longer officially exists; in 1964 the government changed the name to General Pánfilo Natera in honor of a revolutionary general. Nevertheless, residents still refer to the community almost exclusively as La Blanca and use the official name only when it is demanded, such as in the case of airmail delivery, yet even then they write "La Blanca" in parentheses.[50]

According to Andrea, La Blanca's tradition of immigration to the United States was established during the bracero program, with men either returning to the federal initiative whenever they could do so or venturing outside it for better-paying jobs.[51] This began a migrant social network as men returned and told their friends and family about opportunities, enticing some to join them on the next trip. Little by little, more men made the trip north and returned with savings to live on for a few months or to slowly build and add to their houses. Eventually the trip north became the path to economic advancement to such an extent that those who did not participate were seen as unenterprising. According to Andrea, "the people that do not go to the United States live in poverty, they are conformists and do not move from there."[52] This perception was reinforced by the fact that everyone in town had at least one relative, often more, living in the United States, and could subsequently tap into knowledge and financial resources to make their maiden voyage *al Norte*. These ties often meant that a new migrant might have a place to stay, connections to employment opportunities, or even people to lend him or her money to make the trip.

Today, La Blanca is little different from the place it was when Javier and Andrea immigrated to Pico Rivera. According to its former residents, it is a small town with narrow roads, some paved with cobblestones or other material, but most of them dirt, a community where sheep and donkeys from the *ranchos* still wander about. It has a "*presidencia*" (city government offices) and a "*jardin*" (the town square), but little commerce. There are three elementary schools and one junior high and high school each. Traditionally, homes in La Blanca are made from adobe; about 70 percent of all the houses in the municipality are made from this, with the rest consisting of a variety of stones.[53] Notably, houses financed with US dollars are built with more expensive materials and contain newer appliances.

In 2000, 21,689 people—10,424 men and 11,265 women—lived in the municipality. A 1990 estimate placed La Blanca's population at about 3,500.[54] In contrast, residents estimated the year-round population to be between 8,000 and 10,000, with the number ballooning up to nearly 20,000 when people return for the Christmas season and the celebration of the community's patron saint, Santa Ana, on July 26.[55] Thus, residents believe that at any given point, at least half of the townspeople reside on the northern side of the US-Mexico border and that the town's year-round population appears to be overrepresented by youths under sixteen and the elderly.[56] Their observations are backed up by the 2000 census numbers for the municipality, which counted only 3,370 people working, 11,345 inactive, and almost 7,000 people unaccounted for.

Furthermore, between 1985 and 2005 there were only 648 births in the municipality.[57] Five years later, the population had decreased to 21,398, with 10,246 men and 11,152 women.[58] Overall, La Blanca's population decline fits in with statewide patterns. In 2000, Zacatecas led Mexican states in the numbers of immigrants that left for the United States: 48 out of every 1,000 people left, in contrast to the national average of 16 per 1,000.[59] A growing number of municipalities in Zacatecas have had negative population growth. In the 1980s the number was 24; by 1999 it was 34 out of 57.[60]

Andrea immigrated to the United States after she married Javier. They went to Pico Rivera because several members of his family lived there, mainly at the Samoa Apartments, or *los Samoas*. It made sense for her to go to the United States, since they were newlyweds and she could take care of household duties such as cleaning and cooking. For her part, Andrea was familiar with the expectations that came in marrying a young migrant man in the 1980s. It was no longer the case that men would marry but leave their wives in town; wives were instead joining their husbands in the United States. She looked forward to spending time with her husband but did not know they would share a two-bedroom apartment with two other men, and sometimes four, to save money on rent. She also did not expect to cook and clean for all of them. This situation was not ideal for either Javier or Andrea. He wanted to provide an apartment for the two of them, but that was nearly impossible given his low wages. Still, they made a life for themselves, eventually having two children. In *los Samoas* they found a community of immigrants from Mexico, El Salvador, Peru, and Nicaragua.

Pico Rivera: Suburban, Working-Class Apartments

Pico Rivera, approximately eleven miles southeast of Los Angeles on the southern edge of the San Gabriel valley, was an overwhelmingly majority Latina/o suburb with a population in 1990 of 59,177.[61] In the late 1980s several families from La Blanca lived in Pico Rivera, more specifically, in the Samoa Apartments. The apartment complex in the mid-1980s and 1990s consisted of working-class families, mostly immigrants from Mexico along with a handful of other Latin Americans, and only a few US-born Latina/o and white people. There were varying configurations to the living arrangements of tenants. Javier and Andrea, for example, rented a two-bedroom apartment but used only one room in order to rent out the other bedroom and sometimes the living room. Other apartments were occupied solely by single and married immigrant men, and still others had nuclear or extended families. On average, adult male and female tenants were in their mid-thirties. The couples, many of whom were married, often had young children, though there were also older parents with teenagers, some of whom were US born. The length of US residence ranged from new arrivals to inhabitants of a decade, with their entrance into the country varying from overstaying a visa to undocumented passage.

The women and men living the apartment complex worked throughout the Los Angeles area in a variety of jobs at warehouses, light manufacturing plants, and service sector businesses, with recent, undocumented immigrant women often working in sweatshops. Despite their steady employment and dreams for homeownership, the $165,000 median home value of homes in Pico Rivera and similar figures in surrounding areas precluded many of them from ever being able to afford a mortgage payment.[62] Sometimes having enough money to pay the $600 to $1,200 monthly rent was hard enough and did not allow for much saving.

The California recession of the early to mid-1990s made the situation dramatically worse.[63] The economic downturn hit everyone hard; many lost their jobs and were unable to find other employment that offered a decent salary, not to mention benefits. If they could, they tapped into their unemployment benefits while working jobs that paid meager earnings, worked as many as four part-time, low-wage jobs, and did their best to make it through the next month. With no end to such struggles in sight, people began following leads from friends and relatives about jobs in other parts of California or looking for cheaper rents, better pay, or both; some even ventured outside of the state.

Moving to the South

In 1994 Javier's brother, a resident of La Blanca and *los Samoas*, found his way to Fort Smith, Arkansas. He quickly found a job in a poultry processing plant. He learned that one-bedroom apartments were as cheap as $230; in other words, they were affordable for someone making a working-class salary. He told Javier about these opportunities and encouraged him to make the trip.[64] Moving was not in Javier and Andrea's plans, but when

Javier could not find work that paid more than the $6.50 an hour he earned as a forklift driver, they decided to find out whether the rumors about the plethora of jobs in Arkansas were true. He, Andrea, and their two children moved to Fort Smith in 1995. Javier found a job on his first day in the same poultry processing plant where his brother worked, and also an affordable apartment that their family would not have to share. Andrea and Javier were soon contributing to the buzz in their social network about the opportunities in the state called Arkansas. My own parents, Jesús and Enriqueta, received such a phone call.

My family had lived in *los Samoas* since 1985. It was where my mother, brother, and I arrived when we joined my dad in the United States five years after he left Mexico. Jesús arrived in Los Angeles in 1980 from Guanajuato, Mexico, and within a few months found a job at a manufacturing company; he worked there until the company filed for bankruptcy in the early 1990s. What followed was a cycle in which the company got bought out by another, which in turn went bankrupt and was bought out, and so on. Each new management cut salaries and personnel. By then, Jesús had some seniority, so he was employed until the last company filed for bankruptcy. For the next couple of years he worked through unemployment agencies, taking a severe pay cut, and drew on his unemployment benefits. My mother, who had never worked in the United States, took a part-time job in retail, but the situation had no end in sight. Then Javier and Andrea called to let them know that what they had all heard about Fort Smith was true—there were jobs, and housing was cheap.

Jesús made a trial trip to Arkansas because he thought people often exaggerated the opportunities in other places and he did not want to move us without being sure that what La Blanca's social network said was true. He took the bus and arrived at Javier and Andrea's apartment. The next day, Javier took him to the poultry plant where he worked, and Jesús got a job on the spot. He worked for a few months before calling my mom and telling her that we were moving. By then my brother was enrolled at a university, and he stayed in California while my mother and I joined my dad in Fort Smith in late 1995, along with other people from Los Angeles, *los Samoas*, and La Blanca. By this time a snowball effect had led many people to Fort Smith, where we found a nascent but growing Latina/o community. Many of the arrivals were immigrants who had already lived for a long time in the United States, as well as an increasing number of recent immigrants from Mexico who no longer bothered going to or through California but headed straight to Arkansas.[65] After word of the job opportunities and low cost of living in Arkansas spread through the social network, another hub in the US migrant network was established. Additionally, La Blanca's social networks reported that *"no checan papeles"* ("they don't check papers," i.e., legal documentation) was a widespread policy among the *polleras*. For at least some of the initial immigrants moving from California to Arkansas, the lax enforcement of immigration documents was not a draw because they had become legal permanent residents through the Immigration Reform and Control Act of 1986. But it was very important for those who were undocumented or who wished to emigrate from Mexico but had no legal means to do so. What was central to everyone was the low cost of living and the possibility of homeownership on a working-class salary.

When I asked Andrea why they left California, she said it was "due to high rents and low salaries," the same reply that I received from most of the people I interviewed.[66] In Fort Smith as in California, Javier was the sole economic provider for the family; in Arkansas, however, his family could live on its own without the economic necessity of sharing their living quarters with other people. Jesús was able to become the sole provider again, and we moved into a one-bedroom apartment (as opposed to the studio we rented in *los Samoas*) and paid $230 per month.

The recession forced a lot of people to leave a comfortable and familiar space for unfamiliar territory, and for many men and women there was no question that they would have returned to California if they could have had the economic advancements and job security there that they had in Arkansas. However, one advantage that Fort Smith offered over Los Angeles was *tranquilidad*. This is a word that frequently came up in my interviews; it literally means "tranquil," but the majority of my respondents connect it with the absence of violence, specifically gangs ("no hay pandillas") and other bad influences.[67] *Tranquilidad* is also something Latina/o immigrants have discussed with other scholars in Georgia and North Carolina. Rebecca M. Torres, E. Jeffrey Popke, and Holly M. Hapke interviewed 136 Latinas/os in rural Greene County, North Carolina, and the most frequent response to the open-ended question of "What do you like about living in Greene County?" was *tranquilo*. The authors go on to note that to the migrants it means a variety of applications of "peaceful" or "calm," including fewer gangs and less crime, noise, traffic, and overpopulation, as well as less danger of being harassed by local police or detained by immigration officers.[68] Latina/o parents who moved to Dalton, Georgia, sought to leave impoverished neighborhoods in Los Angeles and Houston and have a safer environment and better schools for their children.[69] Many immigrant parents in Arkansas had heard horror stories about youth *que se descarrilan* (who went down the wrong path) or knew parents who had struggled with their kids over gang activity, alcohol abuse, drug use, and premarital sex and sought to avoid these struggles in their own families.

Many parents liked Pico Rivera, as did mine, because as a suburb it largely lacked the rough and "bad" neighborhoods they associated with other parts of Los Angeles. Nevertheless, they sought to limit their children's exposure to "bad influences," and in Arkansas those were also largely lacking. In the beginning, it was because mostly single men lived there, and then it was a lot of young families with very young children, but eventually teenagers who had lived in Southern California or other larger US urban areas began moving with their families and, according to most Latinas/os, bringing their gang affiliations with them. Many Mexicans argue that they arrived first and no gang activity existed until the arrival of Salvadorians a few years later.[70] In the mid-1990s, Fort Smith also lacked the problems stemming from urban disinvestment that were prevalent in Los Angeles. The city was definitely divided into working-class, middle-class, and upper-class areas as well as concomitant white and Black areas, but the "bad" part of town was simply working-poor with very affordable apartments. This area was fairly close to downtown, and it was also where Latinas/os began to concentrate. Before them, Asian refugees had congregated in this area for transitional housing, living there to save enough money to move to nicer apartments or even to rent or buy a house in another part of town.

"Life Is Worth Living in Fort Smith"

Fort Smith, which borders the state line with Oklahoma, was the third-largest city in Arkansas, following Little Rock and North Little Rock. City officials touted Fort Smith's wholesome environment as ideal for raising children, while also citing the low unemployment rate and a cost of living that was generally 12 to 14 percent below the national average as proof of its economic opportunities.[71] In fact, Ray Baker, the longtime mayor, frequently proclaimed, "Life is worth living in Fort Smith, Arkansas." The dynamic growth of the Latina/o community in the 1990s can be observed most remarkably in school district enrollment figures between 1990 and 2004 (chart 4.4). In 1990, Latina/o pupils made up only 1 percent of district enrollment, but by 2000 enrollment had grown to 11 percent, and by 2004 it stood at nearly 20 percent, with more than 2,000 Latinas/os among the total population of 12,871 students.

In the public schools, educators formed opinions about these students

Figure 4.1. Downtown Fort Smith; author photo.

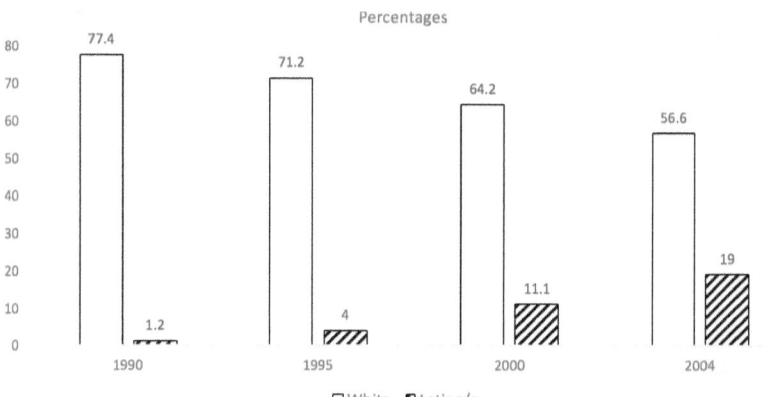

Chart 4.4. Fort Smith Public Schools enrollment of Latina/o and white students, 1990–2004

and the ethnic and racial groups they represented. I interviewed a variety of people to get a more complete picture of the changes that occurred over the past thirty years. A comment from Anna, a white educator in Fort Smith, lays bare the processes at play and how students were racialized in relationship to each other. Anna worked in the local public schools for most of her career and had seen and experienced the demographic changes in the area.

> The one thing that I noticed immediately when we began to enroll what I would call "the wave" of Hispanics was that they were the easiest of all the races to talk to or to get information from. They didn't have the reticent or the reserved nature of the Asians nor did they have any chip on their shoulders as the Blacks. The one thing that I remember specifically is that they all seemed very glad to be here. And they seemed to be very grateful to be here. . . . They were all cooperative. The Asians were all cooperative if you exclude the Laotian males which can be very uncooperative or some of the Laotian females that could be very uncooperative.[72]

There are at least three issues at work here. First, the racialization of Latinas/os is grounded in local and state histories that are specific to place. Anna "triangulated" the position of Latinas/os in relationship to Southeast Asians and African Americans, two groups of color that preceded them in the school district.[73] She also engaged in what Natalia Molina calls "racial scripts," a term that "emphasize[s] the ways in which we think, talk about, and act toward one racialized group based on our experiences with other groups whose race differs from our own."[74] Anna made sense of Latinas/os and their behaviors based on her experiences with Asian and Black students, even though the latter do not represent an immigrant group that is learning a foreign language or adapting to a new place. In this case, the behavior of Latinas/os was a welcomed difference from that of Asian refugees or African Americans.

Anna also commented that in the 1970s many of the teachers and students had cultural misunderstandings because Vietnamese and Laotian students would not look at the teacher when he or she was speaking, a behavior Arkansas educators believed was disrespectful. Eventually, a cultural translator explained that the opposite was true—Southeast Asian students were showing deference precisely by not making eye contact with their teachers—and eventually students understood how teachers wanted them to behave. But not all Asians occupied the same racial terrain, as is clear in her distinction between what she believed to be Laotians' difficult behavior and that of more pleasant Asian students (there were also small numbers of Hmong, Thai, Cambodian, and Chinese immigrants).

The second issue is about whiteness as the unmarked but always looming category against which Latina/o students, as well as Asians and African Americans, are judged. In this quote, and indeed throughout our lengthy conversation, Anna did not explicitly compare students of color to white students, yet they needed to be sufficiently cooperative, grateful, and pleasant in order to achieve some level of inclusion or assimilation. Anna reinforced the idea that Black students were resentful without sufficient cause by not acknowledging their experiences with systemic racism and prejudice. She singled out Laotians, male and female, for their "uncooperative" behaviors, and in doing so racialized them more akin to Black students due to their alleged bravado. Unlike meek Vietnamese, difficult Laotians, or resentful Black students, she saw Latinas/os as very happy, cooperative, and compliant, and in this way perhaps racialized them as more similar to white students, at least in the early stages of demographic change. The racialized position of Latinas/os in the public schools can be understood only by accounting for the positions of the other racial and ethnic groups.

The third issue is the stratified setting in the school system that favored some students but negatively impacted others. The ways in which Chicanas/os and other students of color were racialized helped to condition their experiences at school and with school officials. In essence, students could find some level of inclusion if they were communicative, cooperative, and grateful. If they behaved otherwise, they were seen as less than desirable students. This meant that internal fissures such as legality, language proficiency, and comportment were exacerbated by school officials seeking out "exceptional" students in whom they were willing to invest extra time and effort. I returned to Arkansas in the summer of 2012 to conduct more interviews, and during that visit several recent high school Latina/o graduates from different school districts told me they had to find information about college admissions and finances on their own—even though the flagship campus of the University of Arkansas was just forty-five minutes away. Moreover, many of them were not encouraged to pursue a college education, but were instead expected to drop out of high school or to pursue no further education after their high school graduation.

These issues have similarities with the well-documented experiences of Chicanas/os in the Southwest during earlier time periods.[75] Public school officials have rarely encouraged Chicana/o students to pursue higher education, and when they have, it is often to encourage single students they determine are gifted enough to be worthy of their investment. Those students then receive guidance on how to successfully exit the maze that is often public K–12 education. In short, in schools and in the community, Latinas/os and Chicanas/os have to be the right kind of person, one deemed "good," to be granted some semblance of belonging or opportunity to succeed.

The identity formation of Latinas/os in Arkansas is different from that of their counterparts in states such as California or Texas because the history of those places was vastly different, shaped largely by the Mexican American War and Mexico's massive territorial loss. Mexicans have been in those places for a long time. That history, that presence, matters very much for the regional racial formation of Chicanas/os and for the political struggles and gains achieved since 1848. Moreover, California and Texas in the twentieth century were traditional states of immigrant reception where hundreds of thousands of documented and undocumented Mexican immigrants as well as other Latin Americans arrived in search of better lives.

In contrast, Mexican immigrants and Latinas/os in the South were often constructing their identities in areas where Mexicans had little history and where racial and ethnic diversity was new and varied. In Arkansas, Latinas/os learned to negotiate their position in a field of ethnic populations that included Mexican immigrants but also Salvadorans, Puerto Ricans, Vietnamese, Laotians, Cambodians, and educated and often middle-class Latin American immigrants who increasingly serve as a kind of managerial class or as cultural brokers between Mexican and Chicana/o working-class communities and the established white communities. And, of course, even in areas where the African American community is small or not present, Latinas/os define themselves in relationship to Black people and Blackness. Though Latinas/os have received the bulk of the attention in terms of the changing South, there are growing Asian immigrant and Asian American communities throughout the region whose experiences also fissure along lines of ethnicity and class.[76]

In 2000 the median family income in Fort Smith was $41,012, with the median value of homes at $74,200, almost half of what it was in Pico Rivera.[77] Smaller yet still nice homes were available for about half that sum and thus were within the reach of immigrants, working-class people, and even single-income households. Manufacturing is an extensive resource and economic base for Fort Smith, which is home to poultry processing plants, furniture factories, refrigerator and air conditioner manufacturing, and liquor producers. Major corporations such as Whirlpool, Rheem, Trane, Georgia-Pacific, Gerber, Kraft-Planters, and Tyson Foods have operations in Fort Smith. The city is also home to the national headquarters of corporations such as Baldor Electric, Arkansas Best, OK Foods, and Golden Living, the country's largest nursing home health-care provider. In 2004, eleven of the nineteen top employers listed by the city were manufacturing companies, while the remainder consisted of healthcare, education, and government institutions.[78] In 2007 the list grew to twenty-two companies; this time twelve were manufacturing or industrial employers. The poultry company OK Foods was first, with 4,748 jobs, followed by Whirlpool, with 3,000 and Baldor Electric, with 2,262. In total, the twelve manufacturing/industrial companies hired 16,224 workers and held more than 60 percent of the employment opportunities of all of the companies on the list.[79]

The industrial bases for the Fort Smith and Fayetteville-Springdale-Rogers Metropolitan Statistical Areas were diverse in the 1990s, but Latinas/os initially found the most opportunities in the poultry industry. According to the *Economist*, Latinas/os saved the industry and created the economic boom. The causality might not have been so direct had Latinas/os not moved to the South at a time when the poultry companies were desperate for workers to keep up with nationwide demand. If Latinas/os did not save the entire industry from collapse, they facilitated its expansion. Georgia's agricultural commissioner, Tommy Irvin, concurred, saying the industry would have collapsed without Latinas/os: "It would have to close down. You'd see poultry prices for the consumer shoot out the sky. The Hispanics have saved the industry."[80] By 1994, Tyson's Arkansas workforce of twenty thousand was 18 percent Latina/o.[81] They also helped the area's economic growth, as some immigrants eventually worked in other manufacturing jobs as well as in construction and landscaping, and some of their children entered the service industry. But initially, *polleras* were where they expected to get jobs, while the area's low cost of living and possibility of homeownership completed the picture.

Working in the Poultry Industry: *"No checan papeles"* and Raids

The Latinas/os who arrived in Fort Smith in the 1990s were documented and undocumented immigrants; the latter in particular moved for employment opportunities since La Blanca's social networks were reporting that Fort Smith companies "*no checan papeles.*" This meant the real possibility of steady employment and a weekly paycheck regardless of legal status, something which was increasingly difficult to find in areas like Los Angeles.[82] Sometimes companies hired recruiters to find laborers from Texas, California, or even south of the border. But in the case of La Blanca's people, it was the social network that did the recruiting. One researcher, Steve Striffler, found a similar effect among the Latinas/os he interviewed in northwest Arkansas. When people first heard rumors about work in "chicken" in Arkansas, some made the trek, and then provided more concrete information to their social networks. One of Striffler's interview subjects remarked, "[T]he Christopher Columbus of Arkansas. That's what they call me because I discovered Arkansas for my pueblo (in Mexico)."[83] In 1987 or 1988 he broke a twenty-year pattern of circular migration from his home state to California when a friend, a fellow worker, told him about "chicken" jobs in Arkansas. He said immigrants heard rumors about better jobs all the time, so he decided to go with one son to see if they could find work in Arkansas. "The first day, Tyson hired us. There were ten Mexicans in the plant. Pure gringos. . . . Now it's all Mexican." He told two sons in California to leave immediately for Arkansas. They rented a trailer for the first two years. "Then my sons and I brought our wives and kids. Within four years we bought a house. Then the whole town (in Mexico) stopped going to California and started coming to Arkansas."[84]

It is unclear whether companies at the beginning of Latina/o migration knowingly and willingly hired undocumented workers, or whether the latter duped the former with false documents. In 1993 newspapers within the state began reporting that northwest Arkansas was becoming home to large numbers of undocumented people. According Jessee F. Tabor, chief patrol agent of the New Orleans office of the Border Patrol with oversight of Arkansas, "illegal aliens" were increasingly a "very significant" part of the poultry industry for three interrelated reasons. "First, the 3 percent unemployment rate in Northwest Arkansas means poultry processors are having a heck of a time making up a workforce," Tabor said. "Second, poultry processing and agriculture in general have traditionally drawn a large number of illegals. It's labor-intensive work and there's a very high attrition rate in the work force."[85] According to Striffler, white workers left plants in northwest Arkansas during the area's economic boom of the 1990s. Striffler estimates that by 2000, when he did fieldwork and labored in one of Tyson's northwest Arkansas plants, its workforce was three-fourths Latina/o, with Southeast Asians and Marshall Islanders accounting for most of the remainder of the workers, and very few white people on the lines, though they predominated in management.[86]

Tabor said employers were following the rules: "Employers are doing an excellent job but as long as they have a significant number of illegal aliens, there is a chance that we might arrest a significant number all at one time and it could have a very adverse impact on their operation."[87] With these words he depicted the poultry industry sympathetically by talking about the difficulties they faced in finding workers locally. Based on this logic, the poultry industry was an innocent victim twice over, because the arrest of their workforce would cause them business difficulties. Social networks are important for providing information about local settings, including employment information, but whereas in Tabor's description all Latinas/os are con artists, individuals reported how casually employers checked employment eligibility, including when business owners "*no checan papeles.*"

Soon some Arkansans welcomed federal officers with applause.[88] In 1995 Operation SouthPAW raided worksites throughout Arkansas, Georgia, Tennessee, Alabama, Mississippi, and Louisiana. SouthPAW was a multiagency task force that included the INS, Border Patrol, US Department of Labor, US Public Health Service, and state and local police authorities. By the end of the operation three thousand suspected undocumented workers were caught in those states based on the four-month investigation and tips from the public. In Arkansas the task force raided more than two dozen food-processing (mainly poultry) and light manufacturing plants in September and caught about six hundred undocumented workers. According to federal officials, the wages of those apprehended ranged from $4.50 to $10.50 per hour and averaged $6.05. Based on an average work year of two thousand hours, the officials estimated they opened up between $8.5 and $11 million in salaries for the state's legal workers.[89]

The poultry industry, however, maintained that there were already jobs available beforehand. Archie Schaffer, a Tyson spokesman, said, "The suggestion that any of these Hispanic workers are taking jobs away from Americans is absolutely nonsense. . . . Anybody in Northwest Arkansas or Clarksville or Dardanelle who wants to work, we have the jobs available."[90] Doug Siemens, a spokesman for Simmons Foods, said, "There's a very tight labor market in this area. There is not an easy answer. Jobs are available, and we're looking for workers currently. But we had jobs available before Wednesday. I'm not going to blame INS or say INS is causing us a problem, but this is something we've got to work through."[91] What Siemens came short of suggesting was that the INS should leave poultry companies alone because local people were not available or did not take those jobs.

But Joseph Gavalis, a special agent with the Labor Department's Office of Labor Racketeering, said the deterrent value of the operation was more significant than the number of undocumented workers apprehended. "What difference does it make if we get 200 people and 400 people don't show up for work? We don't count people. We count jobs. That's 600 jobs that can go to Americans. . . . All we want to do is level the playing field—for employees, employers, and businesses."[92] This is a familiar discourse of white victimization, because when Gavalis talked about leveling "the playing field" and about "American" jobs, he implied that the local white workforce was being denied jobs that instead were filled by undocumented immigrants. But the poultry industry claimed white Americans did not want the jobs, and that businesses struggled to find local workers.

But the poultry industry was not alone in responding less than enthusiastically to the raids. Governor Jim Guy Tucker responded to the operation by saying, "Six hundred workers . . . compared to what? . . . The attention has been focused on what seems to me a relatively small number of employees who are illegally working. No one's attention has been given to how many were lawfully there, had their papers, had the proper documentation by their employer and so forth."[93] During Operation SouthPAW, most of the news articles covered "illegal workers" rather than "illegal aliens," a minor but important distinction if for no other reason than that the former designation constructs Latinas/os at the very least as contributing to the economy by their participation in the labor sphere. Likewise, Governor Tucker talked about workers and not people or families, but he did point out that six hundred was a small number compared to the many Latinas/os who worked in poultry processing but were legally in the United States. A year earlier the Hispanic Relations Task Force had estimated that forty-two thousand Latinas/os lived in Arkansas, and thus Tucker had a point.[94] Even if the discussion was limited to undocumented immigrants, a 1993 Border Patrol estimate suggested there were twelve thousand "illegal Mexican aliens" in northwest Arkansas, yet raids at their preferred industry captured only six hundred undocumented immigrants.[95]

During the monthlong coverage of Operation SouthPAW in Arkansas, employers were often praised for their good work in checking that applicants had the correct documentation; none of the Arkansas plants received fines from the raids.[96] Part of the difficulty, according to INS spokesman Ben DeLuca, was that federal authorities "have to prove they [employers] knowingly hired illegal workers. If the illegal workers present fraudulent documents—unless the fraudulent documents were given to them by the employers—it's difficult to prove the employer knowingly hired undocumented workers. . . . There is a lot of document fraud out there that only an immigration officer is able to detect from a valid document."[97] This reasoning portrayed Latinas/os as experts in deception, lawbreakers who took advantage of naïve and unsuspecting employers. If Latinas/os and Mexicans were undocumented, then they had to purchase documents to present to employers, and maybe the latter truly had no idea that some of the credentials were counterfeit.

However, that excuse does not stand, given that businesses began accepting new documents from workers who had been deported only days before. Don Johnson cites an instance where a man was deported after a raid but was able to get back to Arkansas in a few days. He then showed up at his old worksite with new documentation and a different name. No one asked him any questions, and he was rehired. When Johnson asked him why company officials were not curious about his new name, he smiled and said, "They know." Ron Kidd, the INS supervisory special agent for investigations in Memphis, also began to have some doubts: "What I find hard to believe is a personnel office where they hire umpteen thousand people and they see a good Social Security card and good green card, and they accept some of the other cards as being good as well. I find it difficult to believe that they believe these people aren't illegal aliens."[98] Kidd believed the personnel offices had enough experience to know how to differentiate valid from invalid documents, but the human eye is no substitute for searching a government database. Relying on another person to recognize the validity of documents would be erratic—Javier and Jesús still laugh about being turned down for jobs at an employment agency because the interviewer thought their resident alien cards were counterfeit.

Raids took place all over the United States, including in California and Florida, but immigrants who were caught there had a harder time finding a job if they managed to get back. It was a seeming contradiction that undocumented immigrants continued to move to northwest Arkansas while raids were taking place or in their aftermath. However, poultry industry representatives were correct in asserting that there were plenty of jobs—so many that immigrants could risk deportation because they knew that if they were able to get back to Arkansas, they were very likely to find another job almost immediately, sometimes even in the same plant. This is not to say that deportation is not a traumatic event, because it is. It exposes immigrants to premature death, as crossing the border is a grueling endeavor and one where they inherently risk their lives.

Latinas/os, especially resident aliens and naturalized citizens, also reaped the benefits of such a needy labor market and took trips to Mexico for Christmas, their town's fiesta, or other special occasions. Javier and Jesús asked for a leave a couple of different times and were told that the company needed them to work, that they could not leave, and that if they chose to do so, they would lose their jobs and be banned from working at the factory for at least a few months or more. For a few years, Javier, Jesús, and others left their jobs when necessary and were able to find work at other plants upon their return. Of course, if the company paid them a slightly higher wage, then workers had to weigh their options. That took place in the 1990s, but by the end of the decade Latinas/os were reporting through social networks like La Blanca's that there were still jobs in Fort Smith, although poultry companies were increasingly contracting with employment agencies to get their workers. A drawback for workers was that working through an agency paid less than if they were hired by the company itself. The company benefited from the employment agencies because it allowed them to pay less in salaries and to avoid grievances such as workers' compensation claims as well as efforts by workers to participate in or organize a labor union.[99]

A lot of suspicion remained as to whether the poultry industry knowingly allowed people to work without proper documentation, provided workers with a contact that sold them the documents, and even whether they organized human trafficking rings to smuggle workers into poultry plants throughout the United States. As in so many other areas of the poultry industry, Tyson was no exception. Tyson Foods Incorporated was indicted in December 2001 by the federal government for conspiring to smuggle workers into the United States. Following this indictment, former Tyson workers filed a class action suit in 2002 claiming that the company knowingly hired undocumented workers to depress wages.[100]

Smuggling Undocumented Workers and Working Conditions

In December 2001 the federal government sued Tyson Foods after a two-and-a-half-year investigation led by the INS and with the participation of the Department of Agriculture, Social Security Administration, FBI, and US Attorney's Office for the Eastern District of Tennessee. The Justice Department claimed that fifteen of Tyson's plants in nine states had conspired since 1994 to smuggle two thousand undocumented Mexican and

Guatemalan immigrants into the United States and provided them with counterfeit papers so they could work at Tyson plants. The indictment named six managers in the largest case of its kind against a US corporation. The suggestion was that the managers acted on orders from top officials in corporate headquarters.[101]

Amador Anchondo-Rascon moved to Tennessee from Florida after he heard that nurseries there paid better. He then moved to Shelbyville, Tennessee, when he heard that the Tyson plant paid better wages than the nurseries. Like so many others before and after him, he arrived in Tennessee after having already lived elsewhere in the United States. He had worked in Florida's agriculture circuit until his move to Tennessee. When he got to Shelbyville in 1989, there were only a handful of other Mexican immigrants, but over the next decade the Latina/o community grew, and he opened a grocery store to cater to his countrymen. He became a kind of middle man between Latin American immigrants, mainly Mexicans but increasingly Guatemalans, and the white community, serving as a translator in court and for police, taking new arrivals to landlords and used-car dealers to vouch for them, and acting as "a perfect go-between from Tyson plant managers searching for low-wage workers."[102] In the meantime, two local police officers became suspicious of the documents Latinas/os handed them during stops for traffic and other offenses. When questioned, the immigrants would often reply, "Los Tres Hermanos" (the name of Anchondo-Rascon's grocery store). The officers called the INS, and an undercover agent purchased counterfeit documents at the store for $150 each. That marked the beginning of the operation, and in subsequent meetings Anchondo-Rascon told undercover agents that Tyson plant managers frequently asked him to supply undocumented immigrants, paying him between $100 and $200 per worker with corporate checks for "recruitment fees."[103]

Before the case went to jury, the judge dismissed twenty-four of the thirty-six counts against Tyson, including the one about smuggling workers into the United States. One juror was "appalled that the government didn't have more hard evidence."[104] The evidence they had was testimony from former Tyson employees who pled guilty to violating immigration laws and from undercover immigration agents who secretly recorded conversations with Tyson officials. Defense lawyers argued that none of the evidence linked Tyson's corporate management to the crime; company officials were mentioned by other people but were never directly implicated. The jury acquitted Tyson and three managers, and the company maintained that rogue employees had taken matters into their own hands without approval from headquarters. Mark D. Hopson, a lawyer for Tyson, said that Tyson was "the absolute wrong test case for this" because "Tyson was in the 1 percent of employers who volunteered to get on a computerized identification checking system," a government-sponsored program to check for fraudulent documents.[105] The company had enrolled in INS's "Electronic Verification Program" and reported doing so in its 1997 Annual Report, in which they concluded that "the program allows us to verify the validity of team members documentation, thus ensuring our compliance with the law."[106] However, John MacCoon, the assistant US attorney in Chattanooga, said Tyson would sometimes circumvent the system by hiring workers through temporary agencies that did not have access to the system.[107] Hopson was right in referring to the lawsuit as a "test case," because that kind of indictment rarely occurred for such a big company. The Department of Justice stated that it was "committed to vigorously investigating and prosecuting companies or individuals who exploit immigrants and violate our nation's immigration laws," while the INS said it was "committed to enforcing compliance with immigration law," but Striffler points out that "neither agency has done much to protect low-wage workers of any nationality."[108]

Yet the INS and DOJ are not the only government agencies that consistently fail to protect workers. The US Department of Agriculture (USDA), responsible for developing federal policy on farming, agriculture, and food, had intimate connections to agribusinesses. By the late 1970s and most clearly in the 1980s, there was a "revolving door" that led department officials back and forth between positions at the USDA and posts in agribusiness firms. By the 1990s this relationship became even clearer. Brent E. Riffel argues, "Tyson managers formed alliances both in congress and at upper levels of regulatory agencies that allowed them to advance the company's interest under the guise of protecting the consumer or the industry as a whole."[109] In the 1990s a new way to inspect food, Hazard Analysis and Critical Control Point (HAACP), apparently presented a tougher position, "but inspectors quickly noted that it actually weakened controls because each plant was allowed to design its own inspection plan which would then be approved by a largely compliant USDA."[110]

The organization Human Rights Watch described the relationship between federal agencies such as the USDA and the meat industry as follows: "Federal authorities regulate line speed, for example, only in light of two considerations: avoiding adulterated meat and poultry products and not hinder companies' productivities and profits. Workers' safety is a nonfactor."[111] This lack of concern for worker safety led to "extraordinarily high rates of injury. Workers injured on the job may then face dismissal. Workers risk losing their jobs when they exercise their rights to organize and bargain collectively in an attempt to improve working conditions."[112] Managers constantly demand more production and mandate that their people work faster. A woman in northwest Arkansas left for a year to have a baby and returned to find the line producing forty-two birds per minute, as opposed to the thirty-two per minute they had processed when she left. The job's repetitive motions, which can reach up to thirty thousand per day, leave even young people with limited mobility after a few years. One worker testified: "I hung the live birds on the line. Grab, reach, lift, jerk. Without stopping for hours every day. Only young, strong guys can do it. But after a time, you see what happens. Your arms stick out and your hands are frozen. Look at me now. I'm twenty-two years old, and I feel like an old man."[113] By 2000 the Occupational Safety and Health Administration reported that one out of seven poultry workers became injured on the job, and that they were fourteen times more likely to "suffer debilitating injuries stemming from repetitive trauma—like 'claw hand' (in which injured fingers lock in a curled position) and ganglionic cysts (fluid deposits under the skin)."[114]

Working under these conditions is a hard way to achieve upward mobility or homeownership, but many Latina/o immigrants have done just that. Yet whether as undocumented or legalized US residents or citizens, they were always looking for other opportunities, better jobs, and more pay. The poultry industry is one of the lowest-paying employers in the Fort Smith area, and its workers frequently sought to get a foot in the door at companies such as Rheem, Whirlpool, or Gerber, which paid better wages and offered less dangerous working conditions. But those jobs were difficult to obtain.

In the 1990s, if Latinas/os wanted to spend several weeks in Mexico or El Salvador for a Christmas holiday, they had limitations on how long they could be absent. If they were newer employees and had been with a company for less than a year, they were either ineligible for any vacation time or limited to just one or two weeks of absence. Each company had its own policies pertaining to absences, but employers warned Latinas/os that if they were absent at all or were gone longer than their approved vacation time, they would be fired and blacklisted. Throughout most of the 1990s, when Latinas/os chose to spend Christmas holidays in their native countries, they found that they were indeed unable to go back to work with previous employers; however, they could simply go to the next poultry company and get a job there.

Working in the poultry industry was arduous, but in the 1990s workers had greater mobility and more choices than they did a decade or two later. Recent scholarship such as that by Vanesa Ribas, Angela Stuesse, and OXFAM elucidates how employers tightened their control over laborers as the labor market became saturated or the industry reached its production capacity.[115] In the twenty-first century, poultry workers have reported dire and extremely dehumanizing experiences, such as being denied a bathroom break and having to soil themselves in order to keep their job. Supervisors were stingy with bathroom breaks because they knew that sometimes workers said they needed to use the bathroom as a way to have a little bit of an added break.

The economic boom in northwest Arkansas also created demand for housing, which in turn meant a need for construction workers. This work too paid better than the *polleras*, and many men chose to do those jobs instead.[116] Landscaping also grew in tandem with construction and created another employment possibility for Latina/o workers. Javier, for example, worked in landscaping after a friend introduced him to a small-business owner. They got along well, and the boss asked him to recruit reliable workers and put him in charge of the work crew. Javier told Jesús that the pay was much better than poultry—again La Blanca's social networks were at play—and asked him to join the work crew. But Jesús was approaching sixty years of age and thought he would be unable to work eight-, ten-, or twelve-hour days in the Arkansas heat, so he stayed at a Tyson plant where he had worked for several years. Javier did such a good job running the work crew that when the owner sought to expand his business and move to Springfield, Missouri, he asked Javier to join him. In the meantime, Andrea and Javier had saved enough money for a downpayment on a home and had become homeowners. At first Javier turned down his boss precisely because they had finally achieved that goal, but the boss offered to pay him more. So they went to Springfield, where they knew they would find other people from La Blanca who had also moved from Arkansas as they followed leads to better-paying jobs.

Latina/o Diversity, Prejudice, and Racism

The heterogeneity of Latina/o immigrants requires scholars to be careful not to categorize all Latinas/os as Mexicans or as working class. When I conducted interviews and oral histories, I often asked Latinas/os about their experiences with racism and prejudice, and at that time I thought they were going to tell me about white or Black people behaving in a derogatory manner. Yet I heard instead far more about intra-Latina/o tensions than I anticipated. Several of the people I interviewed talked about the racism and prejudice they experienced from white people, but tended to bring up that issue after they first talked about the difficulties between Mexicans and Salvadorans.

Among other things, I asked people to tell me about or describe the Latina/o community in Arkansas. I got a variety of responses. Gustavo, a Mexican immigrant who arrived in the early 1980s, received a bachelor's degree in business administration from the University of Arkansas at Fayetteville. His family owned a business that produces a Mexican foodstuff now distributed throughout northwest Arkansas and Tulsa Walmart stores. Gustavo answered the question by talking about tensions and difficulties within the Latina/o community. He said:

> And like all communities, good people arrive and bad people arrive. . . . But there are some that come from over there and they think they're in a gang or want to create gangs of their own, and that has created a lot of problems here, especially in Fort Smith and Van Buren. It's like I tell people, Americans already look badly upon us, and then we want to call more attention to ourselves and we don't want people to see us in a bad way. And I see that the climate here and in other parts is—then when they say that there was a robbery, or a shot fired—Hispanic. Hispanics. And that, that is giving us a bad name, here. And then sometimes for a few, we all have to pay; you're on the street, they see you Hispanic, and there are some that see us badly.

Gustavo talked about good people and bad people but never said who these "bad" people might be. Gretel, a Colombian immigrant who arrived in northwest Arkansas in the early 1980s and worked for one of the school districts, identified a specific group as problematic:

> Before, we were more united. I don't know what's happening right now—there are a lot of people coming that are pushing us off course, and we don't know what's happening, but before, we were much more united. The second people that started to arrive after Mexicans were the Salvadorians; there's a lot of Salvadorians. It's so much—as a teacher in the public schools—one can see a lot of gangs. We didn't see that seven, eight years ago—one didn't see any of those things. Right now there are a lot . . . a lot of gangs, a lot [of] problems in the public schools between

Salvadorians, Mexicans, and Americans; there are many problems right now.[117]

Gretel stopped short of stating that Salvadorans brought gangs with them, though according to her, there had been no gangs eight years earlier, when the Latina/o population was mostly Mexican. Interviewees often blamed gang activity on Latino youth who had lived in poor neighborhoods of Los Angeles, Dallas, and other metropolitan areas prior to moving to Arkansas.

Genoveva, a Mexican immigrant who worked for many years in the school system, elaborated on the phenomenon by drawing on her experiences in the public schools:

> Unfortunately, I see a lot of problems with Hispanics among each other when they're not from the same country, which I could never understand. . . . I used to go into the schools and saw Salvadorians fighting with the Mexicans, or the Guatemalans fighting with the Salvadorians, and Salvadorians and Mexicans are just enemies. "Are you kidding? You're both Hispanic, you both speak the same language, you have to be united, you can't fight, you already have trouble with everybody else hating you for you to hate each other."[118]

At first I thought that since Gretel and Genoveva referenced school system experiences, this phenomenon might be limited to youth. However, when I asked Gustavo whether segregation existed in Fort Smith, to my surprise he answered, "I think 'yes' because, for example, when I played soccer, I saw that, for example, if you were in a team and the majority of the players were Salvadorian, they wouldn't let a Mexican join the team, and the opposite. Like, we segregate ourselves among ourselves. And I think that there are a lot of conflicts in that." He added, "Salvadorians and Mexicans are just enemies"—a strong statement, and one that does not bode well for intragroup coalitions. If Latinas/os cannot play soccer together, and alliances are breaking down according to national origin, then pan-Latina/o effects in the region are that much more uncertain and unpredictable politically, culturally, or socially than one might expect.

The other responses that I received to the question of segregation were in the affirmative, but people often cushioned their assertion. Interviewees usually did this by speaking of self-segregation, often using the example of immigrants living close to people they knew. After such answers, I asked whether segregation was solely of our own making or if there was something more to it. Though they were each aware of which side of town particular people lived in, they thought of such a development in terms of economics or class mobility. For example, Genoveva said:

> Yeah, yeah. I do believe that. Blacks seem to stay to one area. Hispanics—Mexicans, Salvadorians, Guatemalans, whatever—they tend to because, for example, it's just like when you first find someone that lives in a different state and you go to that state because you have a friend there. Housing is no different. People will tend to go where there is already a Hispanic homeowner and they will just gravitate toward that complex or whatever and before you know it the complex is all Hispanic or all Black. And I think we do a lot of self-segregation. . . . Well, some of it is not intentional; a lot of this has to do with your income. I think that you're limited in choices, and if one complex has very inexpensive rent, then that's probably where you're going to go because you can't afford a $600-a-month beautiful complex or the homes in Fianna Hills [a wealthy neighborhood]. A lot of itself, a lot of it is out of the need to be able to afford where you live.

Celia, a Puerto Rican immigrant in her mid-thirties, arrived in the city in the mid-1990s. She also worked in the school district. When I asked her whether segregation exists in Fort Smith, she said,

> Oh yeah. Mm hm. It sure does. And I don't think it's only, not only for the Hispanics but for the black community and the lower income. I think it exists everywhere. I mean it's subtle, you don't see it, but for example, you see that there's neighborhoods, and you see, you see who lives where and . . . I would say it's both. Self-segregation I would see, for example, when they come over here they already have families or the acquaintances and they want to stay together because that's their comfort zone. But I also think, the way the housing is, I would say the land, the mortgages, how they are in different parts of the city, that helps segregate. Like I said, it's subtle, but if you're only getting minimum pay you're not going to be able to afford a house in one side of the city because of the amount of money that you're making.

Enrique, a Cuban in his fifties, had lived most of his life in the South, including almost thirty years in Fort Smith. He was one of a handful of Latina/o doctors or other such professionals in the city, though he noted that except for him and a woman, most people in this group were not immigrants themselves or even the children of immigrants. The first thing Enrique did when I asked about segregation was to sigh. Then he said,

> That's a tough question. I think that probably the minorities aren't being allowed, even though there's not a strong effort, I think just the way culture is that still the minorities, whether it's Hispanics or African American or Asian, they have to work harder to get the education . . . So I don't know that you would say that, you know, it's driven, discriminatory segregation, but I think we've still got a long ways to go until we're all blended in, assimilated as a culture, the way I see it.

Of everyone I asked, he was the only one who did not fall back on an economic explanation, but notably he hinted at assimilation as a possible answer to segregation.

When I asked them if they had ever experienced racism in Arkansas, many of the people I interviewed answered in the affirmative, proceeded to give examples, and downplayed the incidents or attributed them to the ignorance or fear of others. Celia, for example, said that racism exists everywhere; one can find people that want to help and others that do not, but often those who do not like immigrants lack education. Gretel had a somewhat similar take and spoke about an incident that took place at the local junior college in 1985:

> Once at the university there was a student . . . a colleague once made a comment because I was Hispanic. . . . It affected me a lot because I left the classroom running and didn't return to class. . . . Everyone's entitled to their own opinion, you know, but sometimes they are comments that people say only to say them, to make you feel bad. . . . The redneck that made that comment that we shouldn't be in this state. That we had come to take away their work opportunities. . . . It was a comment of poor taste. I ran into the guy a year later and he apologized. But the damage was already done, right?

Gretel categorized the guy as a "redneck" and thus also bought into stereotypes, in this case of poor white men. She also downplayed the incident by concluding it was a comment made in poor taste, despite her recognition that the remark was very hurtful and that such comments are meant to hurt people.

Early on in my conversation with Gustavo, he said he had never experienced racism or had people look down on him. But when I asked him explicitly about the issue, he contradicted himself, because he did have anecdotes. Recall that he had said, "Americans already look badly upon us and then we want to call more attention to ourselves and we don't want people to see us in a bad way." His experiences with racism were tied to language issues, racist stereotypes, and racial profiling, though he did not provide excuses for racist actions. He said the following when I asked him directly about racism:

> Then there were times when I'd go here and people to talk to me, but they talk to me as if I didn't speak English. And when I answer them, they're like, "Whoa." And then right away they change their way, like when you speak, when you go to a government office, they're a little despotic. ... There are people that tell me, 'You don't sound Hispanic, you speak English well.' And sometimes I tell them, 'I can speak it even better than you, you know.' Because they stereotype us, that because we're Hispanic, we aren't educated and that we are all drunks during the weekends, and all that. They don't think that there are people like us that are improving ourselves, that went to college.

Of the Latinos interviewed, Ricardo was the most outspoken and least apologetic about his experiences. Ricardo was a Mexican man in his early forties, married, and a father of three. He had moved to Fort Smith about twenty years earlier from East Los Angeles, where he had lived since his teenage years. Like many other people, he worked in the poultry industry for several years before getting a break in another occupation. When I asked Ricardo about racism, he said:

> In all aspects. In the labor aspect, in general, in whatever place I go. ... An example. An American trying to talk to you in Spanish all the time. I'm not ashamed. In public places. If you're interested, this might be interesting—I consider that I've been more of an object of racism on the part of older people, the elderly than of young people. Of the third age. People of Anglo-Saxon origin, the White race. ... Did you write down racism in law enforcement agencies, it exists. If you have a car that gives you away as Hispanic I think there's more ... I have seen people that work in American restaurants, people of Hispanic origin that receive commentaries from the people, from the clients of the restaurant, saying, "What are you doing here? Return to your country."

I asked him why Latinas/os stayed if we experience racism, and he said, "Because we don't have anywhere to go. ... We prefer to be objects of discrimination before returning to Mexico. I don't know if it's called discrimination, but I think there's a very closed mind locally on the part of the white race." Despite these difficulties, the Latina/o community in northwest Arkansas continues to thrive. However, the intraethnic fissures continue to expand.

Conclusion

Many Latina/o immigrants worked at least a few years in *polleras* out of necessity. The social networks ensure that the circulating information is up to date—social contacts rank poultry plants or warn workers not to go to certain ones unless their situation is dire. In 2003, Tyson managers told Human Rights Watch, "It is a myth that we are trying to bring in Hispanic employees at the expense of local workers, that we want Hispanic workers so we can exploit or mistreat them. That is absolutely untrue, total nonsense. The increase of Hispanic workers in our plants is a result of us needing workers and Hispanic workers needing jobs."[119] That last part of the statement is correct; Latina/o immigrants, undocumented and legalized, discovered the poultry industry at a time when it was desperate to grow to meet national demand for chicken. The industry would be willing to exploit any worker, from any part of the world, but immigrants that are undocumented have an immense vulnerability that the industry exploits. A plant manager in the South straightforwardly told Striffler, "I don't want them after they've been here for a year and know how to get around. I want them right off the bus."[120] Tyson threatens to fire workers (and follows through) if they protest changes in the workplace or hint at organizing a union.[121] A Tyson worker from a Rogers plant said:

> Tyson always gets rid of workers who protest or who speak up for others. When they jumped from thirty-two chickens a minute to forty-two, a lot of people protested. The company came right out and asked who the leaders were. Then they fired them. They told us, "If you don't like it, there's the door. There's another eight hundred applicants waiting to take your job." They are the biggest company so what they do goes for the rest.[122]

Indeed, Peterson Farms (in Rogers) sent a notice to its third-shift sanitation crew that any worker who was organizing a strike would be fired.[123]

Managers knew there was a willing labor pool to replace laborers that complained about the working conditions, but Tyson lost about $4,000 for every worker it had to retrain, and the industry average of nearly 100 percent turnover per year made this costly.[124] At the same time, John Sampier, the mayor of Rogers for thirteen years, sought to integrate Latinas/os into the community. The Rogers Chamber of Commerce came up with a plan in 1994 that placed a high priority on "the integration of the Hispanic community" throughout the city to "keep Rogers a desirable place to live."[125] As part of the endeavor, the chamber encouraged developers to build affordable housing, and they got the area's largest bank to provide mortgage loans for two-worker immigrant families who earned more than seven dollars per hour at the area's poultry plants.[126]

Despite a seemingly inexhaustible workforce, poultry plants in Rogers still had high turnover rates, and some were considering relocating until Sampier's efforts kicked in. Arvest Bank participated in the endeavor by establishing a financial literacy training program at plants, while the plants provided the classroom space for paid workers to take classes on US banking and homeownership.[127] Arvest Bank also created a program to help immigrants establish credit history, which in turn helped qualify them for home mortgages. The program provided 586 loans with no defaults in eight years. The effort earned $26 million for the bank, and the poultry plants' turnover rate dropped from 200 to 15 percent from 1992 to 1999.[128] According to Sampier, by 1998, 40 percent of the city's forty-five hundred Latinas/os were homeowners.[129] In this way, the poultry industry was a key factor in efforts to smooth over tensions between Latina/o immigrants and white Arkansans while keeping a much-needed supply of laborers.

Tyson, after invoking the notion that "America's labor force has historically been fueled by newcomers," put it to their stockholders as follows: "Tyson Foods has accepted a responsibility to these communities [the ones experiencing changes] by making a vigorous commitment of human and financial resources to assist in assimilating the newcomers in our workforce into American culture and society."[130] The company went on to say that it had "initiated and sponsored" multicultural centers and forums and helped community organizations to provide various services such as English as a second language and citizenship classes as well as opening opportunities for teachers to achieve ESL accreditation. It also provided translation and interpretation services to law enforcement, schools, and health care providers. The company's report closed by noting that it also participated in the Electronic Verification Program, thus ensuring compliance with the law. In other words, Tyson was being a good corporate citizen to immigrants and to longtime residents.

Tyson supported Sampier in his run for reelection against Steve Womack, who ran on a strong anti-immigrant platform; Womack won. The election will be discussed more fully in the next chapter, but for now it suffices to say that the poultry industry's privileged status began to wane as Arkansans noted how important Tyson and other plants were for drawing Latinas/os to their neighborhoods. Tyson, like other poultry companies, had for the most part been allowed to dictate how they got rid of the immense chicken waste, with dire consequences for the area's waterways. The company faced increasing scrutiny for its waste management practices, but it was the connection to the racial and ethnic diversification of the northwest area of the state that made Arkansans leery of Tyson Foods Incorporated.

CHAPTER 5

"Northwest Arkansas's No. 1 Societal Concern": "Illegal Aliens," Acts of Spatial Illegality, and Political Mobilizations

The 1990s was a period of great change for northwest Arkansas, as it went from being an overwhelmingly white area to one that had tens of thousands of Latinas/os. Two central questions guide this chapter: How did the community and state respond to the presence of Latinas/os? How did the responses racialize Latinas/os? I understand racialization as the process by which institutions and individuals form, establish, invoke, adapt, reformulate, and strengthen racial meanings. This happens in different and interconnecting spheres that include juridical, legislative, economic, political, cultural, and social interactions. Some of these are formally part of the state, others are not; at different points in time individuals either cooperate with the state's efforts or do not. As Latinas/os made Arkansas home, as they rented apartments, bought houses, sent their kids to school, attended church, bought cars, shopped for clothes and groceries, and worked at *polleras*, they caught the attention of the statewide press and community members who talked about "aliens," "illegals," "illegal aliens," and "illegal Mexicans."

Although the responses to them varied, Latina/o immigrants were overwhelmingly constructed as "illegal aliens." The discourse of "illegal aliens" racialized all Latinas/os as undocumented, criminal, and Mexican. Informed by Mae Ngai's and Nicholas De Genova's work, I argue that the construction of Latina/o immigrants as "illegal" became a defining characteristic; it ceased being one part of a whole and became the whole that defines the parts.[1] In other words, Arkansans began to work from the premise that all Latinas/os are "illegal" and Mexican. It is a myopic vision that does not allow for the heterogeneity among immigrants with varying legal statuses (undocumented, temporary resident, permanent resident, and naturalized citizen) and migrants who are native-born

US citizens. Moreover, their supposed undocumented status marks them as criminals or people with tendencies to break the law. The construction of Latina/o immigrants as "illegal aliens" draws on notions of citizenship, belonging, and exclusion. This discourse is about the parameters and preservation of community at a variety of scales, including the local and national. Moreover, it is a racialized discourse that marks Latina/o bodies, particularly Mexicans, as foreigners and outsiders. As critical geographers point out, debates about community are about identity and space, place, race, and landscape. One can approach these relationships as constantly changing and dynamic and thus define a community as amorphous, its outlines constantly moving. Or, one can attempt to make static the definition of community and who belongs, reifying and reproducing markers of separation. I argue that the articles concerning Latinas/os in the *Arkansas Democrat-Gazette* are attempts to construct community in the latter sense. To maintain this strict definition, behaviors are monitored to ensure they conform to the norm. However, when new people arrive and are seen as "foreigners," their conduct is scrutinized much more intensely. And if the larger community has the power to do so, it will find ways to police behaviors and/or enact laws in order to protect and preserve its desired lines of community and identity.

White Arkansans policed their community borders based on who belonged (white people) and who did not (Latinas/os); consequently, nearly all behaviors of Latinas/os were understood as "acts of spatial illegality." I define this as any instance in which Latinas/os do not break the white community's laws, customs, or social norms, yet their activity is constructed as objectionable and illicit, and their mere presence is a violation of community. It is when Latinas/os engage in the same behaviors as their white neighbors, with accepted comportment such as going to the park with their family, but their acts are constructed as objectionable and as bringing a taint to that place. In other words, because Latinas/os are racialized as "illegal aliens," their use of spaces can be considered a violation even when it does not depart from the laws or social norms that govern the white community. The result is that Latinas/os themselves become illicit within those spaces.

The reactions toward Latina/o immigrants also mobilized grassroots responses from the Arkansas electorate, especially in the Third Congressional District. In 1997 Dan Morris, a Rogers resident, formed Americans for an Immigration Moratorium (AIM). The following year the mayor of Rogers, John Sampier, a seventeen-year incumbent who had led efforts in northwest Arkansas to incorporate Latinas/os into the area, lost a reelection bid to Steve Womack, an alderman who ran on an anti-immigrant campaign. By 2001 Gunner DeLay, a Republican from Fort Smith, declared "illegal immigration" the "defining issue" in the district. Most politicians responded harshly toward Latinas/os, though in 2000 Governor Mike Huckabee eventually welcomed them to the state as "friends and neighbors," and by 2005 some Black legislators attempted to create opportunities for undocumented students to pay in-state tuition in Arkansas's state colleges and universities.

I begin the chapter by laying out the theoretical framework of Latinas/os' racialization as "illegal aliens" and follow it with an analysis of newspaper stories that demonstrate how Arkansans made sense of these new southerners. From there I explore Latinas/os in public space and the construction of their activities as spatial acts of illegality. The last half of the chapter investigates nativist responses and political mobilizations in northwest Arkansas and how these issues reached statewide politics. The final section addresses the future of Latinas/os in Arkansas.

Racialization and "Illegal Aliens"

As Mae Ngai argues, US immigration has created "illegal aliens," and Mexicans have emerged as emblematic of this juridical status.[2] More importantly, illegal status came to define the racialized contours for Mexicans and, by extension, other Latinas/os assumed to be Mexican. In a similar fashion, Nicholas De Genova also argues that one key aspect in the racialization of Latinas/os, particularly Mexicans, is the discursive and legal power of illegality that serves to racialize all Mexicans in particular ways.[3] While it is true that some Latinas/os in Arkansas were undocumented immigrants, many were also US legal residents, naturalized citizens, and, among the younger generation, US-born nationals. The inability of most Arkansans to fathom that many of the new arrivals were legally present demonstrates the power of spatial illegality and its effects for racialization.

Jonathan Xavier Inda renders the construction of "illegal aliens" in ethical terms. Ultimately, Inda argues that "'illegal' immigrants—typically imagined as criminals, job takers, and welfare dependents—have essentially been constructed as imprudent, unethical subjects incapable of exercising responsible self-government and thus as threats to the overall well-being of the social body."[4] As we shall see, in Arkansas the threat to the "social body" took place at different scales—community, state, and nation.

Fabian, a public school employee, recalled that in northwest Arkansas there was initially "a lot of resistance from a lot of teachers, but there were also a lot of teachers that wanted to make this work. On top of all that you throw in to the mix the fact that there were undocumented people and you are 'a law abiding citizen' and there's a moral fight in your mind."[5] Some teachers verbalized their dislike of and prejudice toward Latina/o students by complaining to Fabian about "his kids." "There was a [teacher] who was about to retire, that lady, forget about it, I felt that what she felt was a *hatred*. She would say, '*Your kids are doing this!*' and '*Your kids!*'" Clearly, then, the consequences of Latinas/os being constructed as undocumented, illegal, or lawbreakers had repercussions throughout different spheres in northwest Arkansas.

In this chapter I focus on how implications of foreignness, criminality, and ultimately illegality defined the process of racialization for Latinas/os and affected their use of private and public spaces. Initially, white residents often complained about Latinas/os for simply being in and making use of front yards and parks, engaging in the same type of activities that white residents undertook. I argue that the "illegal" dimension occurs even if Latinas/os do not break the laws, customs, or social norms of the community, state, or nation. Instead, because Latinas/os are racialized as "illegal aliens," their use of spaces is deemed a violation even if it does not break the law. In addition, Latinas/os themselves become illicit within those spaces. The mere presence of people racialized as undesirable was felt by the white community as a violation, and turned the former's occupancy of those places into objectionable, illicit acts, or acts of spatial illegality.

Making Sense of Latinas/os: "We Just Don't Run Across This Every Day"

In the 1990s, Latinas/os came to Arkansas from various places, but 70 percent had Mexican ancestry, and the next largest group had Central American, especially Salvadoran, origins.[6] The estimates about the number of undocumented immigrants in the area varied widely. According to a US Border Patrol estimate in 1995, about 30 to 40 percent of Latinas/os in Arkansas were undocumented.[7] However, some scholars argue that the undocumented population constituted about 10 percent based on state data, INS estimates, and community and religious organizations.[8] The percentage of undocumented Latinas/os in Arkansas is not important to this project. What is vital is the material force that the construction of Latinas/os as "illegal aliens" exerted in the process of racialization.

Arkansans that encountered Latinas/os at parks, in stores, on the playground, or in other public spaces could not identify their legal status, but operated under the assumption that all Latinas/os were "illegal" and that all "illegals" were Mexican.

Even if the higher estimate of the number of undocumented people is correct, it does not change how Arkansans made sense of Latinas/os. The best indicator as to the relationship between race and documentation is that white and Black immigrants generally are not assumed to be undocumented or necessarily immigrants. White immigrants in particular can skirt being recognized as such—in public they are just white people unless they speak their native language or have other markers, such as dress, that indicate their origin. Black immigrants are often constructed as African Americans, unless they too have markers that suggest otherwise. Asians, both immigrants and US-born citizens, are often seen as foreigners, though not necessarily undocumented.[9] Because Latinas/os can be of any race, lighter-skinned Latinas/os with more European features are not necessarily identified and racialized as Latinas/os unless other markers are present, such as speaking Spanish or being with Latinas/os that have darker complexions and more indigenous or African features. Most of the Latina/o immigrants who moved to Arkansas in the 1990s were native Spanish speakers with darker complexions and more indigenous features, so they were frequently identified as Mexicans and "illegal aliens."

Arkansans in the northwest part of the state had experienced limited personal interactions with Mexican immigrants before the late 1980s, but they had been exposed to national debates and discussions about Mexicans and undocumented immigration and already had firm ideas as to what the federal government needed to do: close the border and deport them all. In 1975, when some Arkansans were sponsoring Vietnamese refugees, C. L. Justin of Winslow in Washington County wrote to Governor David Pryor and told him that the United States would have more than enough room for Southeast Asian refugees if lawful and unlawful Mexican immigrants were barred from entering the country. As Justin saw it, the number of unemployed Americans matched the number of undocumented Mexican immigrants, creating a causal relationship such that if the latter were denied entry into the country, the former would be employed. Moreover, if undocumented Mexicans were not in the country, then there would be plenty of room for Southeast Asian refugees. For Justin, the national body was damaged by the voluminous numbers of Mexican immigrants:

> When we note that the number of unemployed Americans is estimated at 6 to 10 million, and then see that there are thought to be 6 to 10 million

persons entered here illegally from Mexico, ought we not to take some actions? This is in addition to now 400,000 a year entering legally.

If we can curtail this, in fact stop all legal and illegal immigration from that one country alone, will we not have ample room for the perhaps 100,000 refugees from Indo-China, who need our help to save their lives.[10]

During the Mariel boatlift, some Arkansans objected to aiding any "aliens." E. S. Gates of Siloam Springs in Benton County wrote to Governor Bill Clinton to vehemently object to helping Cubans, arguing, "We are overpopulated and under-employed now, and people around here are really angry that 'refugees' are invading the United States on every side and we want it stopped. Also illegal aliens. We want Mexican and all other illegal aliens deported. . . . these aliens populate like flies and cost us far more tax money to keep them than to deport them."[11] Drexel Atkinson from Little Rock wrote, "I protest the lack of enforcement of U.S. immigration laws and the flood of aliens in the U.S. from Cuba and Asia. In addition to this we have immigrants coming in from South America and Mexico both legally and illegally."[12] He pledged not to vote for any federal official if aid to refugees continued and to contact people in Arkansas and other states, thereby suggesting that he was going to start a grassroots anti-immigrant, antirefugee movement. At a time when immigration was not a major issue in Arkansas and the people in question were not from Mexico, Arkansans nonetheless centered their objections and fears on Mexican immigrants, regardless of status. Although Gates and Atkinson recognized that undocumented people could be from other countries, by mentioning Mexico by name they demonstrated that Mexican immigrants were the primary targets of their fears and apprehensions. Their anxieties were likely heightened during the 1980s, when the national immigration conversation focused on the millions of undocumented people in the United States and the Immigration Reform and Control Act of 1986 was passed to allow many people to legalize their status.

By the 1990s, articles about Latinas/os had begun to appear in newspapers with increasing frequency, especially as these immigrants began to settle in the state. Beginning with the first few stories printed in the 1990s about Latinas/os, we can see an evolution in the way they were portrayed, as the focus shifted from legal migrant workers to undocumented Hispanics to "illegal aliens."[13] The latter construction proved to be long-lasting as the Latina/o community grew.

In May 1990 the *Arkansas Gazette* published "Migrants Fill Summer Niche," which focused on men (they were the only ones mentioned while wives waited elsewhere) who worked on fish farms during the spring and summer in Lonoke County. The story said that Jack Wheat, the mayor of the town of Lonoke, counted "35 to 50 migrant workers from Spanish-speaking countries," including Mexicans and Guatemalans. Wheat added that the work "demands a lot of manual labor and they're legal immigrants. The demand here is so great seasonally that apparently there are not enough people in the area to fill the jobs."[14] Employers liked the migrants because they were quick learners and did not "need breaks for summer vacations or summertime football practice." Wheat eased any local anxieties by addressing two key issues: that these workers were not taking jobs from Americans workers, and that they were not undocumented immigrants.[15]

The story also included a picture of two men laughing, with a caption that read, "LIGHT MOMENT: Juan Negrete, a migrant worker from Mexico, shares a light minute with his friend and coworker Roy Lewis, during a lunch break. Migrant workers are in demand in Lonoke in the summer." The picture captured camaraderie between the men as they shared a friendly moment in the lunchroom over their shared struggle of getting through the workday. The reporter began the story by recounting an instance in the lunchroom in which Negrete told Lewis about a home remedy for a sore throat. The story suggested that workers such as Negrete brought "Spanish 101" and "cultural lessons" to Lonoke, as well as money spent at a local Walmart on items like gold chains, charms, earrings, and watches. Jewel Ashmore, a Walmart employee, said the migrants' presence "makes my job a whole lot more interesting. And it has been educational for me—I can count to 10, and learned the words 'dinero' for money and 'agua' for 'water.'" The story ended by citing various other things that Arkansans had learned from migrants—such as foods like "beans, rice, hot peppers and tortillas"—while observing that the townsfolk were "eager to make friends," and that Negrete enjoyed "going to high school baseball games with Lewis."[16]

The sketch of these Latina/o migrants was short, but it covered a variety of topics and hinted at the newcomers' diverse origins. It stated that migrants were legally present in the country, that they were hard workers who learned quickly, and that they were available to work at times when local workers wanted to take time off or do other activities. As migrant workers, they presumably left when their labor was no longer needed; they were disposable workers. They were also consumers who spent money in the local economy or deposited it in local banks as they saved to buy a truck, although some sent money home to wives and parents. The report read like a human interest story in which immigrants and locals teach each other about their culture and language. After all, baseball is "America's pastime."

The story about Lonoke stood in contrast to the *Democrat-Gazette*'s next report, "Immigration Officials Arrest Hudson Workers," which appeared in the newspaper almost two years later. The story concerned workers at Hudson Foods, a poultry plant in Noel, Missouri, a short drive across the state line. Its focus was the ongoing INS raids in the area's poultry plants to "check for illegal aliens, most of whom are Hispanic." The reporter wrote that several workers from the area's poultry plants claimed the INS made surprise inspections in northwest Arkansas poultry plants in those weeks, though no other story appeared stating that undocumented immigrants were found. To relate the raid in Missouri to Arkansas, the journalist wrote that "the Hispanic population in Northwest Arkansas has grown at such a clipping rate" that police officers in towns such as Rogers were required to learn Spanish, while Tyson Foods had started offering Spanish classes to supervisors "to accommodate the growing Hispanic workforce."[17] Unlike the previous Lonoke article, this story presented no human face. It was about the INS, the poultry industry, and "illegal aliens, most of whom are Hispanic." No estimates are given for the growth of Latinas/os, though the implications are clear: they get in trouble with local police departments and they work in the poultry industry. They were no longer described as legal migrant workers; now they were "illegal" permanent workers, and no friendly moment is depicted between coworkers at poultry plants.

If there was some doubt as to their activities after they presumably crossed the border, the next story made it clear they were not beyond breaking the law (again). On May 28, 1992, a story appeared in the *Democrat-Gazette* titled, "Osceola Wants Aliens off Its Hands; INS Refuses to Take Penniless 11 Held in Break-in." According to the article, the police department in the northeast Arkansas town of Osceola arrested eleven "illegal aliens" after receiving a call that "Spanish-looking people" were breaking into a truck. The eleven people arrested were accused of stealing a battery and cables, as well as shoplifting food. "We just don't run across this every day. The numbers we were dealing with kind of caught my attention," said the town's police chief, Phil Johnson. The Osceola Police Department in Mississippi County called the Little Rock and Memphis INS offices to have the men deported, but were told to let them go because employed "illegal aliens" were "the lowest level" on the Border Patrol's list. Jim Hipple, the agent in charge of the Border Patrol in Little Rock, said, "That [the undocumented men] sounds like Osceola's problem to me." He noted that the agency could pick them up and send them back to Mexico, but he added, "Those offenses are the least of our worries. We are dealing with [other] criminal adult illegal aliens who commit heinous crimes, or those of a serious type." Osceola's mayor, Dick Kennemore, was surprised at the response. "I couldn't believe it," Kennemore said. "Here President [George H.] Bush is sending the Haitians back, we are spending huge amounts of money on a super collider, and they told me to just let them go."[18]

Jessee F. Tabor, the chief patrol agent with the Border Patrol's New Orleans office, said the article misrepresented the agency and that it was "normal procedure not to interfere until local disposition has run its course." However, Arthur Pugh, an Osceola police captain, stood by city officials, saying, "That's the first time a law enforcement agency told me to let loose a criminal." Four of the eleven suspects were sixteen-year-old boys who were transferred to the county's juvenile authority and released to relatives living in Alabama "who are U.S. residents." The remaining men, ages seventeen to twenty-three, were released on their own recognizance.[19] One adult and one juvenile were charged with theft for taking battery cables, but the Border Patrol had no plans to deport them to Mexico.[20]

In the Southwest, the INS and then the Border Patrol historically had exercised latitude in terms of how they enforced immigration laws. For example, as far back as 1910, officials let Mexican immigrants enter the United States even though there were statutes on the books that prevented the entry of those "likely to become a public charge" or who were infirm, whose morality was in question, or who were seeking to work as contract laborers. F. W. Berkshire, the supervising inspector at El Paso, told his superior in Washington that "all of the Mexican aliens of the laboring class" could be denied entry under the "likely to become a public charge" statute, but they both knew that the Mexicans could find transportation to areas where they would find employment.[21] As George Sánchez put it, "Both American officials and entering aliens understood that it was the labor needs of the American Southwest that defined Mexican immigration to the United States and not laws drawn up in Washington."[22] In her study of the Border Patrol, Kelley Lytle Hernández argues that "the U.S. Border Patrol's rise in the U.S.-Mexico borderlands not only evolved according to economic demands and nativist anxieties but also operated according to the individual interests and community investments of the men who worked as Border Patrol officers."[23]

According to US policy, the Border Patrol is responsible for removing undocumented people from the country, yet at various points in time its officers have chosen to overlook those laws because they understand the service that able-bodied workers provide, usually to agriculture. This proved to be the case in Arkansas, with the regional offices unconcerned about the eleven employed undocumented Mexicans, but the local law enforcement officers were more alarmed because they were unaccustomed to seeing such large numbers of Latinas/os. Moreover, the agencies had differing hierarchies of criminality: the Border Patrol viewed undocumented people as a low priority unless they committed serious crimes, whereas for the local police department, the fact that the men had broken the law by crossing the border was reason enough to cast them as threatening criminals.

At this moment in which various institutions working at different scales decide whether to uphold federal laws, the seeming contradiction in their approaches can be found in Mayor Kennemore's comment about the United States actively turning away and returning (some) people who are trying to enter the country while simultaneously allowing others to remain. Kennemore invoked the example of Haitians because in that moment they were national news. In 1991 a military coup d'état unseated the democratically elected president, Jean-Bertrand Aristide, and in the aftermath, thousands of Haitians took boats, arrived on US soil, and sought to enter seeking asylum. On May 24, 1992, President Bush ordered the Coast Guard to intercept all Haitians at sea and return them without determining the legitimacy of their claims for asylum.[24]

Haitians have historically been denied equal treatment in seeking asylum. The federal government argued that they were economic migrants rather than political refugees, despite evidence of persecution under the repressive regimes that had ruled the country since the late 1950s. The unfair treatment of Haitians continued in the 1990s. For example, in December 1992 when a Cuban pilot diverted a plane to Miami after gagging and handcuffing the co-pilot and the security guard, he and all the Cubans were given the opportunity to stay in the United States if they so wished. A few months later, a Haitian man also diverted a plane to Miami, but he was accused of piracy, jailed, and threatened with a twenty-year sentence.[25] In 1995 President Clinton changed long-standing policy toward Cubans during the so-called *balsero* crisis (from the Spanish "*balsa*," for "raft," i.e., boat people), when many poor and working-class islanders fled for the United States. The administration ordered Cuban *balseros* to be intercepted at sea and repatriated to Cuba, yet those who reached US soil were allowed to stay and begin their paperwork for legal entry. Mariel

Cubans in 1980 and *balseros* in the 1990s had similar backgrounds and differed from the first waves of Cubans who arrived in the United States after Castro took power, and for whom special legislation was enacted. The exiles in the 1960s were part of the island elite and were largely of European ancestry, while Cubans in the last two decades of the twentieth century were largely working-class people with more African ancestry. Clinton's abrupt change on Cuban admission policy might have reflected a fear of poor immigrants of color. At the same time, Cubans that reached US soil were allowed to stay. This policy stood in sharp contrast to procedures that remove others who attempt to reach the United States in a similar fashion, such as Haitians and Dominicans.[26]

The incident in Osceola took place only four days after President Bush essentially closed the US border to Haitians, yet the federal agencies were unwilling to deport the handful of undocumented men already in Arkansas. Ngai notes that "the illegal alien cannot be constituted without deportation—the possibility of threat of deportation, if not the fact."[27] This happens because the state has a system in place to detain and deport individuals. It is a looming threat that may, in fact, never take place. Yet the threat alone can leave psychological and cultural consequences in the form of "community vulnerability and isolation, and the use of undocumented workers as a highly exploited and reserve labor force."[28] According to De Genova, "what makes deportability so decisive in the legal production of migrant 'illegality' and the militarized policing of nation-state borders is that some are deported in order that most may remain (un-deported)—as workers, whose particular migrant status may thus be rendered 'illegal.'" This maintains a labor force as "a distinctly disposable commodity" and "keeps a cheap labor reserve."[29] For Kennemore, the Osceola incident was a moment of rupture and contraction, because he knew that the US president was returning thousands of Haitians to their country but was told to allow a handful of men to continue their undocumented journeys. What Kennemore and Pugh did not understand were the purposes these men served by remaining in the United States; they were going to be, if they had not already been, a cheap and disposable workforce.

Work was central to the construction of Latinas/os, but as the community grew and women and children joined their husbands and fathers, Latinas/os expanded their activities beyond the work in *polleras*.[30] They moved into a variety of neighborhoods and entered into an assortment of daily activities. The three newspaper articles in the 1990s that talked about Latinas/os suggest that Arkansans were quite accepting of migrant workers as people who would toil the land or water when necessary, but then would leave after the season had passed. Learning how to say "*dinero*" and count to ten in Spanish was all right, as was learning about "rice, beans, and red peppers," but once Latina/o immigrants began to find permanent work in the poultry industry, once they put down roots in Arkansas as they rented and bought homes, they were no longer curiosities and were constructed instead as "illegal aliens." While newcomers are supposed to adapt to their surroundings, not everyone was pleased with the participation of Latinas/os in ordinary activities. The next section demonstrates how their uses of public and private spaces such as housing, front yards, and motor vehicles were deemed spatial acts of illegality.

Contours of Spatialized Illegality and Public Space

Only a year after the eleven undocumented Mexicans caught the attention of the Osceola Police Department, Julieanne Miller reported that "Northwest Arkansas is encountering a large influx of illegal Mexican aliens the past 16 months." By her estimations, "12,000 illegal Mexican aliens" in the area had led federal authorities to conduct raids in Fort Smith. After the raids, "citizen complaints" led the US Border Patrol to return to search apartments in working-class neighborhoods on the city's north side. According to Miller, "the complaints regarded overcrowded residences or illegal aliens using public facilities. Almost all of the illegal aliens survived in dirty, squalid living conditions in low-rent housing near their jobs or in the downtown areas of Fort Smith and Van Buren."[31]

The remark presented two issues. The first concerns "overcrowded" housing or non-normative behaviors that painted Latinas/os as unsanitary, unhygienic, poor, and living too many to an apartment. The comment on the type of housing they occupied made it seem as if unhygienic living conditions should have been expected from people who inhabited the lower strata of society; this impression contributed to their racialization. Overcrowding is presented as a cultural trait in these stories because there is no suggestion that Latina/o immigrants live in this manner as a means to save rent money or that it is a temporary solution until they have saved enough to live on their own or buy a house. Instead, their housing patterns are pathologized as something threatening to the rest of society, especially through descriptions of their supposedly filthy living quarters.

The second part of the remark was a complaint about "illegal aliens using public facilities." In other words, the objection was about supposedly undocumented people *using* public facilities as opposed to the *mis-*

use of them. However, it is impossible to visually or aurally identify undocumented immigrants, since they can be of any phenotype, and people legally present in the United States can also speak Spanish. White Arkansans rejected the patronage and participation of Latinas/os in the community and, I argue, constructed their activities as spatial acts of illegality precisely because the group often did not break social rules or norms in their use of public amenities or while engaged in other activities. Being in public view increasingly became a loaded issue for Latinas/os, as many Arkansans objected to their presence.

Concerns about housing were rampant in relation to Latinas/os, and in 1994 Springdale residents and several members of the Springdale City Council knew "how to handle overcrowded housing caused by a growing Hispanic population: Hire an officer with a gun."[32] They proposed that the lawman go door to door to enforce housing codes. According to Mike Rodman, a reporter for the *Arkansas Democrat-Gazette*, the debate was part of what many considered "Northwest Arkansas' No. 1 societal concern: how to deal with an influx of Mexicans." Springdale residents complained about "too many Mexicans living in the same house," leading to "unhealthy conditions" and "slumlike conditions." Alderman Howard Cook said that the officer needed to be "forceful, carry a weapon and be tied to the Police Department," because in enforcing the law he would "eventually run into a drug deal." The presence of Latinas/os was cause for distress, not only because they supposedly broke sanitary norms through their living arrangements, but also because, according to Cook, they were drug dealers. Here we see the conflation of living arrangements with a person's character, as everyone who shares an apartment with more people than the norm becomes a drug dealer. Cook went beyond racializing Latinas/os as undocumented, unhealthy, or unsanitary. Inda argues that the construction of immigrants as "illegal" also serves to substantiate the belief that they will break other laws and create crime.[33] The Springdale alderman demonstrated this process quite clearly by failing to cite any evidence to support his claim.

Complaints about housing extended beyond the occupation of certain structures to issues about the use of space within private property. In June 1994, Springdale resident Karen Wolf complained that "they [Latinas/os] congregate in the front yard instead of in the back yard like normal people.... There's loud music late at night, and it's like they're trying to take over. If they would just stay inside it wouldn't bother me, but it's very unnerving."[34]

Wolf's anxieties about Latinas/os were built on two factors—

abnormality and visibility. First, Latinas/os are viewed as abnormal because they have different habits in congregating with friends and family; instead of using backyards "like normal people," they use front yards. Presumably this behavior trespasses the boundaries of a social norm likely established through custom and not law. Also at stake is a norm regarding public or semipublic space, because front yards are easily seen from the street and sidewalk, allowing the public to view occurrences on private property. The second issue is about visibility: if Latinas/os were inside their houses, and therefore essentially invisible, then there would not be a problem. In this instance, for Latinas/os to be visible in a public space breaks an expectation of invisibility and a social norm that excludes them from definitions of community. These transgressions amount to "taking over," or becoming an overpowering force that drastically changes the environment.

Although Wolf also complained about loud parties, her statement demonstrated the extent to which an everyday activity became suspect when a particular behavior was deemed non-normative in comparison to the behavior Wolf and other white residents engaged in.[35] Wolf did not say what (else) Latinas/os were doing to try to "take over," or state whether a determinate number of Latinas/os would be acceptable. Instead, the presence of *some* Latinas/os in her neighborhood was alarming enough to make her feel menaced and unnerved. Wolf simply did not like the sight of Latinas/os, since for her own reasons and according to her logic she would have no problem if they were inside—completely out of sight—and virtually locked in their homes. In this scenario, the acts of spatial illegality by Latinas/os would be muted if they were hidden behind closed doors and kept out of public view.

In moving to Arkansas, Latinas/os moved into the "Natural State," the Arkansas motto as proclaimed on license plates. This nickname suggests a high regard for outdoor activities such as fishing, bike riding, or visiting the state's many parks and waterways. Yet some Rogers residents complained of "heavy Hispanic patronage of parks, lakes, and streams in the area." Dana McCoy, who had moved to Rogers from California five years earlier, said, "I don't have a problem with anybody being at places. . . . It's just that things have changed so much. You go over to Prairie Creek on a weekend now, and it feels like almost all is Hispanic."[36] This comment is particularly significant, because one strong objection to Latinas/os regarded their lack of assimilation. McCoy herself said, "I don't see Hispanic people trying to meet people halfway here. Some aren't making an effort to adapt," yet she found an Arkansan activity like going to the park on a weekend to be an objectionable behavior when practiced by Latinas/os.[37] McCoy, like Wolf, complained about the use of public space and suggested that if the park had not "changed so much," then everything would have been fine. Of course, for the park to remain what it was, it would have had to remain overwhelmingly white.

Complaints about the use of public and private space demonstrated the nativist responses of many Arkansans, who did not object to similar activities by those they deemed insiders or citizens. What McCoy, Wolf, and others objected to was the change in scenery, if you will; they did not like seeing Latinas/os, people deemed "illegal aliens" and outside of *their* community, using public space, regardless of their right to do so. For Latinas/os, going to the park in Rogers on a sunny afternoon became an act of spatial illegality.

Exclusionary responses were not limited to housing or the use of park space. In November 1996, Alberto and Bertha De La Torre filed the proper paperwork with Springdale to open a club geared toward Latinas/os. They were given a license to operate such a business, but after neighbor complaints about "loud Mexican music" and "handguns," the city informed the De La Torres in February 1997 that their permit was being revoked. According to the city, someone had made a mistake in authorizing such an establishment in the area, and the permit was invalidated on the grounds that it violated zoning laws. Significantly, this was the second business venture the couple had engaged in that was curtailed. Prior to opening the club, they had organized dances at the Springdale Rodeo Grounds, only to have the Rodeo of the Ozarks, the organization that ran the grounds, halt their activities. According to John Gladden, a board member, the dances were being held every weekend with no opportunities for other community groups to use the venue, so they limited "profit-making ventures to one use a year" in order to make it "more beneficial to the whole community."[38] In one instance, "loud Mexican music" served as the cloak behind which Latinas/os were rejected and denied their rights as ethnic entrepreneurs to cater to their clientele. In the other case, the De La Torres' rights as citizens or members of a community were denied because their events were detrimental "to the whole community." Both of these instances constituted acts of spatial illegality, as Latinas'/os' use of public space was perceived as a threat to the larger community.

Struggles over issues of space continued ten years after Latinas/os moved to Rogers and first realized they were closely monitored and targeted in public spaces as they engaged in daily activities. By 2001 local Latina/o leaders and the Mexican American Legal Defense Fund

(MALDEF) had received a barrage of complaints about racial profiling. In one case, Miguel Lopez, thirty-six, and Nora Virginia Lopez, forty-five, were driving home with their kids in July 2000 when they passed a police vehicle heading in the opposite direction. The police passed them, turned around, followed them, and without motive pulled the couple over. Two uniformed officers and a plainclothes person approached the Lopezes; one asked for immigration papers and questioned them while the other two searched the car without permission. The officers left without issuing a citation.[39] That the officers asked for immigration documentation made it clear they sought to apprehend "illegal aliens."

By March 2001 the Rogers Police Department faced a class-action racial profiling lawsuit. Joe Berra of the San Antonio office for MALDEF and Gary Kennon of Bentonville filed the suit in Western District Court in Fayetteville. Three Rogers residents, including the Lopezes, claimed they were illegally stopped, detained, and asked for identification. The suit named the police chief, Tim Keck; the mayor, Steve Womack; the Rogers Police Department; the city; and fifty officers listed as John Doe. Keck said he had met with Latina/o community leaders four times in the year prior to hear complaints but did not see any unconstitutional or bad policy. His response was, "In this business, if you're doing your job right, somebody's going to be unhappy because you're enforcing the law."[40] According to MALDEF, "Rogers police have been unlawfully targeting Latinos for stops, searches, and investigations in a form of racial profiling, frequently linked to the improper entanglement by local police in immigration enforcement."[41]

These events exhibited two developments: the institutionalization of discrimination aimed at Latinas/os, and their fight for rights despite having no Latina/o elected public officials. As MALDEF pointed out, "some anti-Latino and anti-immigrant bias has unfortunately made its way into local structures of government. This was the first serious challenge by the Latino community to this type of discrimination by government officials in the area."[42] The alleged actions by police officers were based on "fears and unfair perceptions" of newcomers. According to Berra, "Latinos stopped by Rogers police are being asked to show immigration documents or social security cards. . . . Local police have been misguided into thinking they can somehow control the growing Latino population by holding over them the threat of immigration enforcement." Berra's description of police behavior demonstrated that the construction of Latinas/os as "illegal aliens" continued, as they continued to be stopped and asked to prove their legal status and right to be in the country. In this way, police officers attempted to enforce the imaginary border of their community by weeding out people they deemed undesirable. For at least a decade, Latina/o use of roads in Arkansas was seen as an act of spatial illegality, with officers ultimately violating constitutional rights in demanding immigration documents.

The lawsuit was settled in 2003 after an agreement was reached between MALDEF and the City of Rogers.[43] It provided that the Rogers Police Department must publish a general order regarding "prohibition and prevention of racial/bias profiling" in its "Policy and Procedures" manual. "The order prohibits officers from engaging in profiling persons based on race, national origin, citizenship, religion, ethnicity, age, gender or physical or mental disability for the purpose of initiating law enforcement action—except to determine whether a person matches a specific description of a particular suspect." Among other processes, the settlement also established a means of tracking racial profiling and an ad hoc monitoring/advisory committee. Perhaps the most significant part of the agreement was that it ensured that "local police enforcement of federal civil immigration laws will be strictly prohibited, because this is what led to the racial profiling of Latino citizens and immigrants alike."[44] The ruling was an important win for immigrants, particularly following the 9/11 attacks, when anti-immigrant sentiment was severe at the national level.

Historically, law enforcement agencies enforced city, county, state, or national/federal laws, but they had no authority outside of their jurisdiction. In terms of immigration and its laws, a police department had to call the Border Patrol or the INS if they realized a suspect was an undocumented immigrant. Community activists and police officers tried to let immigrants know that their legal status was irrelevant if they had experienced a crime, that police officers were not immigration officials and would not deport them. This stance also aided investigations, because crimes went unreported if immigrants feared that contacting the police might lead to their own deportation.

As the immigration debate once again became heated after 9/11, some politicians and law enforcement officials thought it made sense for local officers to aid the federal government in capturing undocumented people. In 2003 there were efforts to expand the reach of federal authorities by using local and state agencies to enforce immigration laws as part of the "war on terror" enacted by President George W. Bush. The federal government used the Immigration and Nationality Act's Section 287(g), added through the Illegal Immigration Reform and Immigrant Responsibility Act of 1996, which provided for the "performance of immigration officer functions by state officers and employees."[45] The provision authorized the

Department of Homeland Security to enter into agreements with local law enforcement agencies so they could enforce immigration laws as long as officers received training and were supervised by Immigration and Customs Enforcement (ICE).

By February 2005 two Republicans, Representatives Jeremy Hutchinson and Timothy Hutchinson, proposed House Bill 1012, which sought the participation of Arkansas State Police officers in ICE's 287(g) training program.[46] The Hutchinson brothers' bill passed and became Act 907 of 2005, making Arkansas the third state, after Florida and Alabama, to participate in the program. By September 2007 four northwest Arkansas law enforcement agencies—the Benton County Sheriff's Office, the Rogers Police Department, the Washington County Sheriff's Office, and the City of Springdale Police Department—had signed the memorandum of agreement that defined the scope and limitations of their authority.[47]

In this situation, northwest Arkansas law enforcement agencies eagerly signed up to help the federal government police US borders and, in the process, attempt to halt the changes occurring in their community. At first it might be surprising that southern officers would be so willing to participate in a federal program, given their traditionally fierce independence and antifederalism. Upon closer inspection, however, we can see that this was just another way of obtaining federal largesse. The state actors finally got what they wanted—the authority to check immigration documents and attempt to remove people from the United States.

For northwest Arkansans, the change from an overwhelmingly white area to one with Latina/o immigrants and migrants was too much to bear. The change in their public spaces brought on by the presence of Latinas/os was objectionable. Consequently, they mobilized by strictly enforcing zoning laws, dictating what kinds of events could be held at a venue for community organizations, and policing Latinas/os as they drove to work, school, and shopping centers, as well as eventually obtaining the authority to check for immigration documents. Their efforts to curb the area's diversification did not stop there, however. They mobilized grassroots nativist responses similar to those in California and Arizona and took the debate over "illegal aliens" to the local and state political arenas.

Nativist Responses and the Political Mobilizations

Nativism, Americans' efforts to define themselves and the United States in a narrow way that excludes foreigners, usually the most recent ones, has long been present in the country. As Peter Schrag argues, many of the men foundational to the US government and nation were nativists. Benjamin Franklin worried about Germans and wrote various pieces foretelling the doom to come if they were not excluded from the nascent nation. Later, once the German problem was averted, other outsiders took their place—Irish, Italians, Jews. The fears and complaints were the same: their culture was too different, they would not assimilate, they would be detrimental to our way of life, they would usher in the end of the United States (as we know it).[48] In the United States there is also a relationship between nativism and racialization, because complaints are aimed at people constructed as racially different from the mainstream. When the United States was predominantly British in its heritage, other Europeans were deemed too different to assimilate based on characteristics used to define races. Over decades, and in relationship to the perceived threat posed by African Americans, the social construction of Irish, Italians, and Jews as being of different racial stock was altered, and these groups came to be included as "white" in the United States.[49] Today, descendants of Germans, Italians, and Jews as well as Native Americans and African Americans contribute to the new chorus of nativist fears about "Third World" immigrants.

At the turn of the twenty-first century, nativist fears, mobilizations, and organizations were extensive. In June 1997, Dan Morris, a Rogers resident who had moved to Arkansas in 1988 from New Mexico, formed Americans for an Immigration Moratorium (AIM). The group proposed a five-year halt on immigration, a more selective policy in admitting new immigrants, and more assimilation of "Hispanics" into the region's culture. Morris also wanted immigrants to be unable to sponsor family members who wanted to join them in the United States. He said that his experiences in New Mexico and California had convinced him that a heavy flow of immigrants caused more crime, poorer schools, and lower property values.[50] Local law enforcement officials, however, reported that Latina/o growth had not created more crime and that Latinas/os were often blamed for crimes they did not commit.[51] Morris's wife was so displeased by this response that she threatened to leave the area. In a letter to John Sampier, the mayor of Rogers, in March 1997, she wrote that longtime residents would leave the region if Latina/o growth continued. Some Rogers residents in fact did move out of neighborhoods where Latinas/os were buying and renting homes.[52]

As Morris's case suggests, white migrants who moved from other states brought their racial ideologies and prejudices with them to northwest Arkansas. Morris made it clear that his beliefs about dangers posed by immigrants had led him and his wife to leave the Southwest and move to northwest Arkansas. In a letter to the *Arkansas Democrat-Gazette*, A. Lee Smith stated that he and his family had left California because of immigrants and added that Florida had been "ruined" as well.[53] Even in 1980, Carroll L. Gates of DeQueen in Sevier County said she had moved to Arkansas from Arizona in 1964 because Arkansas was not "overpopulated," adding that relatives in Miami said Cubans had "ruined" the city.[54] More research is needed to determine how many white migrants with negative ideas about immigrants became active in the grassroots mobilizations of the late 1990s and 2000s and whether the most outspoken Arkansans were transplants from other states, like Smith, Gates, and the Morrises.

In July 1998, AIM allied with five other anti-immigrant organizations in support of federal legislation to enact a five-year moratorium on immigration, running a two-week radio, television, and newspaper ad campaign in Arkansas.[55] According to Morris, "the law-abiding, tax-paying citizens are being forced to finance what many believe is the destruction of their own community." He also argued that promoting immigration to fill low-wage jobs was like "committing national suicide."[56] Morris was also concerned about how many "illegal aliens" were "drug smugglers, terrorists, carriers of disease, thieves, and murderers."[57] In the anti-immigrant groups' construction, Latina/o immigrants were a threat to the national body and to Arkansas communities. The group racialized Latinas/os as criminals and a threat to safety, child rearing, finances, and health. As Inda points out, this framework constructs immigrants, particularly Latinas/os and Mexicans, as a threatening horde, public burdens whose excessive population growth causes urban sprawl and the problems associated with "inner cities," such as "overcrowded housing," unemployment, wage depressions, and crime.[58]

Morris was not the only migrant from the United States who felt immigrants were a peril. A. Lee Smith of Hot Springs, in central Arkansas, wrote to the *Arkansas Democrat-Gazette* after the editors asked readers whether the number of immigrants to the United States should be cut.[59] Smith stated that California and Florida had been ruined by immigrants of any legal status who came from various parts of the world; noticeably, however, he did not mention Europeans, Canadians, or any other white immigrants. He deployed familiar tropes of white victimization, abuse of the system, overcrowding, and an overall threat to the nation and its electoral politics. His solution was to use any military and pseudo-military outfit to deport any and all "illegal" immigrants. And to protect himself from accusations of racism, he argued he was not the only one to feel that way and was "justified" because his father was three-fourths Native American:

> Your request for opinions on the immigration problem hit a nerve with my family. We left California for this very reason.
>
> Illegal immigration has ruined California and Florida. The homes of many of our relatives in Marysville and Downey, Calif., are practically unsalable because they are surrounded by Vietnamese and Hispanic and God only knows what else.
>
> Minorities outnumber Native Americans and Caucasians badly. If you think they are here just to work, think again. They came with printed booklets telling them how to get welfare and food stamps and hospitalization.
>
> Many illegal immigrants voted in the last election. We are being flooded here in Hot Springs with illegals: Hispanic, Chinese, Vietnamese, Central Americans, Iranians. There are 18 living in one small two-bedroom house.
>
> I want every illegal alien rounded up and deported. If they come back give them six months of hard labor. I don't care if they have been here six months or 40 years if they came illegally. Use the Marines, Army, Air Force, Coast Guard, National Guard, police and Boy Scouts, but catch everyone and deport them.
>
> Stop all immigration for at least 10 years. Congressmen and senators should pay attention: We will note accordingly. If I were the only one in our community who felt this way, I would think it was only me, but my friends and most people I talk to agree with me. Let the illegals and all immigrants build their own country.
>
> I feel justified in feeling this way. My dad was three-quarter Cherokee, American Indian.[60]

Smith deployed his race and ethnicity as a shield; his Indian background was supposed to make evident that he could not be racist because he was a person of color. At the same time, if anybody had a right to defend this land, it was Native Americans, the people who lived here prior to European conquest.

Smith's response might, at first, seem the ranting of a disgruntled individual, but it had remarkable similarities to another nativist response. In April 1999 the Washington County (Arkansas) Republican Women adopted a resolution that called for tighter limits on legal immigration and more effective enforcement against undocumented immigration:

> Whereas the escalating influx of legal and illegal immigrants into Arkansas since the 1980s and particularly during the 1990s — most from the

Third World—is of grave concern to the state's residents. . . . Whereas residents' concerns are directly ascribed to cultural and language tensions, overcrowded schools, loss of American jobs and consequent assurance that local wages remain low due to overwhelming hire of immigrants, gangs, increasing crime, graffiti, and urban sprawl, all resulting in massive expenditures of taxes to deal with these problems and a continual erosion of the traditional American way of life.[61]

Significantly, the group objected to both legal and undocumented immigration, but they singled out so-called Third World immigrants, suggesting that it was principally racial and class characteristics that contributed to the erosion of the "traditional American way of life." And like Morris and AIM, the Republican Women believed immigrants were a threat culturally, linguistically, and criminally. Notably, the resolution emanated from within the ranks of one of the major US political parties and sought to push institutional responses to Latina/o immigrants. The Washington County Republican Women's resolution and AIM's complaints about immigrants parallel the logic and words used in 1994 to pass Proposition 187 in California and Proposition 200 later in Arizona. Inda posits, "It [racialized nativism] constructs a marked division between the dominant traditions and ways of life of the United States and the cultures of the Third World immigrants. Given their cultural difference, the latter populations are often construed as incompatible with and as a threat to the integrity of the national body."[62]

The United States has experienced long moments of nativism, and the turn of the twenty-first century was such a time, with politicians and scholars alike fanning the flames. Patrick Buchanan, who tried in 1992 and 1996 to secure the Republican nomination for president and eventually ran for that office under the Reform Party, is a pillar of the conservative Right and nativist mobilizations. Buchanan follows in the footsteps of prior nativists by decrying how "immigrant invasions imperil our country and civilization." But beyond talking about how the United States will no longer have a white majority, he paints a picture not just of "illegal aliens" but of enemies within the country—"tens of thousands are loyal to regimes with which we could be at war, and some are trained terrorists sent here to murder Americans."[63] To Buchanan, every nonwhite immigrant is the epitome of a criminal—a terrorist—who threatens (white) Americans' safety and culture. Samuel P. Huntington, a professor at Harvard University, holds Latinas/os responsible for threatening "to divide the United States into two peoples, two cultures, and two languages."[64]

He cites the failure of Latinas/os to assimilate "Anglo-Protestant values that built the American dream. The United States ignores the challenge at its peril." Again, immigrants, especially Mexicans, threaten the coherence of the country, the legacy and culture of a great nation founded by "overwhelmingly white, British, and Protestant" settlers. Huntington posits that "the most powerful stimulus to such white nativism will be the cultural and linguistic threats whites see from the expanding power of Hispanics in U.S. society."[65] In other words, Latinas/os are at fault for making white nativists react with such vehemence. Northwest Arkansas's racial and ethnic diversification in the 1990s began to show some of these strains, and anti-immigrant sentiments increasingly began to shape local and regional political campaigns.

The area is a Republican corner in an otherwise solidly (conservative) Democratic state, but native Arkansans are not the only ones responsible for this shift. From the 1960s onward, the area became the adopted home of many white retirees from the Midwest. According to Brooks Blevins, Ozarkers reacted to the arrivals with curiosity and sometimes even resentment, though both eventually came to a live-and-let-live accord. These midwesterners brought more religious diversity to the Protestant area as well as their Republican beliefs, which contributed to making "northwest Arkansas a stronghold of republicanism" in the late twentieth century. Blevins suggests that these white midwestern retirees might have been responsible for electing John Paul Hammerschmidt as the first post-Reconstruction Republican congressman in 1966, and for sending Tim Hutchinson to Washington as the first post-Reconstruction Republican senator thirty years later.[66] They would also shape the area's political response to Latinas/os, though more research needs to be conducted to determine whether there were differences between how native Ozarkers and midwestern migrants reacted to Latinas/os. What is clear is that anti-Latina/o sentiments began to play out in the political arena.

In the Rogers mayoral election of 1998, John Sampier, a seventeen-year incumbent, lost to a former alderman, Steve Womack. Womack ran on a platform of "zero tolerance" for undocumented immigrants, depicted Sampier as supporting "illegal immigration," and insisted that legal immigrants "speak the language" and conform to community norms.[67] However, when Latinas/os engaged in standard behaviors such as going to the park on weekends, white Arkansans objected to their presence and constructed their acts as spatial illegality. Nonetheless, Sampier posited that the "right" behaviors and language spoken would lead to immigrants' acceptance, as long as they were not "illegal."

In contrast to Womack, Sampier had been at the forefront of attempts to incorporate Latinas/os and had been cochairman of the Governor's Hispanic Relations Task Force. In Rogers, he supported efforts to support English as a Second Language programs in the public schools and placing paraprofessionals in the classroom to more quickly address the needs of Spanish-speaking students who did not need to "sacrific[e] their culture or native language."[68] In response to the letter written by Morris's wife in which she claimed that longtime residents would leave if the Latina/o growth continued, he replied: "If unhappy longtime residents or any others are discontented for unchristian, racist attitudes and choose to leave for such reasons, then I believe my city will be the better for their departure."[69] During the election, however, the majority of Rogers's residents decided it was time for him to leave office.

In another election, in 2001, Gunner DeLay, a Republican from Fort Smith, said at a forum sponsored by the Washington County Republican Women that "illegal immigration" was the "defining issue in the race" for the Arkansas Third Congressional District. DeLay claimed the issue needed an immediate remedy, and he said he would consider using the military to secure the US-Mexico border.[70] The other candidates considered undocumented immigration to be important but asked voters to remember that Latina/o growth in the area was also due to legal immigration and to Spanish-speaking US citizens.[71] Ultimately, DeLay lost the race to John Boozman of Rogers. Boozman then joined the Congressional Immigration Reform Caucus, which proposed denying citizenship to US-born children of undocumented immigrants.[72]

In 2005 Jim Holt, a Republican state senator from Springdale, announced the formation of Protect Arkansas Now, which was modeled after the Arizona group that successfully lobbied to pass Proposition 200.[73] Joe McCutchen of Fort Smith, the chairman of the organization, said President George W. Bush was not protecting the nation from "Mexican invaders" and that "no society can withstand this type of invasion, particularly Third Worlders, who are uneducated and very poor."[74] Holt proposed the Arkansas Taxpayer and Citizen Protection Act, which would halt state spending on undocumented immigrants. Some of the wording was copied from the Arizona legislation and argued that Arkansas was a "safe haven" for "illegal immigrants." Among other provisions, the law would have required state employees to report suspected immigration violations or face misdemeanor charges.[75] The bill died in that session, but the issues have not disappeared.

Conclusion

Governor Huckabee, to his credit, eventually helped to propose an initiative aimed at aiding undocumented immigrants. In 2005 he and Representative Joyce Elliot, a Democrat from Little Rock, proposed House Bill 1525, which would allow undocumented immigrants who attended at least three years of high school and graduated from an Arkansas school to qualify for in-state tuition and taxpayer-funded scholarships at state universities. Huckabee compared the situation to the Central High School crisis, which he said might have been a legacy to be proud of if the state had handled it differently. Elliot, a Black woman, compared the situation of undocumented pupils to the struggles of Black students in the 1950s. When she addressed the Arkansas House, she recalled her childhood in the state and said she grew up "with the boot of the government on my back and I was a mere child."[76] This image suggested that the federal government attempted to keep her down and that she did not want undocumented students to face a similar situation if they were denied a college education. The proposed bill passed the House but fell five votes short in the Senate.[77] The alliance in Arkansas between a white man and a Black woman, the former representing what might be the epitome of privilege in the United States and the latter the struggles for gender and racial equality, and their invocation of African American struggles for equal opportunities, drew upon historical legacies of oppression and injustice.

In 2005 the Arkansas legislature began to address what it meant to have Latinas/os who were not just undocumented workers but also college-age students. Representative Sam Ledbetter, a Democrat from Little Rock, supported Bill 1525 in part because he believed that students who did not receive an education would be more likely to commit crimes and be sent to prison, where the state would have to pay for their stay. Representative Bill Pritchard, a Republican from Elkins who opposed the bill, worried that if approved, the legislation would encourage other "illegal aliens" to move to Arkansas. Elliot responded that she doubted immigrants would see the state as "the promised land," but even if they moved to Arkansas to take advantage of the law, legislators had to keep in mind that children did not break the law.[78] These positions broadly represent the fears present in states throughout the country as legislatures take a stand and attempt to police their communities and the nation not just by deporting undocumented Latinas/os, but by creating a hostile environment with the hope that immigrants will move out, or never move in at all.

Conclusion: Race, Plantation Bloc, and Nuevo South

In 2000 Mike Huckabee, the Republican governor of Arkansas, offered a few words of encouragement to Latinas/os attending the second Cinco de Mayo Festival in downtown Little Rock's River Market: "We have a very special word for you today. That word is 'welcome.' We think it's very important Arkansans roll out the red carpet for our Hispanic friends and neighbors."[1] Huckabee did not refer to "illegal aliens," "illegal workers," or even solely to Latinas/os, but rather to "friends and neighbors," making his speech a significant departure from the discourse of many politicians in the South and Southwest who have fanned anti-immigrant and nativist sentiments against Latinas/os. This warm greeting, however, was couched within a larger goal, a statewide "Hispanic Assimilation Program" to begin with a $50,000 study supposedly focused on the needs of Latina/o Arkansans, but which would emphasize workplace language skills that ultimately might be more beneficial to employers who could communicate more fluently and efficiently with a growing workforce. The festival's attendees were a mixed crowd, and Huckabee also had some reassuring words for white Arkansans: "People who are Anglo should not feel threatened or anything other than positive about this. . . . I think there are some prejudices to overcome. But I feel like all of us are immigrants at some time." He went further, invoking values commonly held throughout the Bible Belt by saying that Arkansans should learn from Latinas/os' devotion to God and family. In a region historically shaped by Indian removal and chattel slavery as well as by vicious anti-Black racial cleansing, sundown towns, and Japanese American internment camps, such an affable gesture toward Latinas/os was at odds with previous efforts to remove or contain racial difference. Indeed, Huckabee's welcome was a decade late, since Latina/o migrants and immigrants who had started moving to Arkansas in substantial numbers in the 1990s were greeted in ways that were reflected by an article in the state newspaper of record which proclaimed them "Northwest Arkansas's No. 1 societal concern."[2]

In 2001, Huckabee continued to push Arkansans to accept Latinas/os through religious understanding while simultaneously invoking the history of prior racial discrimination against African Americans. He addressed the Arkansas Baptist State Convention Annual Meeting, where he received a standing ovation when he said that his fellow Christians had a second chance to make amends for the "evil and wrong" done to African Americans by welcoming Latinas/os:

> We as Christian people—even we as Baptist people—we have made some horrible mistakes over the last couple of hundred years in the way we dealt with African-Americans, and even the very way racism was preached and advertised with a twisted version of God's word. . . . We'd better look at the curve ahead. Arkansas has (one of the) largest growing Hispanic populations in the country. God might be giving us a second chance to do right. . . . I'm not saying to support illegal activity. . . . I'm saying act like loving Christian people.[3]

Huckabee's remarks revealed the contentious social positioning of Latinas/os in Arkansas at the turn of the twenty-first century. Some Arkansans lauded Latinas/os for upholding traditional family values; within this paradigm they respected and admired the focus on family and religious devotion and found common ground with their state's newest generation of immigrants. Simultaneously, however, Arkansans began to think of Latinas/os as linked to "illegal activity," namely as undocumented people or "illegal aliens" who broke the law. In calling on Baptists and Christians to act lovingly toward the newcomers, Huckabee explicitly positioned Latinas/os in relation to African Americans as an oppressed group and white people as oppressors and racists. When he suggested that the "evil and wrong[s]" against Black people were in the past, he elided ongoing struggles and failed to locate Latinas/os as only the newest group in Arkansas who deserved equal treatment but did not receive it. After all, only ten years earlier African American Arkansans had fought to end school segregation and to gain true electoral voting power through court-ordered redistricting.

The Continued Power of the Plantation Bloc

The changing racial and ethnic landscape in places that were overwhelmingly white throughout most of the twentieth century begs the question of why Arkansas has not enacted punitive anti-immigrant legislation like Alabama or Georgia, especially when we consider the dynamic growth of the Latina/o and immigrant communities. In 2005 Arkansas passed House Bill 1012, which allows law enforcement agencies to participate in section 287(g) of the Illegal Immigration Reform and Immigrant Responsibility Act of 1996 and has made life more difficult and scary for undocumented Latinas/os. But given the area's regional history, why has legislation not been more punitive?

One answer is the legacy of the "good ol' boys" system—a system that still allows a lot of state matters to be resolved at informal lunches and within social circles. The system can still function in Arkansas because the state remains small in population, as does the business community, despite a few major economic actors like Walmart and Tyson Foods—the business community is still small enough that a few business leaders can call governors, senators, and representatives and persuade them to keep certain legislation from moving forward. The Reverend Steve Copley, chair of the Arkansas Friendship Coalition (AFC), said that his organization's "sole mission" is to prevent "state legislation that's punitive towards immigrants from passing in Arkansas because we feel like it's up to the federal government, the constitution's pretty clear. . . . It's an interesting coalition when you think about it, but [it's] about that one issue of not seeing [Arkansas become] an Arizona or an Alabama."[4] The AFC formed in the fall of 2007, after Allen Leverette, the publisher of the *Arkansas Times*, talked to Gordon Garlington, a Presbyterian minister and an acquaintance—their mothers attended church together. Garlington told Leverette to get in touch with Reverend Copley. So Garlington, Leverette, and Copley went to lunch:

> Oklahoma had just happened and it was just beginning to bubble up, so we had lunch, and what was interesting was, at the table sitting next to us were two attorneys and a lady that was at the Clinton school at the time talking about the same thing, and we quickly joined forces. And we had to decide who we needed as members in order to really launch this.

The Oklahoma law he refers to was a punitive anti-immigrant bill that sought to push people to leave the state. The bill made it "illegal to knowingly transport illegal immigrants, creates state barriers to hiring illegal workers and requires proof of citizenship before a person can receive government benefits."[5] The Oklahoma Supreme Court upheld most of the law in June 2011.

In establishing the organization, Garlington, Leverette, and Copley thought about who would "be the players interested in seeing immigrant communities protected. We come a different way—for religious figures it's a moral issue, for the business community . . . [it was about] who was interested in seeing folks who were here protected." The founding board members included representatives from Tyson Foods, the Associated General Contractors, the Clinton School of Public Service, the *Arkansas Times* and *El Latino* newspapers, and the Arkansas affiliate of the American Civil Liberties Union, as well as a restaurateur, a contracting firm, a member of the League of United Latin American Citizens (LULAC), and religious leaders. When I asked Reverend Copley how the AFC operated and organized, he said it is a voluntary organization that monitors what is on the legislative session, forms committees, decides who is going to "visit" with legislators, and then starts "visitin' with the speaker of the house and senate pro tem."

The AFC is clear in its purpose and accepts that in other areas of worker and immigrant lives, its members might have different ideas about whether changes need to be implemented. "We also realize this is the issue that we're solely working at because there are other issues that can arise—how workers are treated, whether they're paid minimum wage, whether health and safety laws are followed because many folks in there might be on opposite sides of that debate, and I think many folks understood that," said Copley. He himself chaired the committee that successfully advocated for an increase in the state's minimum wage. The AFC also facilitates other alliances; for example, some of its members support the Arkansas DREAM Act and "visit" with legislators and others to advocate for its passage. Although the AFC is an official organization with a website, the page has a minimum amount of information, and the AFC functions not by organizing grassroots support but by "visiting" with people—legislators—because, as Copley puts it, "it's a small enough state that folks begin to know one another." It remains to be seen how much longer this "good ol' boys" system can succeed, and as full of contradictions as the AFC is, its members have—at least in part—helped to prevent the kinds of punitive anti-immigrant legislation present in other parts of the South.

The Nuevo South is the newest manifestation of the New South—a regime built on white supremacy, the exploitation of racial difference, and increasingly on legal statuses (citizen, refugee, undocumented, nonimmigrant), which is why some of the newest coworkers on the poultry lines in northwest Arkansas are Marshall Islanders, a highly vulnerable community due to their legal status. As "nonimmigrants" they are authorized to work in the United States and have valid social security numbers, but there is no path to permanent US residency and thus no path to US citizenship. Much like undocumented immigrants, they can attain permanent US residency in only three ways: (1) have an adult US-citizen child who petitions for a parent and can be financially responsible for them; (2) obtain a US visa through a (very limited) lottery system; or (3) serve in the US military to "earn" their residency and subsequent citizenship. Today, Springdale is home to the largest Marshallese community outside the Marshall Islands.

By 2010 the Latina/o population in Arkansas had reached almost 200,000, 6.4 percent of the state's population.[6] In the previous decade Latinas/os had driven Arkansas's diversification—they accounted for 41 percent of the overall population growth and, in this southern state, made up 83 percent of youths of color.[7] There are areas and districts with substantial Latina/o communities, such as Senate District 7 in Washington County, where Latinas/os make up almost one-third of the population.[8] In the same decade, the Asian population grew by nearly 80 percent to constitute 1.2 percent of all Arkansans. The Third Congressional District, however, was no longer defined as the northwest quadrant. Had the congressional lines from 1990 and 2000 remained in place, that district would have had a significant Latina/o base. In fact, the Latinas/os who lived in Springdale, Rogers, Fayetteville, and Fort Smith accounted for more than 30 percent of all Latinas/os in Arkansas in the first decade of the twenty-first century.

By then the popular construction of Vietnamese immigrants had changed to become something akin to that of the "model minority." This shift did not happen in isolation, nor was it simply the result of their achievements since 1975. Rather, the transformation in the racialization of the Vietnamese is directly connected to the placement and arrival of other people—Cubans in 1980, and ethnic Mexicans, both migrants and immigrants, in the 1990s. When Vietnamese refugees arrived in Arkansas, they probably did not know they were stepping into a situation that would be framed through old and powerful antagonisms which had shaped regional identities since the nineteenth century. They probably did not realize that their racialization was anchored in the intersection of national and local fears and anxieties. Nor could they anticipate that despite their tenuous reception, they would become, at least in the abstract, model subjects, or that their adaptation to their southern home would be used as an archetype to belittle other newcomers. As Asian and Latina/o communities grow in the region, the way they are defined and racialized by southerners will make regional racial formation important as a focal point of analysis for multifaceted understandings of race and ethnicity across places in the US South. Today, Arkansas is more multiracial and multiethnic than it was in the previous century. Racial meanings are thus being contested and created in a field that is more diverse and complex. The South can no longer be defined, if indeed it ever could, through a racial binary. As scholars, we need to pay attention to how migrants, immigrants, and refugees—and reactions to them—are altering regional racial mores, meanings, and understandings.

Notes

Introduction

1. Mike Trimble, "Last, Sad Effort Gets Underway in First Welcome," *Arkansas Gazette* (Little Rock), May 3, 1975, A1.
2. Peggy Robertson, "Governor Greets First 71 Refugees," *Arkansas Gazette*, May 3, 1975, A1.
3. Editorial, "A Welcome to the Refugees," *Arkansas Gazette*, May 3, 1975, A4.
4. Robertson, "Governor Greets First 71 Refugees."
5. Bob Lyford and Freddie Nixon to Rob Wiley, memo, October 14, 1980, box 2, folder 2 ("Cuban Refugees/Fort Chaffee—Memos & Notes"), Bill Clinton State Government Project, unprocessed papers, William J. Clinton Presidential Library and Museum, Little Rock, Arkansas (hereinafter cited as BCSGP). Please note that I accessed the BCSGP before it was processed and formally organized; I include the folder titles for this archive so that other scholars can locate the correct folders for their own research.
6. William Clinton, statement to the press, May 7, 1980, box 2, folder 15 ("Cuban Refugees/Fort Chaffee—File 12"), BCSGP.
7. Personal interview, July 17, 2012. Throughout this book I will use pseudonyms to protect interviewees' identities.
8. Ibid.
9. James W. Loewen, *Sundown Towns: A Hidden Dimension of American Racism* (New York: Touchtone, 2005), 48, 204-205, 285; Guy Lancaster, *Racial Cleansing in Arkansas, 1883-1924: Politics, Land, Labor, and Criminality* (Lanham, MD: Lexington Books, 2014).
10. D. R. Stewart, "Rich in Jobs, Northwest Arkansas Becomes Mecca for Illegal Aliens," *Arkansas Democrat-Gazette* (Little Rock), March 4, 1993, sec. D.
11. Ibid.
12. James W. Loewen, *The Mississippi Chinese: Between Black and White* (Long Grove, IL: Waveland, 1971); Malinda Maynor Lowery, *Lumbee Indians in the Jim Crow South: Race, Identity, and the Making of a Nation* (Chapel Hill: University of North Carolina Press, 2010); Helen B. Marrow, *New Destination Dreaming: Immigration, Race, and Legal Status in the Rural American South* (Stanford, CA:

Stanford University Press, 2011); Helen B. Marrow, "New Immigrant Destinations and the American Colour Line," *Ethnic and Racial Studies* 32, no. 6 (2009): 1037–1057; Khyati Y. Joshi and Jigna Desai, *Asian Americans in Dixie: Race and Migration in the South* (Urbana: University of Illinois Press, 2013); Irene Browne and Mary Odem, "'Juan Crow' in the Nuevo South? Racialization of Guatemalan and Dominican Immigrants in the Atlanta Metro Area," *Du Bois Review* 9, no. 2 (2012): 321–337; Perla M. Guerrero, "A Tenuous Welcome for Latinas/os and Asians: States' Rights Discourse in Late 20th Century Arkansas," in *Race and Ethnicity in Arkansas: New Perspectives*, ed. John Kirk (Fayetteville: University of Arkansas Press, 2014), 141–151; Perla M. Guerero, "Chicana/o History as Southern History: Race, Place, and the U.S. South" in *A Promising Problem: The New Chicana/o History, ed. Carlos Kevin Blanton* (Austin: University of Texas Press, 2016), 83–110.

13. Leslie Bow and John Howard have each written nuanced histories about Asians in other parts of Arkansas. See Leslie Bow, *Partly Colored: Asian Americans and Racial Anomaly in the Segregated South* (New York: New York University Press, 2010); John Howard, *Concentration Camps on the Home Front: Japanese Americans in the House of Jim Crow* (Chicago: University of Chicago Press, 2008).

14. For this project, northwest Arkansas includes the following counties: Benton, Washington, Crawford, Sebastian, Carroll, Madison, Franklin, Boone, Marion, Newton, Johnson, and Pope. In 1990 and 2000 these counties also formed the state's Third Congressional District, making it a coherent entity for political analysis.

15. Guerrero, "A Tenuous Welcome."

16. The "yellow peril" trope began in the nineteenth century and was popularized through William Randolph Hearst's newspapers. Although "yellow peril" is Asian-specific, similar tropes have been strategically deployed against African Americans, Native Americans, and Latinas/os.

17. "Two Decades Later, Mariel Boat Lift Refugees Still Feel Effects of Riot," *Los Angeles Times*, May 5, 2001, sec. A.

18. US Bureau of the Census, *Profiles of General Demographic Characteristics, Arkansas* (Washington, DC: Government Printing Office, 2000); US Bureau of the Census, *Profiles of General Demographic Characteristics, Arkansas* (Washington, DC: Government Printing Office, 2010).

19. W. E. B. DuBois, *Black Reconstruction in America, 1860–1880* (1935; repr., New York: Free Press, 1998); C. Vann Woodward, *Origins of the New South, 1877–1913*, 2nd ed. (Baton Rouge: Louisiana State University Press, 1971).

20. Clyde Woods, *Development Arrested: The Blues and Plantation Power in the Mississippi Delta* (New York: Verso, 1998), 6.

21. William Kandel, "Meat-Processing Firms Attract Hispanic Workers to Rural America," accessed January 10, 2014, http://www.ers.usda.gov/amber-waves/2006-june/meat-processing-firms-attract-hispanic-workers-to-rural-america.aspx#.Uwvpa15RHVU.

22. Steve Striffler, *Chicken: The Dangerous Transformation of America's Favorite Food* (New Haven, CT: Yale University Press, 2005), 95.

23. Julie M. Weise, *Corazón de Dixie: Mexicanos in the U.S. South since 1910* (Chapel Hill: University of North Carolina Press, 2015), 127.

24. Striffler, *Chicken*, 95.

25. Start Hall, "Re-Thinking the 'Base-and-Superstructure' Metaphor," in Papers on *Class, Hegemony, and Party: The Communist University of London*, ed. Jon Bloomfield (London: Lawrence and Wishart, 1977), 44–48.

26. Neil Smith, *Uneven Development: Nature, Capital, and the Production of Space* (New York: Blackwell, 1984), xiii.

27. See Tomás Almaguer, *Racial Fault Lines: The Historical Origins of White Supremacy in California* (Berkeley: University of California Press, 1994); Neil Foley, *The White Scourge: Mexicans, Blacks, and Poor Whites in Texas Cotton Culture* (Berkeley: University of California Press, 1997); David Montejano, *Anglos and Mexicans in the Making of Texas, 1836–1986* (Austin: University of Texas Press, 1987).

28. Michael Omi and Howard Winant, *Racial Formation in the United States: From the 1960s to the 1990s*, 2nd ed. (New York: Routledge, 1994).

29. Claire Jean Kim, "The Racial Triangulation of Asian Americans," *Politics and Society* 27, no. 1 (1999): 105–138.

30. Natalia Molina, "The Power of Racial Scripts: What the History of Mexican Immigration to the United States Teaches Us about Relational Notions of Race," *Latino Studies*, suppl. Race and Blackness in the Latino/a Community 8, no. 2 (2010): 157.

31. Wendy Cheng, *The Changs Next Door to the Díazes: Remapping Race in Suburban California* (Minneapolis: University of Minnesota Press, 2013), 10.

32. Colleen Lye, *America's Asia: Racial Form and American Literature, 1893–1945* (Princeton, NJ: Princeton University Press, 2005); Lisa Lowe, *Immigrant Acts: On Asian American Cultural Politics* (Durham, NC: Duke University Press, 1996).

33. Lowe, *Immigrant Acts*, 18, 4.

34. Ibid., 5.

35. Lye, *America's Asia*, 8.

36. Lowe, *Immigrant Acts*, 19.

37. Ibid., 4.

38. Lye, *America's Asia*, 5.

39. Lowe, *Immigrant Acts*, 8.

40. Mae M. Ngai, *Impossible Subjects: Illegal Aliens and the Making of Modern America* (Princeton, NJ: Princeton University Press, 2004), 4.

41. Ibid., 58.

42. Nicholas De Genova, "Migrant 'Illegality' and Deportability in Everyday Life," *Annual Review of Anthropology* 31 (2002): 419–447.

43. Ngai, *Impossible Subjects*, 7–8.

44. Ibid., 2.

45. Evelyn Nakano Glenn, *Unequal Freedom: How Race and Gender Shaped American Citizenship and Labor* (Cambridge, MA: Harvard University Press, 2002).

46. Ibid., 53.

47. Ibid., 54.

48. Ibid., 53–54.

49. Jonathan Xavier Inda, *Targeting Immigrants: Government, Technology, and Ethics* (Malden, MA: Blackwell, 2006).

50. Ibid., 108.

51. Ibid., 177.

52. Montejano, *Anglos and Mexicans*; Foley, *White Scourge*; Almaguer, *Racial Fault Lines*; Nicholas De Genova and Ana Y. Ramos-Zayas, "Latino Rehearsals: Racialization and the Politics of Citizenship between Mexicans and Puerto Ricans in Chicago," *Journal of Latin American Anthropology* 8, no. 2 (2003): 18–57; Nicholas De Genova and Ana Y. Ramos-Zayas, *Latino Crossings: Mexicans, Puerto Ricans, and the Politics of Race and Citizenship* (New York: Routledge, 2003); Clement Lai, "The Racial Triangulation of Space: The Case of Urban Renewal in San Francisco's Fillmore District," *Annals of the Association of American Geographers* 102, no. 1 (2012): 151–170; Lilia Fernández, *Brown in the Windy City: Mexicans and Puerto Ricans in Postwar Chicago* (Chicago: University of Chicago Press, 2012); Anthony Ocampo, "Are Second-Generation Filipinos 'Becoming' Asian American or Latino? Historical Colonialism, Culture and Panethnicity," *Ethnic and Racial Studies* 37, no. 3 (2014): 425–445; Eric Tang, "A Gulf Unites Us: The Vietnamese Americans of Black New Orleans East," *American Quarterly* 63 (March 2011): 117–149; Cheng, *The Changs Next Door to the Díazes*; Natalia Molina, *How Race Is Made in America: Immigration, Citizenship, and the Historical Power of Racial Scripts* (Berkeley: University of California Press, 2014).

53. Using the snowball sampling method, I could not locate any Cubans who had been in Fort Chaffee and remained in Arkansas. A reporter found that only about twelve Cubans remained in the state; see "Two Decades Later." For an in-depth study about Cubans and the Mariel boatlift, see Susana Peña, *¡Oye Loca!: From the Mariel Boatlift to Gay Cuban Miami* (Minneapolis: University of Minnesota Press, 2013).

54. Jennifer Stump, "Huckabee Announces Hispanic Program at LR Festival," *Arkansas Democrat-Gazette*, May 8, 2000.

Chapter 1: New South to Nuevo South

1. Jacqueline Froelich and David Zimmermann, "Total Eclipse: The Destruction of the African American Community of Harrison, Arkansas in 1905 and 1909," *Arkansas Historical Quarterly* 58, no. 2 (1999): 131–159.

2. Ibid., 148–156.

3. Gordon Morgan, *Black Hillbillies of the Arkansas Ozarks* (Fayetteville: Department of Sociology, University of Arkansas, 1973).

4. Jay Jay Wilson and Ron Wallace, *Black Wallstreet: A Lost Dream* (Long Island City, NY: Seaburn, 2004); James Hirsch, *Riot and Remembrance: The Tulsa Race War and Its Legacy* (Boston: Houghton Mifflin, 2002).

5. W. E. B. Du Bois, "Of Work and Wealth" (1920), republished in *Darkwater: Voices from Within the Veil* (Mineola, New York: Dover Publications, 1999), 47–62.

6. Quotation in Kimberly Harper, *White Man's Heaven: The Lynching and Expulsion of Blacks in the Southern Ozarks, 1894–1909* (Fayetteville: University of Arkansas Press, 2010), 32.

7. James W. Loewen, *Sundown Towns: A Hidden Dimension of American Racism* (New York: Touchstone, 2005), 204.

8. James W. Loewen, "Sundown Towns and Counties: Racial Exclusion in the South," *Southern Cultures* 15, no. 1 (Spring 2009): 22–47.

9. Loewen, *Sundown Towns*, 139.
10. Morgan, *Black Hillbillies*.
11. Brooks Blevins, *Hill Folks: A History of Arkansas Ozarkers and Their Image* (Chapel Hill: University of North Carolina Press, 2002), 212.
12. Harper, *White Man's Heaven*.
13. Bruce Schulman, *From Cotton Belt to Sunbelt: Federal Policy, Economic Development, and the Transformation of the South, 1938-1980* (New York: Oxford University Press, 1991), ix.
14. Robin D. G. Kelley, "Foreword," in *Remembering Slavery: African Americans Talk about Their Personal Experiences of Slavery and Emancipation*, ed. Ira Berlin, Marc Favreau, and Steven F. Miller (New York: New Press, 2007), vii.
15. David Roediger, *The Wages of Whiteness: Race and the Making of the American Working Class*, rev. ed. (New York: Verso, 1999), 13.
16. Clyde Woods, *Development Arrested: The Blues and Plantation Power in the Mississippi Delta* (New York: Verso, 1998), 45, 40, 2.
17. Kelley, "Foreword," vii; Woods, *Development Arrested*, 6.
18. C. Vann Woodward, *Origins of the New South, 1877-1913*, 2nd ed. (Baton Rouge: Louisiana State University Press, 1971).
19. Woods, *Development Arrested*.
20. Schulman, *From Cotton Belt to Sunbelt*; Gavin Wright, *Old South, New South: Revolutions in the Southern Economy since the Civil War* (New York: Basic Books, 1986); Numan V. Bartley, *The New South, 1945-1980* (Baton Rouge: Louisiana State University Press, 1995); George B. Tindall, *The Emergence of the New South, 1913-1945* (Baton Rouge: Louisiana State University Press, 1967); James C. Cobb, *The Selling of the South: The Southern Crusade for Industrial Development, 1936-1990*, 2nd ed. (Urbana: University of Illinois Press, 1993).
21. Cobb, *Selling of the South*.
22. John Egerton, *Speak Now against the Day: The Generation before the Civil Rights Movement in the South* (New York: Knopf, 1994).
23. Ira Katznelson, *When Affirmative Action Was White: An Untold History of Racial Inequality in Twentieth-Century America* (New York: Norton, 2005).
24. Bartley, *The New South*; Wright, *Old South, New South*.
25. Cobb, *Selling of the South*, 63.
26. Ibid.
27. Ibid., 2.
28. Cobb, "The Emergence of the Sunbelt South," chap. 7 in ibid.
29. Ibid., 280.
30. David Goldfield, "The Changing Continuity of the South," review of Schulman, *From Cotton Belt to Sunbelt*, *Reviews in American History* 20, no. 2 (1992): 233.
31. Woods, *Development Arrested*; Cobb, *Selling of the South*; Wright, *Old South, New South*; V. O. Key, *Southern Politics in State and Nation* (New York: Knopf, 1949); Woodward, *Origins of the New South*.
32. Key, *Southern Politics in State and Nation*.
33. Ibid.; Woodward, *Origins of the New South*, chaps. 3 and 12; Schulman, *From Cotton Belt to Sunbelt*.
34. Blevins, *Hill Folks*, 199.
35. Ibid., 5, 14-18.

36. Ibid., 19; Bethany Moreton, *To Serve God and Wal-Mart: The Making of Christian Free Enterprise* (Cambridge, MA: Harvard University Press, 2009), 10–11.
37. Blevins, *Hill Folks*, 29.
38. Ibid., 39.
39. Ibid., 39, 52.
40. John B. Boles, *The Great Revival: Beginnings of the Bible Belt* (Lexington: University Press of Kentucky, 1996), 44.
41. Blevins, *Hill Folks*, 53.
42. Ibid., 56; Moreton, *To Serve God and Wal-Mart*, 10–11.
43. Blevins, *Hill Folks*, 204.
44. Ibid., 26.
45. Ibid., 61, 42, 96.
46. Ibid., 105, 163–166.
47. Brent E. Riffel, "The Feathered Kingdom: Tyson Foods and the Transformation of American Land, Labor, and Law, 1930–2005" (PhD diss., University of Arkansas, 2008), 205.
48. Blevins, *Hill Folks*, 166–168.
49. Moreton, *To Serve God and Wal-Mart*, 1.
50. Ibid., 89.
51. Ibid., 106–107.
52. Jack Bass and Walter De Vries, *The Transformation of Southern Politics: Social Change and Political Consequence since 1945* (New York: Basic Books, 1976), 25, 96, 104. See also Alexander P. Lamis, *The Two Party South*, expanded ed. (New York: Oxford University Press, 1988), chap. 9; Blevins, *Hill Folks*, 205–206.
53. V. O. Key, "Arkansas: Pure One-Party Politics," in Key, *Southern Politics in State and Nation*, chap. 9.
54. Bass and De Vries, *Transformation of Southern Politics*, 25.
55. Ibid., 87–88.
56. Froelich and Zimmermann, "Total Eclipse," 138.
57. Moreton, *To Serve God and Wal-Mart*, 14–15.
58. Bass and DeVries, *Transformation of Southern Politics*, 5.
59. Ibid., 28.
60. Jeannie M. Whayne, "Dramatic Departures: Political, Demographic, and Economic Realignment," in *Arkansas: A Narrative History*, ed. Jeannie M. Whayne et al. (Fayetteville: University of Arkansas Press, 2002), 375; Blevins, *Hill Folks*, 205–206.
61. Blevins, *Hill Folks*, 198–199.
62. Ibid., 206.
63. Ibid., 212.
64. Warwick Sabin, "The White Place: A Good Home and Little Isolation in Northwest Arkansas," *Arkansas Times* (Little Rock), February 3, 2005, sec. A. According to the Southern Poverty Law Center, Harrison is home to an active chapter of the Knights of the Ku Klux Klan (KKK); in 2010 the state as a whole had twenty-three active hate groups based on white supremacist ideals, ranging from the KKK to neo-Confederates to neo-Nazis to those with a Christian identity. Harrison and its surrounding towns are home to six such organizations; see "Active

KKK Groups," *Southern Poverty Law Center*, accessed March 27, 2010, http://www.splcenter.org/get-informed/intelligence-files/ideology/ku-klux-klan/active_hate_groups, and "Arkansas Hate Map," *Southern Poverty Law Center*, accessed March 27, 2010, http://www.splcenter.org/get-informed/hate-map#s=AR.

65. US Bureau of the Census, *Profiles of General Demographic Characteristics, Arkansas* (Washington, DC: Government Printing Office, 2000).

66. Sabin, "The White Place."

67. Marjorie Rosen, *Boom Town: How Wal-Mart Transformed an All-American Town into an International Community* (Chicago: Chicago Review Press, 2009).

68. Ann Markusen, *Regions: The Economics and Politics of Territory* (New York: Rowman and Littlefield, 1987), xi.

69. Ibid., 6.

70. C. Vann Woodward, *The Strange Career of Jim Crow*, 3rd rev. ed. (New York: Oxford University Press, 2002).

71. John A. Kirk, "The 1957 Little Rock Crisis: A Fiftieth Anniversary Retrospective," *Arkansas Historical Quarterly* 66, no. 2 (2007): 91.

72. Ibid., 92.

73. Ibid.

74. Ben F. Johnson III, "After 1957: Resisting Integration in Little Rock," *Arkansas Historical Quarterly* 66, no. 2 (2007): 258–283.

75. Johnson, "After 1957," 280, 281, 283, 282n36; Grif Stockley, *Daisy Bates: Civil Rights Crusader from Arkansas* (Jackson: University Press of Mississippi, 2005), 296–297.

76. Stockley, *Daisy Bates*, 283.

77. Amendment 44 quoted in John Brummet, "Rid State of Bogus Amendment," *Arkansas Gazette* (Little Rock), October 5, 1990, sec. B.

78. Tony A. Freyer, "Politics and Law in the Little Rock Crisis, 1954–1957," *Arkansas Historical Quarterly* 66, no. 2 (2007): 154.

79. Mark Oswald, "Segregation Act Resurfaces," *Arkansas Gazette*, September 23, 1990, sec. A.

80. Jerry Dean, "Arkansas Segregation Vote Close," *Arkansas Gazette*, November 8, 1990, sec. B.

81. Max Brantley, "Darker Side to Close Vote on Racist Law," *Arkansas Gazette*, November 11, 1990, sec. B.

82. Kirk, "The 1957 Little Rock Crisis," 100. For a detailed discussion of the members of the Capital Citizens' Council in Little Rock, see Graeme Cope, "'Honest White People of the Middle and Lower Classes'? A Profile of Capital Citizens' Council during the Little Rock Crisis of 1957," *Arkansas Historical Quarterly* 61, no. 1 (2002): 37–58.

83. Numan V. Bartley, "Looking Back at Little Rock" (1966), republished in *Arkansas Historical Quarterly* 66, no. 2 (2007): 114.

84. Johnson, "After 1957," 277, 281.

85. Andrew Brill, "*Brown* in Fayetteville: Peaceful Southern School Desegregation in 1954," *Arkansas Historical Quarterly* 65, no. 4 (2006): 339, 338, 340, 342.

86. Judith Kilpatrick, "Desegregating the University of Arkansas School of Law: L. Clifford Davis and the Six Pioneers," *Arkansas Historical Quarterly* 68, no. 2 (2009): 124.

87. Phoebe Godfrey, "Bayonets, Brainwashing, and Bathrooms: The Discourse of Race, Gender, and Sexuality in the Desegregation of Little Rock's Central High," *Arkansas Historical Quarterly* 62, no. 1 (2003): 55.

88. Ibid., 45.

89. Douglas S. Massey and Chiara Capoferro, "The Geographic Diversification of American Immigration," 25–50; Mark A. Leach and Frank D. Bean, "The Structure and Dynamics of Mexican Migration to New Destinations in the United States," 51–74; and Katharine M. Donato et al., "Changing Faces, Changing Places: The Emergence of Nonmetropolitan Immigrant Gateways," 75–98; all in *New Faces in New Places: The Changing Geography of American Immigration*, ed. Douglas S. Massey (New York: Russell Sage Foundation, 2008).

90. Charles Hirschman and Douglass S. Massey, "Places and Peoples: The New American Mosaic," in Massey, *New Faces in New Places*, 4–10; William Kandel and Emilio A. Parrado, "Industrial Transformation and Hispanic Migration to the American South: The Case of the Poultry Industry," in *Hispanic Spaces, Latino Places: Community and Cultural Diversity in Contemporary America*, ed. Daniel D. Arreola (Austin: University of Texas Press, 2004), 255–276; Steve Striffler, *Chicken: The Dangerous Transformation of America's Favorite Food* (New Haven, CT: Yale University Press, 2005); Michael J. Broadway, "From City to Countryside: Recent Changes in the Structure and Location of the Meat- and Fish-Processing Industries," in Donald D. Stull, Michael J. Broadway, and David Griffith, *Any Way You Cut It: Meat Processing and Small Town America* (Lawrence: University Press of Kansas, 1995), 17–40; Griffith, "*Hay Trabajo*: Poultry Processing, Rural Industrialization, and the Latinization of Low-Wage Labor," in ibid., 129–152; Rebecca M. Torres, E. Jeffrey Popke, and Holly M. Hapke, "The South's Silent Bargain: Rural Restructuring, Latino Labor and the Ambiguities of Migrant Experience," in *Latinos in the New South: Transformations of Place*, ed. Heather A. Smith and Owen J. Furuseth (Burlington, VT: Ashgate, 2006), 37–68; James D. Engstrom, "Industry and Immigration in Dalton, Georgia," in *Latino Workers in the Contemporary South*, ed. Arthur D. Murphy, Colleen Blanchard, and Jennifer A. Hill (Athens: University of Georgia Press, 1999), 44–56; Greig Guthey, "Mexican Places in Southern Spaces: Globalization, Work, and Daily Life in and around the North Georgia Poultry Industry," in ibid., 57–67; Emilio A. Parrado and William Kandel, "New Hispanic Migrant Destinations: A Tale of Two Industries," in Massey, *New Faces in New Places*, 99–123.

91. Andrew Wainer, "The New Latino South and the Challenge to Public Education: Strategies for Educators and Policymakers in Emerging Immigrant Communities" (Los Angeles: Tomás Rivera Policy Institute, University of Southern California, 2004); William A. Kandel and Emilio A. Parrado, "Hispanic Population Growth and Public School Responses in Two New South Immigrant Destinations," in Smith and Furuseth, *Latinos in the New South*, 111–134; David Griffith, "New Midwesterners, New Southerners: Immigration Experiences in Four Rural American Settings," in Massey, *New Faces in New Places*, 179–210; Regina Cortina, "MexAmerica and the Global American South," paper presented at the Navigating the Globalization of the American South conference, University of North Carolina–Chapel Hill, 2005.

92. Raymond Mohl, "Latinization in the Heart of Dixie: Hispanics in Late-Twentieth-Century Alabama," *Alabama Review* 87, no. 4 (2002): 243–274; Mohl,

"The *Nuevo* New South: Hispanic Migration to Alabama," *Migration World Magazine* 30, no. 3 (2002): 14–18.

93. ACLU, "Crisis in Alabama: Immigration Law Causes Chaos," accessed June 30, 2014, https://www.aclu.org/crisis-alabama-immigration-law-causes-chaos.

94. Leon Fink, *The Maya of Morganton: Work and Community in the Nuevo New South* (Chapel Hill: University of North Carolina Press, 2003).

95. James C. Cobb and William Stueck, eds., *Globalization and the American South* (Athens: University of Georgia Press, 2005).

96. Ibid., xv.

97. Fran Ansley and Jon Shefner, eds., *Global Connections and Local Receptions: New Latino Immigration to the Southeastern United States* (Knoxville: University of Tennessee Press, 2009); Jon Shefner and Katie Kirkpatrick, "Introduction: Globalization and the New Destination Immigrant," in ibid., xv–xl.

98. Jamie Winders, *Nashville in the New Millennium: Immigrant Settlement, Urban Transformation, and Social Belonging* (New York: Russell Sage Foundation, 2013).

99. Jamie Winders, "Changing Politics of Race and Region: Latino Migration to the US South," *Progress in Human Geography* 29, no. 6 (2005): 683–699; Winders, "Bringing Back the (B)order: Post-9/11 Politics of Immigration, Borders, and Belonging in the Contemporary US South," *Antipode* 39, no. 5 (2007): 920–942; Winders, "New Directions in the Nuevo South," *Southeastern Geographer* 51, no. 2 (2011): 327–340; Winders, "Re-Placing Southern Geographies: The Role of Latino Migration in Transforming the South, Its Identities, and Its Study," *Southeastern Geographer* 51, no. 2 (2011): 342–358; Winders, "Representing the Immigrant: Social Movements, Political Discourse, and Immigration in the US South," *Southeastern Geographer* 51, no. 4 (2011): 596–614.

100. Winders, "Changing Politics." For some exceptions, see Barbara Ellen Smith, "Across Races and Nations: Social Justice Organizing in the Transnational South," in Smith and Furuseth, *Latinos in the New South*, 235–256; Helen B. Marrow, "Hispanic Immigration, Black Population Size, and Intergroup Relations in the Rural and Small-Town South," in Massey, *New Faces in New Places*, 211–248; Paula D. McClain et al., "Racial Distancing in a Southern City: Latino Immigrants' Views of Black Americans," *Journal of Politics* 68, no. 3 (2006): 571–584; and Angela Christine Stuesse, "Globalization 'Southern Style': Transnational Migration, the Poultry Industry, and Implications for Organizing Workers across Difference" (PhD diss., University of Texas at Austin, 2008).

101. Winders, "Changing Politics," 689.

102. Angela C. Stuesse and Laura E. Helton, "Low-Wage Legacies, Race, and the Golden Chicken in Mississippi: Where Contemporary Immigration Meets African American Labor History," *Southern Spaces*, December 31, 2013, accessed January 10, 2014, southernspaces.org/2013/low-wage-legacies-race-and-golden-chicken-mississippi#sthash.To5sN74e.dpuf.

103. Julie M. Weise, *Corazón de Dixie: Mexicanos in the U.S. South since 1910* (Chapel Hill: University of North Carolina Press, 2015).

104. Ibid., 85.

105. Miranda Cady Hallett, "'Better Than White Trash': Work Ethic, *Latinidad* and Whiteness in Rural Arkansas," *Latino Studies* 10, no. 1–2 (2012): 81–106.

106. Hallett mentions once that Laotians moved to Danville in the 1970s and

1980s but does not mention them again, nor does she talk about the size of the community or how their presence affects local racialized dynamics.

Chapter 2: Yellow Peril in Arkansas

1. Peggy Robertson, "Governor Greets First 71 Refugees," *Arkansas Gazette* (Little Rock), May 3, 1975.
2. "Arkansas: A Temporary Home," *Arkansas Gazette*, May 3, 1975.
3. Mike Trimble, "Last, Sad Effort Gets Underway in First Welcome," *Arkansas Gazette*, May 3, 1975, A1.
4. Lipman also addresses the legal designation used to define Vietnamese people. They were, at least initially, not refugees but "parolees" who were granted temporary admittance to the United States and needed sponsors to leave the camps. She makes the point, however, that in written government and media documents, the group was usually described as refugees. More importantly, this is how Vietnamese people understood themselves; thus, I use "refugees" to refer to the group. Jana Lipman, "A Refugee Camp in America: Fort Chaffee and Vietnamese and Cuban Refugees, 1975-1982," *Journal of American Ethnic History* 33, no. 2 (2014): 57-87.
5. Eric Tang, "A Gulf Unites Us: The Vietnamese Americans of Black New Orleans East," *American Quarterly* 63 (March 2011): 117-149.
6. Wendy Cheng, *The Changs Next Door to the Díazes: Remapping Race in Suburban California* (Minneapolis: University of Minnesota Press, 2013), 10.
7. Fear of Asian people within economic and cultural spheres has a history in the United States that dates back to the late nineteenth century, while the racialization of Asians as physically and intellectually different from white people and the intersection of anti-Asian fears and nativism predominate during economic downturns. Although "yellow peril" is Asian-specific, similar tropes have been strategically deployed against African Americans, Native Americans, and Latinas/os. For more on yellow peril, see Colleen Lye, *America's Asia: Racial Form and American Literature, 1893-1945* (Princeton, NJ: Princeton University Press, 2005); Lisa Lowe, *Immigrant Acts: On Asian American Cultural Politics* (Durham, NC: Duke University Press, 1996). For discussions of the ways in which Asians have been racialized across space and time, see Nayan Shah, *Contagious Divides: Epidemics and Race in San Francisco's Chinatown* (Berkeley: University of California Press, 2001); Roger Daniels, *Prisoners without Trial: Japanese Americans in World War II* (New York: Hill and Wang, 1993).
8. "Two Decades Later, Mariel Boat Lift Refugees Still Feel Effects of Riot," *Los Angeles Times*, May 5, 2001; Susana Peña, *¡Oye Loca! From the Mariel Boatlift to Gay Cuban Miami* (Minneapolis: University of Minnesota Press, 2013).
9. Jennifer Stump, "Huckabee Announces Hispanic Program at LR Festival," *Arkansas Democrat-Gazette* (Little Rock), May 8, 2000.
10. Claire Jean Kim, "The Racial Triangulation of Asian Americans," *Politics and Society* 27, no. 1 (1999): 105-138.
11. Maranda Radcliff, "Fort Chaffee," *Encyclopedia of Arkansas History and Culture*, July 2008, accessed May 27, 2010, http://www.encyclopediaofarkansas.net/encyclopedia/entry-detail.aspx?entryID=2263.

12. W. J. Bennett Jr. et al., *Center Valley*, Archeological Assessment Report No. 217 / Fort Chaffee Cultural Resource Report No. 17 (US Army Corps of Engineers, Little Rock District), July 24, 1995, 5.

13. US Congress, Eleventh Report of the Preparedness Subcommittee of the Committee on Armed Services, *Investigation of the Preparedness Program*, 82nd Cong., 1st sess., 1951, 6.

14. Merrill R. Pritchett and William L. Shea, "The Afrika Korps in Arkansas, 1943-1946," *Arkansas Historical Quarterly* 37, no. 1 (Spring 1978): 3-22.

15. Quotation in Russell Bearden, "Life inside Arkansas's Japanese-American Relocation Centers," *Arkansas Historical Quarterly* 48, no. 2 (Summer 1989): 169-196.

16. Quotation in William C. Anderson, "Early Reaction in Arkansas to the Relocation of Japanese in the State," *Arkansas Historical Quarterly* 23 (Autumn 1964): 195-211.

17. Quotation in Pritchett and Shea, "The Afrika Korps in Arkansas," 8.

18. C. Calvin Smith, "The Response of Arkansans to Prisoners of War and Japanese Americans in Arkansas, 1942-1945," *Arkansas Historical Quarterly* 53 (Autumn 1994): 340-366.

19. Ibid.

20. Pritchett and Shea, "The Afrika Korps in Arkansas," 3-22.

21. Bennett, *Center Valley*, 5.

22. US Army Corps of Engineers, St. Louis District, "Supplement to the 1994 Archives Search Report for Camp Chaffee," *Defense Environment Restoration Program for Formerly Used Defense Sites*, September 2002, 2-1.

23. Bennett, *Center Valley*, 5.

24. Ibid.

25. Ibid.

26. Catherine A. Lutz, *Homefront: A Military City and the American Twentieth Century* (Boston: Beacon, 2001).

27. "Politics Key to the Fate of Camp's Last Cubans," *New York Times*, January 4, 1982, sec. A.

28. For more information about sundown towns in the United States, see James W. Loewen, *Sundown Towns: A Hidden Dimension of American Racism* (New York: Touchstone, 2005); for the case of Harrison, see Jacqueline Froelich and David Zimmermann, "Total Eclipse: The Destruction of the African American Community of Harrison, Arkansas in 1905 and 1909," *Arkansas Historical Quarterly* 58, no. 2 (1999): 131-159.

29. George M. Marsden, *Fundamentalism and American Culture*, 2nd ed. (New York: Oxford University Press, 2006), 244, 237, 234-239.

30. Brian Stanford Miller, "Car Tags and Cubans: Bill Clinton, Frank White and Arkansas' Return to Conservatism" (PhD diss., University of Mississippi, 2006), 49.

31. Marsden, *Fundamentalism and American Culture*, 231-232, 239-246.

32. Miller, "Car Tags and Cubans," 88; Bethany Moreton, *To Serve God and Wal-Mart: The Making of Christian Free Enterprise* (Cambridge, MA: Harvard University Press, 2009), 1.

33. Manning Marable, *Race, Reform, and Rebellion: The Second Reconstruction and Beyond in Black America, 1945-2006*, 3rd ed. (Jackson: University Press of Mis-

sissippi, 2007); Clive Webb, ed., *Massive Resistance: Southern Opposition to the Second Reconstruction* (New York: Oxford University Press, 2005).

34. Numan V. Bartley, *The Rise of Massive Resistance: Race and Politics in the South during the 1950s* (Baton Rouge: Louisiana State University Press, 1999); George Lewis, *Massive Resistance: The White Response to the Civil Rights Movement* (London: Hodder Arnold, 2006); Francis M. Wilhoit, *The Politics of Massive Resistance* (New York: G. Braziller, 1973).

35. Kevin M. Kruse, *White Flight: Atlanta and the Making of Modern Conservatism* (Princeton, NJ: Princeton University Press, 2005); Matthew D. Lassiter, *The Silent Majority: Suburban Politics in the Sunbelt South* (Princeton, NJ: Princeton University Press, 2006).

36. "Plan Reported to Use Chaffee," *Arkansas Gazette*, April 25, 1975.

37. "Fort Chaffee Just One Possibility as Refugee Camp, Pentagon Says," *Arkansas Gazette*, April 26, 1975.

38. Roy Bode, "Use of Fort Chaffee Confirmed," *Arkansas Gazette*, April 29, 1975.

39. Caroline L. Brendel to David Pryor, May 3, 1975, box 67, folder 29, manuscript collection 336, David Hampton Pryor Papers, Special Collections Department, University of Arkansas Libraries, Fayetteville; hereinafter DHPP. For letters that express similar sentiments, please see this folder.

40. David Pryor to constituents supportive of Vietnamese refugees in Arkansas, 1975, box 67, folder 29, DHPP.

41. *Dumas (AR) Clarion* quoted in "The Arkansas Press: Those Vietnamese Refugees at Fort Chaffee," *Arkansas Gazette*, May 11, 1975.

42. *Yell County Record* (Danville, AR) quoted in ibid.

43. Donald T. Critchlow, *The Conservative Ascendancy: How the GOP Right Made Political History* (Cambridge, MA: Harvard University Press, 2007), 176.

44. *Northwest Arkansas Times* (Fayetteville) quoted in "The Arkansas Press: Those Vietnamese Refugees at Fort Chaffee."

45. "Procedures Set Up for Relief Agencies to Route Refugees," *Arkansas Gazette*, May 28, 1975.

46. Ibid. A close look at US history demonstrates that freedom and liberty have been the rights of only a small percentage of the nation's population. For two excellent analyses, see Evelyn Nakano Glenn, *Unequal Freedom: How Race and Gender Shaped American Citizenship and Labor* (Cambridge, MA: Harvard University Press, 2002) and Mae M. Ngai, *Impossible Subjects: Illegal Aliens and the Making of Modern America* (Princeton, NJ: Princeton University Press, 2004).

47. "Exhibit A: Refugees Resettled into Society as of December 20, 1975," in a proposal from Reverend Tom Adkinson, associate minister at Lakeside United Methodist Church, Pine Bluff (AR), February 26, 1976, box 92, folder 19 ("Vietnamese/English Education Proposal, 1976"), DHPP.

48. US Census Bureau, "Table 195: Citizenship and Year of Immigration for Foreign-Born Persons by Country of Birth 1980," *1980 Census of Population, Chapter D, Detailed Population Characteristics, Part 5, Arkansas* (Washington, DC: US Department of Commerce, 1981), 8. These numbers do not include foreign-born persons from China, Hong Kong, India, Iran, Israel, Japan, Korea, Lebanon, the Philippines, Thailand, or Turkey.

49. "Exhibit B / Printout Dated 31 Dec. 1975 and Released through Governor's Office," in Adkinson proposal, February 26, 1976, DHPP.

50. I did not find that white Arkansans thought it was unfair for African Americans to receive unemployment, food stamps, or other benefits. However, several brought up other people of color whom they perceived as foreigners to the nation without regard to citizenship status, such as ethnic Puerto Ricans, Cubans, or Mexicans.

51. Ernest Dumas, "Chaffee to Provide Transitory Housing, Bumpers, Pryor Say," *Arkansas Gazette*, April 30, 1975; "Labor Force Statistics from the Current Population Survey—Unemployment Rate," Bureau of Labor Statistics, US Department of Labor, July 28, 2016, http://data.bls.gov/pdq/SurveyOutputServlet.

52. Carol Griffee, "Aid for Refugees: Good Intentions Outshine Spite," *Arkansas Gazette*, May 16, 1975.

53. Notes RE: Phil Matthews, box 68, folder 7 ("Vietnamese Refugee Program—Sponsorship M-R") and folder 8 ("Vietnamese Refugee Program—Sponsorship S-Z"), DHPP.

54. "Shoe Firm Wants to Hire 150 Refugees," *Arkansas Gazette*, May 17, 1975.

55. Ibid.

56. Griffee, "Aid for Refugees."

57. May 1975, box 68, folders 1-8, DHPP.

58. Gim Shek to David Pryor, May 5, 1975, box 67, folder 30 ("Vietnamese Refugee Program—Unfavorable"), DHPP.

59. Mrs. [Do Van Thuan], "A Painful Trip," August 20, 1975, Southeast Asia Relocation Collection, Artwork/Photographs, Pebley Center, Boreham Library, University of Arkansas-Fort Smith; hereinafter SEARC.

60. "Procedures Set Up for Relief Agencies to Route Refugees," *Arkansas Gazette*, May 28, 1975.

61. With the exception of one letter, what follows comes from essays written by refugees in an advanced English course at Fort Chaffee. There are enough essays that are thematically similar and dated August 19, 1975, to suggest that all were written that day. The essays also suggest that the teacher asked students to share their stories, how they got to Fort Chaffee, or where they learned English, and each refugee shared different parts of her or his travails. To allow refugees to speak for themselves, I have transcribed the letters with their original spelling, grammar, and capitalization.

62. Dave DeHart, who helped run the radio station at Fort Chaffee, remembers that it began broadcasting in Vietnamese and shortly thereafter in Cambodian, since there were also Cambodians in the camp. Transcript, Dave DeHart oral history interview, by Stacey Kowalski, February 7, 2002, 4, in "Center for Local History and Memory—Fort Chaffee Project," Pebley Center, Boreham Library, University of Arkansas-Fort Smith.

63. Tran Thi Kim Hoa, writing assignment for "Advanced Class, 4:30-6," Fort Chaffee, Arkansas, August 19, 1975, SEARC. Refugees signed into their English class according to Vietnamese custom: surname, middle name(s), given name; their names in the essay reflect the US custom of given name, middle name(s), surname. However, the footnotes reflect how they signed into class or wrote their names on the assignment and what is found in the archive.

64. Ibid.

65. Tran Thi Kim Hoa, letter to Mr. and Mrs. Jerry Turner, September 14, 1975, SEARC.

66. Ibid.

67. [No name given], "My English Study," August 19, 1975, SEARC.

68. Do Van Thuan, "The Some Past Time of My Self," August 20, 1975, SEARC.

69. Mrs. [Do Van Thuan], "A Painful Trip," August 20, 1975, SEARC.

70. Trinh Thi Cam Hong, August 19, 1975, SEARC.

71. David Pryor to John Miller, August 7, 1975, box 68, folder 4 ("Vietnamese Refugee Program—Special Assistance"), DHPP.

72. Ibid.

73. Marcus Halbrook to David Pryor, August 12, 1975, box 68, folder 4 ("Vietnamese Refugee Program—Special Assistance"), DHPP.

74. Statement by David Pryor, August 15, 1975, box 68, folder 4 ("Vietnamese Refugee Program—Special Assistance"), DHPP.

75. "That Golden Door," *Southwest Times Record* (Fort Smith, AR), August 23, 1975, attached to letter from A. DeGroff to the *Southwest Times Record* and carbon copied to Governor David Pryor and John Eisenhower, August 23, 1975, box 67, folder 33 ("Vietnamese Refugee Program—Assistance Offered [3 of 3]"), DHPP.

76. Note from Rick Osborne, Office of the Governor, July 30, 1975, box 68, folder 9 ("Vietnamese Refugee Program—Suggestions and Ideas"), DHPP.

77. Alden E. Roberts, "Racism Sent and Received: Americans and Vietnamese View One Another," *Research in Race and Ethnic Relations* 5 (1988): 75–97.

78. Anna (pseudonym) worked in local public schools for most of her career; personal interview, September 9, 2005.

79. I overheard comments like these in public during the various times that I conducted field research in 2004, 2005, 2008, and 2012, and several interviewees reported that they had heard similar remarks or that other Arkansans confided these observations to them as one white person to another.

Chapter 3: Mariel Cubans as an "Objectionable Burden" and "Illegal Aliens"

1. Bob Plunkett, "What Went Wrong at Fort Chaffee: Behind the Cuban Refugee Crisis," *Arkansas Times* (September 1980): 42–43; the subsequent quotations are from the same source.

2. Ibid., 43.

3. Ibid., 34.

4. B. E. Aguirre, "Cuban Mass Migration and the Social Construction of Deviants," *Bulletin of Latin American Research* 13, no. 2 (1994): 172.

5. Manning Marable, *Race, Reform, and Rebellion: The Second Reconstruction and Beyond in Black America, 1945-2006*, 3rd ed. (Jackson: University of Mississippi Press, 2007); Clive Webb, ed., *Massive Resistance: Southern Opposition to the Second Reconstruction* (New York: Oxford University Press, 2005).

6. Numan V. Bartley, *The Rise of Massive Resistance: Race and Politics in the South During the 1950s* (Baton Rouge: Louisiana State University Press, 1999);

George Lewis, *Massive Resistance: The White Response to the Civil Rights Movement* (London: Hodder Arnold, 2006); Francis M. Wilhoit, *The Politics of Massive Resistance* (New York: George Braziller, 1973).

7. Kevin M. Kruse, *White Flight: Atlanta and the Making of Modern Conservatism* (Princeton, NJ: Princeton University Press, 2005); Matthew D. Lassiter, *The Silent Majority: Suburban Politics in the Sunbelt South* (Princeton, NJ: Princeton University Press, 2006).

8. David Roediger, *The Wages of Whiteness: Race and the Making of the American Working Class*, rev. ed. (New York: Verso, 1999).

9. Dan T. Carter, *The Politics of Rage: George Wallace, the Origins of the New Conservatism, and the Transformation of American Politics* (New York: Simon and Schuster, 1995).

10. Dan T. Carter, *From George Wallace to Newt Gringrich: Race in the Conservative Counterrevolution, 1963-1994* (Baton Rouge: Louisiana State University press, 1996).

11. Joseph Crespino, *In Search of Another Country: Mississippi and the Conservative Counterrevolution* (Princeton, NJ: Princeton University Press, 2007); Donald T. Critchlow, *The Conservative Ascendancy: How the GOP Right Made Political History* (Cambridge, MA: Harvard University Press, 2007); Lisa McGirr, *Suburban Warriors: The Origins of the New American Right* (Princeton, NJ: Princeton University Press, 2001).

12. Clive Webb, "A Continuity of Conservatism: The Limitations of *Brown v. Board of Education*," *Journal of Southern History* 70, no. 2 (2004): 335.

13. Jeffrey R. Dudas, "In the Name of Equal Rights: 'Special' Rights and the Politics of Resentment in Post-Civil Rights America," *Law and Society Review* 39, no. 4 (2005): 723.

14. Ibid., 726.

15. Ibid., 732.

16. Brian Stanford Miller, "Car Tags and Cubans: Bill Clinton, Frank White and Arkansas' Return to Conservatism" (PhD diss., University of Mississippi, 2006), 49.

17. George M. Marsden, *Fundamentalism and American Culture*, 2nd ed. (New York: Oxford University Press, 2006), 231-232.

18. Ibid., 234-239, quotation from 237.

19. Ibid., 239-243, quotation from 240.

20. Ibid., 244-246, quotation from 246.

21. Miller, "Car Tags and Cubans," 88.

22. James T. Patterson, *Restless Giant: The United States from Watergate to Bush v. Gore* (New York: Oxford University Press, 2005), 10.

23. Anthony Campagna, *Economic Policy in the Carter Administration* (Westport, CT: Greenwood, 1995); Patterson, *Restless Giant*, 59.

24. Campagna, *Economic Policy in the Carter Administration*, xi.

25. W. Carl Biven, *Jimmy Carter's Economy: Policy in an Age of Limits* (Chapel Hill: University of North Carolina Press, 2002), 130-144.

26. Diane K. Blair and Joan Roberts, "Acquiescent Arkansas: The 1981 Response to Reaganomics and the New Federalism," *Publius* 12 (1983): 163.

27. Brian Hufker and Gray Cavender, "From Freedom Flotilla to America's

Burden: The Social Construction of the Mariel Immigrants," *Sociological Quarterly* 31, no. 2 (1990): 321.

28. For more about the waves of Cuban exiles, see Silvia Pedraza, "Cuba's Refugees: Manifold Migrations," *Cuba in Transition* 5 (1995); Maria de los Angeles Torres, *In the Land of Mirrors: Cuban Exile Politics in the United States* (Ann Arbor: University of Michigan Press, 1999); Felix Roberto Masud-Piloto, *From Welcomed Exiles to Illegal Immigrants: Cuban Migration to the U.S., 1959-1995* (Lanham, MD: Rowman and Littlefield, 1996).

29. Gastón A. Fernández, "Race, Gender, and Class in the Persistence of the Mariel Stigma Twenty Years after the Exodus from Cuba," *International Migration Review* 41, no. 3 (2007): 612; Pedraza, "Cuba's Refugees," 317-318; Pedraza, "*Los Marielitos* of 1980: Race, Class, Gender, and Sexuality," *Cuba in Transition* 14 (2004): 91.

30. Hufker and Cavender, "From Freedom Flotilla to America's Burden," 327; John Borneman, "Emigres as Bullets/Immigration as Penetration Perceptions of the Marielitos," *Journal of Popular Culture* 20, no. 3 (1986): 73; Susana Peña, "'Obvious Gays' and the State Gaze: Cuban Gay Visibility and U.S. Immigration Policy during the 1980 Mariel Boatlift," *Journal of the History of Sexuality* 16, no. 3 (2007): 485; Susana Peña, *Oye Loca: From the Mariel Boatlift to Gay Cuban Miami (Minneapolis: University of Minnesota Press, 2013)*; Julio Capó, Jr., "Queering Mariel: Mediating Cold War Foreign Policy and U.S. Citizenship among Cuba's Homosexual Exile Community, 1978-1994," *Journal of American Ethnic History* 29, no. 4 (2010): 78-106.

31. Hufker and Cavender, "From Freedom Flotilla to America's Burden," 328.

32. Peña, "Obvious Gays," 485.

33. Pedraza, "Cuba's Refugees," 319.

34. Borneman, "Emigres as Bullets," 83.

35. Ibid., 84.

36. Eithne Luibhéid, *Entry Denied: Controlling Sexuality at the Border* (Minneapolis: University of Minnesota Press, 2002).

37. Lourdes Arguelles and B. Rudy Rich, "Homosexuality, Homophobia, and Revolution: Notes toward an Understanding of the Cuban Lesbian and Gay Male Experience, Part I," *Signs: Journal of Women in Culture and Society* 9, no. 4 (1984): 689; Luibhéid, *Entry Denied*, 78.

38. Arguelles and Rich, "Homosexuality, Homophobia, and Revolution," 689.

39. "Problem Population—Gays," in *Chaffee—Resettlement, Consolidation*, December 3, 1980, p. 58, box 2, folder 7, manuscript collection 870, Alina Fernandez Papers, Special Collections Department, University of Arkansas Libraries, Fayetteville, Arkansas; hereinafter AFP.

40. Peña, "Obvious Gays," 493.

41. Ibid., 483.

42. Plunkett, "What Went Wrong at Fort Chaffee," 39, including Weiss quotation.

43. Warren Brown, "Cuban Boatlift Drew Thousands of Homosexuals," *Washington Post*, July 7, 1980, sec. A.

44. "Problem Population—Gays," 58.

45. Wilford J. Forbush, director, Cuban/Haitian Task Force, to Jack Svahn,

memo, "Fort Chaffee Resettlement Plan," March 10, 1981, p. 4, box 1, folder 5 ("C/HTF: March 3, 1981–March 31, 1981"), AFP.

46. Brown, "Cuban Boatlift Drew Thousands of Homosexuals."
47. Ibid.
48. Peña, "Obvious Gays," 497.
49. Plunkett, "What Went Wrong at Fort Chaffee," 39.
50. Peña, "Obvious Gays," 482.
51. Eithne Luibhéid, "Queer/Migration: An Unruly Body of Scholarship," *GLQ: A Journal of Lesbian and Gay Studies* 14, no. 2–3 (2008): 171.
52. Plunkett, "What Went Wrong at Fort Chaffee," 34.
53. Frederick M. Bohen, director, Cuban-Haitian Task Force, to Eugene Eidenberg, memo, "Monthly Entrant Report for November," December 11, 1980, p. 13, box 1, folder 2 ("C/HTF, Nov 6, 1980-Dec 17, 1980"), AFP.
54. Plunkett, "What Went Wrong at Fort Chaffee," 34.
55. Gastón Fernández, "The Freedom Flotilla: A Legitimacy Crisis of Cuban Socialism?" *Journal of Interamerican Studies and World Affairs* 24, no. 2 (1982): 189. He interviewed 225 Cubans, or 1.5 percent of Fort Chaffee's population, with even distribution across 150 barracks.
56. Plunkett, "What Went Wrong at Fort Chaffee," 34–39.
57. Bob Lyford and Freddie Nixon to Rob Wiley, memo, October 14, 1980, box 2, folder 2 ("Cuban Refugees/Fort Chaffee—Memos & Notes"), Bill Clinton State Government Project, unprocessed papers, William J. Clinton Presidential Library and Museum, Little Rock, Arkansas; hereinafter BCSGP.
58. Editorial, "A Welcome to the Refugees," *Arkansas Gazette*, May 3, 1975, sec. A.
59. Peggy Robertson, "Governor Greets First 71 Refugees," *Arkansas Gazette*, May 3, 1975, sec. A.
60. William Clinton, statement to the press, May 7, 1980, box 2, folder 15 ("Cuban Refugees/Fort Chaffee—File 12"), BCSGP.
61. Alex Stepick, *Pride against Prejudice: Haitians in the United States* (Needham Heights, MA: Allyn & Bacon, 1998), 102.
62. Ibid., 101–103.
63. Carl J. Bon Tempo, *Americans at the Gate: The United States and Refugees during the Cold War* (Princeton, NJ: Princeton University Press, 2008), 182.
64. Stepick, *Pride against Prejudice*, 103.
65. John P. Lagomarcino to Gene Eidenberg, May 30, 1980, p. 1, box 2, folder 15 ("Cuban Refugees/Fort Chaffee—File 12"), BCSGP.
66. Ibid., 1.
67. Ibid., 1–3.
68. Ibid., 2.
69. Ibid., 3.
70. Ben F. Johnson III, *Arkansas in Modern America, 1930-1999* (Fayetteville: University of Arkansas Press, 2000), 188.
71. In subsequent years, statewide newspapers reported on how the Vietnamese adjusted to life in Arkansas, but none mentioned welfare assistance. This is not to say that no Vietnamese family used welfare or food stamps, but if there was widespread use, then newspapers would have reported it.

72. George J. Borjas, "Immigration and Welfare: A Review of the Evidence," in *The Debate in the United States over Immigration*, ed. Peter Duignan and L. H. Gann (Palo Alto, CA: Hoover Institute Press, 1998), 121–144; George J. Borjas and Lynette Hilton, "Immigration and the Welfare State: Immigrant Participation in Means-Tested Entitlement Programs," *Quarterly Journal of Economics* 111, no. 2 (1996): 575–604.

73. White quoted in Miller, "Car Tags and Cubans," 84.

74. Ange-Marie Hancock, *The Politics of Disgust: The Public Identity of the Welfare Queen* (New York: New York University Press, 2004); Carly Hayden Foster, "The Welfare Queen: Race, Gender, Class, and Public Opinion," *Race, Gender, & Class* 15, no. 3–4 (2008): 162–180.

75. Chapter 4 addresses these issues more fully as Arkansas elected officials, political organizations, and nativist grassroots organizations accused the federal government of failing to protect America from massive immigration of people from the Third World.

76. "Tidball" note, May 19, 1980, box 2, folder 12 ("Cuban Refugees/Fort Chaffee—File 15"), BCSGP.

77. "Ft. Chaffee Task Force, Public Affairs SITREP," no. 6–9, 11, May 13–17, 19, 1980, box 2, folder 17 ("Cuban Refugees/Fort Chaffee—File 10"), BCSGP. These included three Cubans identified as Communists, causing a crowd to gather on May 13 that had to be dispersed by MPs. Rocks were thrown at the Cubans, but one hit an MP. There was also an incident involving a soldier and a female prostitute, and one domestic disturbance.

78. Press release, Office of the Governor, May 19, 1980, box 2, folder 12 ("Cuban Refugees/Fort Chaffee—File 15"), BCSGP.

79. Ibid.

80. Jimmie "Red" Jones to Governor, memo, "Assistance to Law Enforcement, Sebastian County," May 19, 1980, box 2, folder 12 ("Cuban Refugees/Fort Chaffee—File 15"), BCSGP.

81. Bob Lyford and Freddie Nixon to Rob Wiley, memo, "Chaffee" timeline, October 14, 1980, box 2, folder 2 ("Cuban Refugees/Fort Chaffee—Memos & Notes"), BCSGP.

82. "Security" notes from meeting at Fort Chaffee, May 27, 1980, box 2, folder 6 ("Cuban Refugees/Fort Chaffee—Memos and Notes"), BCSGP.

83. Lt. Col. A. T. Brainerd quoted in Plunkett, "What Went Wrong at Fort Chaffee," 39.

84. Bob Plunkett, "The New Arkansans: The Cuban Refugees, Revisited," *Arkansas Times* (1981): 22.

85. "Two Decades Later, Mariel Boat Lift Refugees Still Feel Effects of Riot," *Los Angeles Times*, May 5, 2001, sec. A.

86. Plunkett, "What Went Wrong at Fort Chaffee," 39.

87. Aguirre, "Cuban Mass Migration," 168.

88. Fernández, "The Freedom Flotilla," 189; Pedraza, "Cubas's Refugees," 319.

89. Plunkett, "What Went Wrong at Fort Chaffee," 39.

90. "Better Security for Camp Asked as Refugees Flee," *New York Times*, May 28, 1980, 14.

91. US Bureau of the Census, *Characteristics of the Population, Detailed Charac-*

teristics of the Population, Arkansas (Washington, DC: Government Printing Office, 1980); US Bureau of the Census, *General Population Characteristics, Arkansas, Prepared by US Department of Commerce* (Washington, DC: Government Printing Office, 1990).

92. *Chaffee—Resettlement, Consolidation*, December 3, 1980, p. 51, box 2, folder 7 ("C/HTF: Office Papers, Nov. 25, 1980—July 29, 1981"), AFP.
93. Quotation in "Two Decades Later."
94. "Better Security for Camp Asked as Refugees Flee."
95. Plunkett, "What Went Wrong at Fort Chaffee," 39, 41.
96. Ibid.
97. "Better Security for Camp Asked as Refugees Flee."
98. Masud-Piloto, *From Welcomed Exiles to Illegal Immigrants*.
99. Jo Thomas, "Troops Ordered to Arkansas Camp after Refugee Riot," *New York Times*, June 3, 1980, A1.
100. Paul Heath Hoeffel, "Fort Chaffee's Unwanted Cubans," *New York Times*, December 21, 1980, SM 8.
101. Bohen, "Monthly Entrant Report for November," December 11, 1980, p. 10, AFP.
102. Aguirre, "Cuban Mass Migration," 171.
103. John Workman, "Churches, Other Organizations All Hard at Work," *Arkansas Gazette*, May 18, 1980, sec. F.
104. Plunkett, "What Went Wrong at Fort Chaffee," 35, 38.
105. Ibid., 38.
106. Masud-Piloto, *From Welcomed Exiles to Illegal Immigrants*; Aguirre, "Cuban Mass Migration," 170.
107. David Engstrom, *Presidential Decision Making Adrift: The Carter Administration and the Mariel Boatlift* (New York: Rowman and Littlefield, 1997), 147.
108. Plunkett, "What Went Wrong at Fort Chaffee," 39.
109. Masud-Pilot, *From Welcomed Exiles to Illegal Immigrants*.
110. "Por lo visto Uds. se han olvidado por lo que estuvimos pasando en Cuba. Muchos de nosotros fuimos presos y demas está decir que todos conocimos los medios de represión en esas 'Prisiones'. . . . " / "[J]amás fuimos tratados en forma tan respetuosa, tan amable. . . . Nos están tratando como seres humanos, sin distinción de raza ni de clases." / Sin embargo, un grupito de 'Caudillos,' políticos sin causa, enredadores y quien sabe, agentes invisibles de Castro, han planteado la clasificación dentro de la Colonia Cubana que se refugia en el Fuerte." All quotations translated by the author and taken from R.T.B., "La Noche del 26 en el Fuerte Café," *La Vida Nueva*, May 27, 1980.
111. "Es una forma que tienen los Estados de proteger a sus pueblos contra los daños irreparables que siempre ocasionaría una inmigración incontrolada"; C.L.S., "Los Impacientes," *La Vida Nueva*, May 28, 1980.
112. L.G.T., "Cubanos Vigilan y Mantienen Control y Orden," *La Vida Nueva*, June 4, 1980; Ray Robinson, "67 Injured in Fort Chaffee Riot," *Southwest Times Record* (Fort Smith, AR), June 4, 1980, sec. A; Plunkett, "What Went Wrong at Fort Chaffee," 44.
113. Aguirre, "Cuban Mass Migration," 169-174.
114. Quotation in Plunkett, "What Went Wrong at Fort Chaffee," 42.

115. Ibid., 44.
116. "Cuidado Con El Fuego!" *La Vida Nueva*, May 26, 1980.
117. Plunkett, "What Went Wrong at Fort Chaffee," 44.
118. Ibid.
119. Ibid., 35.
120. Ibid., 44.
121. Clinton quoted in ibid., 44–45.
122. Ibid., 45.
123. "'Powderkeg' Ignored," *Southwest Times Record*, June 2, 1980, sec. A.
124. Plunkett, "What Went Wrong at Fort Chaffee," 45.
125. Clinton quoted in ibid., 45.
126. Jack Mosely, "Why Did It Happen?" *Southwest Times Record*, June 2, 1980, sec. A.
127. Kevin Laval, "Breakdown in Communication Denied," *Southwest Times Record*, June 4, 1980, sec. A.
128. Ibid.
129. Robinson, "67 Injured in Fort Chaffee Riot."
130. "Chaffee" note, June 14, 1980, box 1 ("Fort Chaffee-Misc.—Freddie 2 of 2"), BCSGP.
131. Robinson, "67 Injured in Fort Chaffee Riot."
132. Fines F. Batchelor Jr. to Clinton, letter, June 16, 1980, box 2, folder 14 ("Cuban Refugees/Fort Chaffee-File 13"), BCSGP.
133. Ibid., 2.
134. This question is addressed fully in the next section.
135. Clinton to Attorney General Steve Clark, letter, June 18, 1980, box 2, folder 14 ("Cuban Refugees/Fort Chaffee-File 13"), BCSGP.
136. Jesse L. Long to Clinton, letter, June 14, 1980, p. 1, box 2, folder 3 ("Cuban Refugees/Fort Chaffee-Misc. Correspondence"), BCSGP.
137. Ibid., 1–2.
138. Ibid., 2.
139. Clinton to William E. Kell, special agent-in-charge, FBI, letter, June 13, 1980, box 1 ("Fort Chaffee Misc.—Freddie 1 of 2"), BCSGP.
140. Drew S. Days III, assistant attorney general, Civil Rights Division, US Department of Justice to Clinton, letter, September 29, 1980, box 2, folder 8 ("Cuban Refugees/Fort Chaffee—File 19"), BCSGP.
141. Clinton to "All State Police Personnel Involved in the Fort Chaffee Incident," memo, October 31, 1980, box 2, folder 8 ("Cuban Refugees/Fort Chaffee—File 19"), BCSGP.
142. Jesse L. Long to Clinton, memo, June 14, 1980, box 2, folder 3 ("Cuban Refugees/Fort Chaffee-Misc. Correspondence") and copy of citizen complaint to inspector general, US Army, June, 6, 1980, box 2, folder 3 ("Cuban Refugees/Fort Chaffee-Misc. Correspondence"), BCSGP.
143. Clinton to Jesse L. Long, letter, June 18, 1980, box 2, folder 3 ("Cuban Refugees/Fort Chaffee-Misc. Correspondence"), BCSGP.
144. Clinton to Steve Clark, letter, June 17, 1980, box 1 ("Fort Chaffee Misc.-Freddie 1 of 2"), BCSGP.
145. Ibid.
146. Aguirre, "Cuban Mass Migration," 172.

147. "Summary of Inquiry of Attorney General Steve Clark," August 27, 1980, p. 1, box 2, folder 8 ("Cuban Refugees/Fort Chaffee-File 19"), BCSGP.
148. Ibid., 7.
149. Ibid., 1-2.
150. Ibid., 2.
151. Ibid., 3.
152. Ibid., 4.
153. Engstrom, *Presidential Decision Making Adrift*, 162-169.
154. Aguirre. "Cuban Mass Migration," 173.
155. "CDR FORSCOM FT MCPHERSON GA//AFOP-COF//," June 2, 1980, box 1, BCSGP.
156. Ibid., 1.
157. Ibid., 2.
158. Ibid., 3.
159. Aguirre, "Cuban Mass Migration," 165-166; Engstrom, *Presidential Decision Making Adrift*, 139.
160. Aguirre, "Cuban Mass Migration," 166.
161. Ibid.
162. Engstrom, *Presidential Decision Making Adrift*, 186-187.
163. "Chaffee" timeline, October 14, 1980, BCSGP.
164. Peggy Watson, "Remaining Refugees Will Be Assigned to Fort Chaffee," *Arkansas Gazette*, August 2, 1980, sec. A.
165. Bill Terry, "Cubans and Politics," *Arkansas Times* (October 1980): 25; Blair and Roberts, "Acquiescent Arkansas," 164.
166. Clinton to President Carter, letter, September 12, 1980, box 2, folder 2 ("Cuban Refugees/Fort Chaffee—Memos & Notes"), BCSGP.
167. Robert Lyford to Clinton, memo, "Security at Fort Chaffee for Consolidation," August 8, 1980, box 2, folder 1 ("Cuban Refugees/Fort Chaffee—Memos and Notes"), BCSGP.
168. "Chaffee" timeline, October 14, 1980, and "Security at Fort Chaffee for Consolidation," August 8, 1980, BCSGP.
169. "Security at Fort Chaffee for Consolidation," August 8, 1980, BCSGP.
170. Christian R. Holmes quoted in Clinton to Clark, letter, September 19, 1980, p. 1, box 2, folder 9 ("Cuban Refugees/Fort Chaffee—File 18"), BCSGP.
171. Clark quoted in the *Lonoke Democrat*; reprinted in "Steve Clark's Opinion on Security at Fort Chaffee," *Arkansas Gazette*, October 20, 1980, sec. B.
172. Clinton to Clark, September 19, 1980, p. 2, BCSGP.
173. Clark to Clinton, letter, September 25, 1980, pp. 1-2, box 2, folder 9 ("Cuban Refugees/Fort Chaffee-File 18"), BCSGP.
174. Ibid., 2.
175. Ibid.
176. Ibid., 3.
177. Ibid.
178. Ibid., 4.
179. Clark to Clinton, September 25, 1980, p. 4, BCSGP.
180. Clark to Clinton, letter, September 25, 1980, p. 1, box 2, folder 9 ("Cuban Refugees/Fort Chaffee-File 18"), BCSGP.
181. Ibid.

182. Ibid., 2.
183. Ibid., 3.
184. Rudy to Bob Lyford, memo, "Steve Clark and Status of Cubans," October 16, 1980, box 2, folder 9 ("Cuban Refugees/Fort Chaffee-File 18"), BCSGP.
185. Benjamin R. Civiletti, US attorney general, to Clinton, letter, October 22, 1980, p. 1, box 2, folder 8 ("Cuban Refugees/Fort Chaffee—File 19"), BCSGP.
186. Ibid., 1.
187. Clinton to Paul Michel, associate deputy attorney general, US Department of Justice, letter, September 26, 1980, box 2, folder 2 ("Cuban Refugees/Fort Chaffee—Memos & Notes"), BCSGP.
188. "Appendix O: Guidance for State and Local Law Enforcement Agencies," *Joint Security Plan for the Cuban Entrants Processing Center Resettlement Operation*, September 5, 1980 (continually updated), Department of Justice and Department of Defense, box 2, folder 12 ("Cuban Refugees/Fort Chaffee-File 15"), BCSGP.
189. Aguirre, "Cuban Mass Migration," 159.
190. Miller, "Car Tags and Cubans," 96.
191. Gregory Jaynes, "Fort Smith Has Bad Morning After," *New York Times*, February 12, 1982, sec. A.
192. Aguirre, "Cuban Mass Migration," 166.
193. Personal interviews, respectively, August 4, 2004, August 5, 2004, and August 10, 2004.
194. Personal interview, August 5, 2004.

Chapter 4: Latinas/os and *Polleras*

1. Brent E. Riffel, "The Feathered Kingdom: Tyson Foods and the Transformation of American Land, Labor, and Law, 1930-2005" (PhD diss., University of Arkansas, 2008).
2. Class issues were a lesser part of the equation in the Ozarks, historically a low-income area that still had many working-class white people in the 1990s.
3. Anecdotal evidence suggests the migration also included some working-class, native-born Chicanas/os, but more thorough research is needed to determine accurate numbers.
4. Steve Striffler, *Chicken: The Dangerous Transformation of America's Favorite Food* (New Haven, CT: Yale University Press, 2005), 95.
5. Ibid., 97-107.
6. The rejection of and reaction to Latinas/os will be explored fully in the following chapter.
7. David Griffith, *Jones's Minimal: Low-Wage Labor in the United States* (Albany: SUNY Press, 1993), 83-114; Donald D. Stull and Michael J. Broadway, *Slaughterhouse Blues: The Meat and Poultry Industry in North America* (Belmont, CA: Wadsworth, 2004), 1-21, 36-51; David Griffith, Michael J. Broadway, and Donald D. Stull, "Introduction: Making Meat," in *Any Way You Cut It: Meat Processing and Small-Town America*, ed. Donald D. Stull, Michael J. Broadway, and David Griffith (Lawrence: University Press of Kansas, 1995), 1-16; David Griffith, "*Hay Trabajo*: Poultry Processing, Rural Industrialization, and the Latinization of Low-Wage Labor," in ibid., 129-151.

8. William Kandel and Emilio Parrado, "Hispanics in the American South and the Transformation of the Poultry Industry," in *Hispanic Spaces, Latino Places: Community and Cultural Diversity in Contemporary America*, ed. Daniel D. Arreola (Austin: University of Texas Press, 2004), 265.

9. Griffith, *Jones's Minimal*, 100. More research is needed on why these early poultry workers did not spawn a large-scale migration of their peers like the one in the 1990s. The Immigration Reform and Control Act of 1986 and the legalization of millions of Latinas/os provides only a partial answer.

10. Quotation in D. R. Stewart, "'Southpaw' Pinches Illegals—613 in Week," *Arkansas Democrat-Gazette* (Little Rock), September 14, 1995, sec. A.

11. Riffel, "Feathered Kingdom," 259. In 2003 a Tyson manager said that one-third of their line force was Latina/o, but interviews of Tyson workers in northwest Arkansas by Human Rights Watch investigators suggested the majority of the workers were immigrants and that most of the immigrants were Latina/o. See Human Rights Watch, *Blood, Sweat, and Fear: Workers' Rights in U.S. Meat and Poultry Plants* (New York: Human Rights Watch, 2004), 110.

12. *Tranquilidad* literally means tranquility, but for many immigrants it encompassed peace of mind in terms of employment and child rearing and referred to an overall wholesome environment. I will discuss the term and its meanings in more detail in a section below.

13. Joe Crommett, "Voter Strength Stressed," *Arkansas Gazette* (Little Rock), March 23, 1990, sec. B; George Wells, "Redistricting Gives Blacks Bigger Say," *Arkansas Gazette*, October 7, 1990, sec. A.

14. Karen Rafinski, "Racial Mix in Delta Is Shifting," *Arkansas Gazette*, January 27, 1991, sec. B.

15. Karen Rafinski, "Arkansas Population: Gainers and Losers," *Arkansas Gazette*, February 3, 1991, sec. A.

16. Ibid.

17. Elizabeth Lowry, "Hot Springs Mayor Calls Changes 'Wealth Flight,'" *Arkansas Gazette*, February 15, 1991, sec. A.

18. Mark Oswald, "Supreme Court Affirms Redistricting," *Arkansas Gazette*, January 8, 1991, sec. A.

19. Wells, "Redistricting Gives Blacks Bigger Say."

20. Ibid.

21. Phoebe Wall Howard, "Clinton Called 'Arrogant,'" *Arkansas Gazette*, July 31, 1990, sec. B.

22. Mark Oswald, "Supreme Court Affirms Redistricting," *Arkansas Gazette*, January 8, 1991, sec. A.

23. Carla Johnson Kimbrough, "Attempts to Ease Racial Heat Cooling," *Arkansas Gazette*, June 25, 1990, sec. A.

24. Ibid.

25. Deborah Mathis, "Benham Loses His Power, Not His Bigotry," *Arkansas Gazette*, November 2, 1990, sec. B.

26. Michael Arbanas, "Senator Accused of Racial Slur," *Arkansas Gazette*, November 1, 1990, sec. B.

27. Mark Oswald, "Clinton Explains Benham," *Arkansas Gazette*, November 3, 1990, sec. B.

28. Arbanas, "Senator Accused of Racial Slur."

29. James Scudder, "Racism Clear in Vote Count, Group Says," *Arkansas Gazette*, November 14, 1990, sec. B.

30. Ibid. In fact, Arkansans nearly elected Ralph Forbes, a white supremacist and former Nazi, to the office of lieutenant governor in 1990; he was defeated in a run-off election. See John Brummett, "Rid State of Bogus Amendment," *Arkansas Gazette*, October 5, 1990, sec. B.

31. Scudder, "Racism Clear in Vote Count."

32. Michael Arbanas, "Arkansas Lacks Civil Rights Statutes," *Arkansas Gazette*, January 20, 1991, sec. A.

33. Michael Arbanas, "Legislators to Propose Package of Civil Rights Laws," *Arkansas Gazette*, January 18, 1991, sec. B.

34. Max Parker, "House Committee Unanimously Recommends Civil Rights Proposal," *Arkansas Gazette*, March 6, 1991, sec. B.

35. Caroline Decker, "Civil Rights Proposal Being Negotiated at Clinton's Bidding," *Arkansas Gazette*, March 8, 1991, sec. A.

36. Ibid.

37. Caroline Decker, "Chamber Ends Negotiations on Civil Rights Act," *Arkansas Gazette*, March 9, 1991, sec. A.

38. Ibid.

39. "A Civil Rights Fig Leaf," *Arkansas Gazette*, March 11, 1991, sec. B.

40. Caroline Decker, "Rights Study, Not Bill, Backed," *Arkansas Gazette*, March 22, 1991, sec. I.

41. Noel Oman, "Signing of Bill Ends State's Long Holdout on Civil Rights Front," *Arkansas Democrat-Gazette*, April 9, 1993, sec. A.

42. James C. Cobb, *The Selling of the South: The Southern Crusade for Industrial Development, 1936-1990*, 2nd ed. (Urbana: University of Illinois Press, 1993).

43. Julie M. Weise, "Mexican Nationalisms, Southern Racisms: Mexicans and Mexican Americans in the U.S. South, 1908-1939," *American Quarterly* 60, no. 3 (2008): 749-778.

44. More research needs to be done, however, to uncover their histories in order to come up with an accurate demographic profile.

45. There is no way to determine what percentage of the 1980 "Spanish origin" population consisted of ethnic Mexicans.

46. The Census Bureau also changed the questions they asked, making it difficult to determine how many of these Latinas/os were foreign born.

47. From the 1980, 1990, and 2000 censuses. Jeralynn S. Cossman and Edward L. Powers, "Dynamics of Hispanic Population Growth in Arkansas," *Arkansas Business and Economic Review* 33, no. 4 (2000): 2-8; Gazi Shbikat and Steve Striffler, "Arkansas Migration and Population," *Arkansas Business and Economic Review* 33, no. 3 (2000): 1-5.

48. Andrew Wainer, "The New Latino South and the Challenge to Public Education: Strategies for Educators and Policymakers in Emerging Immigrant Communities" (Los Angeles: Tomás Rivera Policy Institute, University of Southern California, 2004), 8.

49. The description of the town is taken from interviews with Andrea and Rodolfo, who are both natives of La Blanca. Both names are pseudonyms, to protect their privacy. Andrea, phone interview, November 7, 2004; Rodolfo, personal

Notes to Pages 124–128 **207**

interview, August 13, 2004; "Gral. Pánfilo Natera," *Turismo Zacatecas*, November 9, 2004, http://www.turismozacatecas.gob.mx/Fiestas.htm.

50. Gobierno de Estado—Zacatecas, "Gral. Pánfilo Natera," September 9, 2009, http://www.zacatecas.gob.mx/Municipios/GpanfilonateraHist.htm.

51. Andrea, phone interview.

52. Ibid.; "La gente que no va a Estados Unidos viven en la pobreza, son conformistas y no se mueven de ahí" (translation by author).

53. Gobierno de Estado—Zacatecas, "Gral. Panfilo Natera—Infraestructura Social Y De Comunicaciones," September 9, 2008, http://www.zacatecas.gob.mx/Municipios/GpanfilonateraInfra.htm.

54. For general information about La Blanca, see "General Pánfilo Natera," Enciclopedia de los Municipios y Delegaciones de México, Estado de Zacatecas, http://www.inafed.gob.mx/work/enciclopedia/EMM32zacatecas/municipios/32016a.html.

55. Andrea, phone interview; Rodolfo, personal interview.

56. Andrea, phone interview; Rodolfo, personal interview.

57. For recent information, see "Resumen municipal: Municipio de General Pánfilo Natera," from the Secretaría de Desarrollo Social, http://www.microrregiones.gob.mx/catloc/LocdeMun.aspx?tipo=clave&campo=loc&ent=32&mun=016.

58. "Población Total, Edad Mediana y Relación Hombres-Mujeres Por Municipio Según Sexo," *INEGI Conteo de Población y Vivienda 2005*.

59. Instituto Nacional de Estadística y Geografía (INEGI), http://www.inegi.org.mx/.

60. Miguel Moctezuma Longoria, "La experiencia de las remesas comunitarias del club de migrantes El Remolino, Zacatecas," in *Enfrentando Globalización: Integración Económica y Resistencia popular en México*, ed. Laura Carlsen, Hilda Salazar, and Timothy A. Wise (Mexico City: Miguel Ángel Porrua, 2003), 227.

61. Eighty-three percent of the population was Latina/o according to the 1990 census; US Bureau of the Census, *General Population Characteristics, California* (Washington, DC: Government Printing Office, 1990).

62. Ibid.

63. Nancy Rivera Brooks, "Area's Rebound Expected to Continue," *Los Angeles Times*, November 26, 1996, pt. D.

64. Andrea, personal interview.

65. Ibid.

66. "Debido al alto de la renta y lo bajo de los sueldos."

67. Personal interviews and surveys, August 2004. In 2004 I conducted about twenty interviews with Latinas/os in Arkansas. Given the small size of the pool, the interviews are not statistically sound, but I occasionally use quotes from them because the comments expressed and the experiences described are supported by other researchers who have studied the migration of Latinas/os to the South.

68. Rebecca M. Torres, E. Jeffrey Popke, and Holly M. Hapke, "The South's Silent Bargain: Rural Restructuring, Latino Labor and the Ambiguities of Migrant Experience," in *Latinos in the New South: Transformations of Place*, ed. Heather A. Smith and Owen J. Furuseth (Burlington, VT: Ashgate, 2006), 51–53.

69. Rubén Hernández-León and Víctor Zúñiga, "Making Carpet by the Mile:

The Emergence of a Mexican Immigrant Community in an Industrial Region of the U.S. Historic South," *Social Science Quarterly* 81, no. 1 (2000): 49-66; Hernández-León and Zúñiga, "Mexican Immigrant Communities in the South and Social Capital: The Case of Dalton, Georgia," *Southern Rural Sociology* 19, no. 1 (2003): 36.

70. Interviews and surveys, August 2004.

71. "Frequently Asked Questions," *Fort Smith Chamber of Commerce*, November 8, 2004, http://www.fschamber.com/goodquestions.asp.

72. Personal interview, September 9, 2005.

73. Claire Jean Kim, "The Racial Triangulation of Asian Americans," *Politics and Society* 27, no. 1 (1999): 105-138.

74. Natalia Molina, "The Power of Racial Scripts: What the History of Mexican Immigration to the United States Teaches Us about Relational Notions of Race," *Latino Studies*, suppl. Race and Blackness in the Latino/a Community 8, no. 2 (2010): 157.

75. Intertwined with these issues are those of bilingual education and curriculum. For a discussion of education and Chicana/o history, see Carlos Blanton, *The Strange Career of Bilingual Education in Texas, 1836-1981* (College Station: Texas A&M University Press, 2004); Guadalupe San Miguel, *"Let All of Them Take Heed": Mexican Americans and the Campaign for Educational Equality in Texas, 1910-1981* (Austin: University of Texas Press, 1987).

76. Eric Tang, "A Gulf Unites Us: The Vietnamese Americans of Black New Orleans East," *American Quarterly* 63, no. 1 (2011): 117-149; Khyati Y. Joshi and Jigna Desai, eds., *Asian Americans in Dixie: Race and Migration in the South* (Urbana: University of Illinois Press, 2013).

77. "Fact Sheet: Fort Smith city, Arkansas," *US Census Bureau*, November 9, 2004, http://factfinder.census.gov/servlet/SAFFFacts?_event=Search&geo_id=01000US&_geoContext=&_street=&_county=&_cityTown=fort+smith&_state=04000US05&_zip=&_lang=en&_sse=on; "Perfect Homes," *Fort Smith Chamber of Commerce*, November 8, 2004, http://www.fschamber.com/perfecthomes.asp.

78. "Frequently Asked Questions," *Fort Smith Chamber of Commerce*.

79. "Top Employers, Fort Smith, Arkansas," accessed October 5, 2008, http://www.fortsmithchamber.org/WhitePapers/WhitePapersDisplay.asp?p1=2043&p2=Y&p9=&Sort=. More research needs to be conducted on Fort Smith's political economy to understand why major corporations have locations in this city.

80. Mark Bixler, "Hiring of Illegals Props Poultry 'Culture,'" *Atlanta Journal-Constitution*, December 23, 2001, sec. A.

81. Mike Rodman, "Springdale Up in Arms over Aliens; Parties, Crowding Spark Call for Additional Police," *Arkansas Democrat-Gazette*, July 24, 1994, sec. B.; D. R. Stewart, "INS Defends Efforts to Weed Out Illegals," *Arkansas Democrat-Gazette*, September 25, 1995, sec. D.

82. Personal interviews and surveys.

83. Gustavo, quoted in Striffler, *Chicken*, 103.

84. Ibid., 103-104.

85. D. R. Stewart, "Rich in Jobs, Northwest Arkansas Becomes Mecca for Illegal Aliens," *Arkansas Democrat-Gazette*, March 4, 1993, sec. D.

86. Steve Striffler, "'We're All Mexicans Here': Poultry Processing, Latino Mi-

gration, and the Transformation of Class in the South," in *The American South in a Global World*, ed. James L. Peacock, Harry L. Watson, and Carrie R. Matthews (Chapel Hill: University of North Carolina Press, 2005), 153–156. Springdale is believed to have the largest concentration of Marshallese in the continental United States. In 2005 a special census counted two thousand, but other estimates put the number past six thousand; see "Film Documents Springdale 'Island,'" *Daily Headlines*, University of Arkansas, May 25, 2006.

87. Stewart, "Rich in Jobs, Northwest Arkansas Becomes Mecca for Illegal Aliens."

88. Stewart, "'Southpaw' Pinches Illegals—613 in Week."

89. D. R. Stewart, "Raids Net 350 Illegals at Plants," *Arkansas Democrat-Gazette*, September 9, 1995, sec. A.; Stewart, "INS Defends Efforts to Weed Out Illegals."

90. "Poultry Firms: INS Raids Don't Level Field on Jobs," *Arkansas Democrat-Gazette*, September 10, 1995, sec. B.

91. Ibid.

92. Ibid.

93. Stewart, "INS Defends Efforts to Weed Out Illegals."

94. Mike Rodman, "Northwest Wants Language Barrier to Add Up in School Formula," *Arkansas Democrat-Gazette*, December 24, 1994, sec. B.

95. Julieanne Miller, "Poultry Jobs Lure Aliens, Agent Says," *Arkansas Democrat-Gazette*, November 5, 1993, sec. B.

96. Don Johnson, "Northwest Passage: Being Illegal—It's a Job," *Arkansas Democrat-Gazette*, March 24, 1997, sec. A.

97. Stewart, "Raids Net 350 Illegals at Plants."

98. Ibid.

99. Human Rights Watch, *Blood, Sweat, and Fear*, 165–166.

100. Wendy Zellner, "Hiring Illegals: The Risks Grow," *Business Week Online*, May 13, 2002, http://www.businessweek.com/magazine/content/02_19/b3782091.htm.

101. Striffler, *Chicken*, 98.

102. Kevin Sack, "Under the Counter, Grocer Provides Workers," *New York Times*, January 14, 2002, sec. A.

103. Ibid.

104. Sherri Day, "Jury Clears Tyson Foods in Use of Illegal Immigrants," *New York Times*, March 27, 2003, sec. A.

105. Quotation in ibid.

106. Tyson Foods, Inc., "The Changing Face of Our Workforce," in *Tyson Foods, Incorporated, Annual Report—1997* (Springdale, AR: Tyson Foods, Inc., 1997), 25.

107. Mark Bixler, "Hiring of Illegals Props Poultry 'Culture,'" *Atlanta Journal-Constitution*, December 23, 2001, sec. A.

108. Quotation in Striffler, *Chicken*, 99.

109. Riffel, "Feathered Kingdom," 26.

110. Ibid., 29.

111. Human Rights Watch, *Blood, Sweat, and Fear*, 24.

112. Ibid., 1.

113. Ibid., 24.
114. Nicholas Stein, "Son of a Chicken Man," *Fortune*, May 13, 2002, 136.
115. Vanesa Ribas, *On the Line: Slaughterhouse Lives and the Making of the New South* (Berkeley: University of California Press, 2016); Angela Stuesse, *Scratching Out a Living: Latinos, Race, and Work in the Deep South* (Berkeley: University of California Press, 2016); OXFAM Report, "No Relief: Denial of Bathroom Breaks in the Poultry Industry" (Boston: OXFAM America, 2016).
116. Riffel, "Feathered Kingdom," 259.
117. Personal interview, August 5, 2004.
118. Personal interview, August 5, 2004.
119. Human Rights Watch, *Blood, Sweat, and Fear*, 108.
120. Quotation in Striffler, *Chicken*, 98.
121. Human Rights Watch, *Blood, Sweat, and Fear*, 77–84. For an in-depth discussion of Tyson's antiunion maneuvers and workplace violations of labor law, see Riffel, "Feathered Kingdom," 173–199.
122. Human Rights Watch, *Blood, Sweat, and Fear*, 80.
123. Ibid.
124. Riffel, "Feathered Kingdom," 259.
125. Quotation in Dick Kirschten, "A Melting Pot Chills in Arkansas," *National Journal* 30, no. 46 (1998): 2728.
126. Ibid.
127. "A Quick Look at U.S. Immigrants: Demographics, Workforce, and Asset-Building," The Immigrant Policy Project of the National Conference of State Legislatures, June 17, 2004.
128. Ibid.; "Bridging the Information Gap: How Bankers Can Help the Hispanic Population Realize the American Dream of Homeownership," Federal Deposit Insurance Corporation, March 22, 2005, https://www.fdic.gov/bank/analytical/fyi/2005/032205fyi.html.
129. Kirschten, "A Melting Pot Chills in Arkansas."
130. Tyson Foods, Inc., "The Changing Face of Our Workforce," 25.

Chapter 5: "Northwest Arkansas's No. 1 Societal Concern"

1. Mae Ngai, *Impossible Subjects: Illegal Aliens and the Making of Modern America* (Princeton, NJ: Princeton University Press, 2004); Nicholas De Genova, "Migrant 'Illegality' and Deportability in Everyday Life," *Annual Review of Anthropology* 31 (2002): 419–447.
2. Ngai, *Impossible Subjects*.
3. De Genova, "Migrant 'Illegality' and Deportability in Everyday Life."
4. Jonathan Xavier Inda, *Targeting Immigrants: Government, Technology, and Ethics* (Malden, MA: Blackwell, 2006), 177.
5. Personal interview, July 17, 2012.
6. Jeralynn S. Cossman and Edward L. Powers, "Dynamics of Hispanic Population Growth in Arkansas," *Arkansas Business and Economic Review* 33, no. 4 (2000): 2–8; Gazi Shbikat and Steve Striffler, "Arkansas Migration and Population," *Arkansas Business and Economic Review* 33, no. 3 (2000): 1–5.

7. Michael Whiteley, "Illegals Find Haven in Ozarks," *Arkansas Democrat-Gazette* (Little Rock), July 23, 1995, sec. A.

8. Cossman and Powers, "Dynamics of Hispanic Population Growth in Arkansas."

9. Colleen Lye, *America's Asia: Racial Form and American Literature, 1893–1945* (Princeton, NJ: Princeton University Press, 2005); Lisa Lowe, *Immigrant Acts: On Asian American Cultural Politics* (Durham, NC: Duke University Press, 1996).

10. C. L. Justin to Pryor, May 1, 1975, box 67, folder 30, manuscript collection 336, David Hampton Pryor Papers, Special Collections Department, University of Arkansas Libraries.

11. E. S. Gates to Clinton, May 11, 1980, box 2, folder 18 ("Cuban Refugees/Fort Chaffee—File 9"), Bill Clinton State Government Project, Unprocessed Papers, William J. Clinton Presidential Library and Museum, Little Rock, Arkansas; hereafter cited as BCSGP.

12. Drexel Atkinson to Clinton, no date, box 2, folder 6 ("Cuban Refugees/Fort Chaffee—Memos and Notes"), BCSGP.

13. These are the stories as they appeared in the newspaper indexes; I have not knowingly omitted a story. The stories were in the *Arkansas Gazette* (Little Rock), which folded in 1992, and the *Arkansas Democrat-Gazette*, which was formed by a merger between the *Gazette* and the *Arkansas Democrat*.

14. Phoebe Wall Howard, "Migrants Fill Summer Niche," *Arkansas Gazette*, May 2, 1990, sec. B.

15. In March the unemployment rate in the county was 6.8 percent, higher than the US rate of 5.2 but lower than the state's average of 7.3 percent; "March Unemployment Rates (Percent)," *Arkansas Gazette*, May 3, 1990, sec. C.

16. Howard, "Migrants Fill Summer Niche."

17. Andrea Harter, "Immigration Officials Arrest Hudson Workers," *Arkansas Democrat-Gazette*, February 14, 1992, sec. D.

18. Larry Young, "Osceola Wants Aliens Off Its Hands," *Arkansas Democrat-Gazette*, May 28, 1992, sec. B.

19. Andy Gotlieb, "Osceola Police Arrest 11 Mexicans in Theft," *Arkansas Democrat-Gazette*, May 30, 1992, sec. B.

20. Ibid.; "11 Illegal Aliens Freed," *Arkansas Democrat-Gazette*, June 11, 1992, sec. B.

21. George J. Sánchez, *Becoming Mexican American: Ethnicity, Culture, and Identity in Chicano Los Angeles, 1900–1945* (New York: Oxford University Press, 1993), 51.

22. Ibid., 51.

23. Kelly Lytle Hernández, *Migra! A History of the U.S. Border Patrol* (Berkeley: University of California Press, 2010), 5.

24. Ruth Ellen Wasem, "U.S. Immigration Policy on Haitian Migrants," *CRS Report for Congress*, January 21, 2005, 3.

25. Alex Stepic, *Pride against Prejudice: Haitians in the United States* (Boston: Allyn and Bacon, 1998), 108.

26. Ted Henken, "Balseros, Boteros, and El Bombo: Post-1994 Cuban Immigration to the United States and the Persistence of Special Treatment," *Latino Studies* 3 (2005): 393–416.

27. Ngai, *Impossible Subjects*, 58.
28. Ibid.
29. De Genova, "Migrant 'Illegality' and Deportability in Everyday Life," 438–440.
30. For more information about the role of work in Latina/o migration and racialization, see chap. 4.
31. Julieanne Miller, "Poultry Jobs Lure Aliens, Agent Says," *Arkansas Democrat-Gazette*, November 5, 1993, sec. B.
32. Mike Rodman, "Springdale Up in Arms over Aliens; Parties, Crowding Spark Call for Additional Police," *Arkansas Democrat-Gazette*, July 24, 1994, sec. B.
33. Inda, *Targeting Immigrants*, 108–112.
34. Rodman, "Springdale Up in Arms over Aliens."
35. James Rojas argues that Latinas/os, particularly immigrants, interact with space differently than white people because the former come from places with social structures that serve different purposes. He posits that Latinas/os use front yards as extensions of the home which are meant to be shared by both those inside the perimeter and those on the sidewalk. Moreover, they use props such as chairs in adapting these spaces to serve multiple needs. See Rojas, "The Enacted Environment: The Creation of 'Place' by Mexicans and Mexican Americans in East Los Angeles" (master's thesis, Massachusetts Institute of Technology, 1991).
36. Michael Leahy, "Northwest Passage: When Cultures Collide," *Arkansas Democrat-Gazette*, March 25, 1997, sec. A.
37. Ibid.
38. Greg Harton, "Springdale Officials Deny Race Played a Role in Order to Close Hispanic Club," *Arkansas Democrat-Gazette*, February 16, 1997, sec. B.
39. Kirstan Conley, "Suit Claims Rogers Police Profile Hispanics," *Arkansas Democrat-Gazette*, March 24, 2001, sec. B. The immigration statuses of the Lopezes are unknown.
40. Ibid.
41. MALDEF (Mexican American Legal Defense Fund), "Latinos to Bring Class Action Lawsuit Alleging Racial Profiling by Police in Rogers, Arkansas," March 23, 2001, http://www.maldef.org/news/press.cfm?ID=48.
42. Ibid.
43. MALDEF, "MALDEF Settles Police Abuse Case in Rogers, Arkansas," November 14, 2003, http://www.maldef.org/news/press.cfm?ID=194.
44. Ibid.
45. US Immigration and Customs Enforcement, "Delegation of Immigration Authority Section 287(g) Immigration and Nationality Act," October 28, 2009, http://www.ice.gov/pi/news/factsheets/section287_g.htm.
46. Jake Bleed, "Bill Would Let State Police Enforce Immigration," *Arkansas Democrat-Gazette*, February 5, 2005, sec. A.
47. "Delegation of Immigration Authority Section 287(g)." As of late October 2009, Georgia, North Carolina, South Carolina, Tennessee, and Virginia each had from two to nine law enforcement agencies participating in the program.
48. Peter Schrag, *Not Fit for Our Society: Immigration and Nativism in America* (Berkeley: University of California Press, 2010).

49. Noel Ignatiev, *How the Irish Became White* (New York: Routledge, 1995); Thomas A. Guglielmo, *White on Arrival: Italians, Race, Color, and Power in Chicago, 1890–1945* (New York: Oxford University Press, 2004); Matthew Frye Jacobson, *Whiteness of a Different Color: European Immigrants and the Alchemy of Race* (Cambridge, MA: Harvard University Press, 1998).

50. Greg Harton, "Shut Door to Aliens, Rogers Group Says," *Arkansas Democrat-Gazette*, June 8, 1997, sec. B.

51. "Immigration, Crime Not Tied, Police Say," *Arkansas Democrat-Gazette*, June 16, 1997, sec. B.

52. Harton, "Shut Door to Aliens"; Leahy, "Northwest Passage: When Cultures Collide."

53. A. Lee Smith, "Stop All U.S. Immigration," *Arkansas Democrat-Gazette*, February 2, 1998, sec. B.

54. Carroll L. Gates to Clinton, May 11, 1980, box 2, folder 18 ("Cuban Refugees/Fort Chaffee—File 9"), BCSGP.

55. The organizations were the Federation for American Immigration Reform, American Immigration Control Foundation, Negative Population Growth's Immigration Reform Project, Population-Environment Balance, and Americans for Better Immigration; Rachel O'Neal, "6 Groups Fighting Influx of Aliens," *Arkansas Democrat-Gazette*, July 29, 1998, sec. B.

56. Ibid.; Laura Kellams, "Immigration Heats Debate at Assembly at Bentonville," *Arkansas Democrat-Gazette*, October 31, 1997.

57. O'Neal, "6 Groups Fighting Influx of Aliens."

58. Jonathan Xavier Inda, "The Value of Immigrant Life," in *Women and Migration: In the U.S.-Mexico Borderlands*, ed. Denise A. Segura and Patricia Zavella (Durham, NC: Duke University Press, 2007), 142–143.

59. Editorial, "Immigration: Should Numbers Be Cut?" *Arkansas Democrat-Gazette*, January 18, 1998, sec. B.

60. A. Lee Smith, "Stop All U.S. Immigration," *Arkansas Democrat-Gazette*, February 2, 1998, sec. B.

61. Editorial, "Immigration Wars: The Latest from the Front," *Arkansas Democrat-Gazette*, August 22, 1999, sec. J.

62. Inda, "The Value of Immigrant Life," 140.

63. Patrick J. Buchanan, *The Death of the West: How Dying Populations and Immigrant Invasions Imperil Our Country and Civilization* (New York: Thomas Dunne, 2002), 2.

64. Samuel P. Huntington, "The Hispanic Challenge," *Foreign Policy* (March–April 2004), accessed June 5, 2009, www.foreignpolicy.com.

65. Ibid.

66. Brooks Blevins, *Hill Folks: A History of Arkansas Ozarkers and Their Image* (Chapel Hill: University of North Carolina Press, 2002), 204–206.

67. Joel Kirkland, "Hispanics Were Issue in Rogers," *Arkansas Democrat-Gazette*, November 6, 1998, sec. B.; Dick Kirschten, "A Melting Pot Chills in Arkansas," *National Journal* 30, no. 46 (1998): 2728.

68. Mike Rodman, "Northwest Wants Language Barrier to Add Up in School Formula," *Arkansas Democrat-Gazette*, December 24, 1994, sec. B.

69. Harton, "Shut Door to Aliens."

70. Doug Thompson, "Illegal Immigration a Priority in 3rd District, Hopefuls Say," *Arkansas Democrat-Gazette*, July 27, 2001, sec. B.

71. Doug Thompson, "Immigration Pushed to Forefront," *Arkansas Democrat-Gazette*, August 5, 2001, sec. B.

72. Laura Kellams, "Boozman Joins Caucus to Reform Immigration," *Arkansas Democrat-Gazette*, February 11, 2002, sec. B.

73. Proposition 200 required people to produce citizenship documents when voting or receiving government and social services, and threatened government employees with misdemeanor charges if they provided services to undocumented people.

74. Laura Kellams, "Arizona Alien Law Fuels State Lobbyists," *Arkansas Democrat-Gazette*, January 22, 2005, sec. B.

75. Laura Kellams, "Senators Research U.S. Law on Aliens," *Arkansas Democrat-Gazette*, January 27, 2005, sec. A.

76. Jake Bleed and Michael R. Wickline, "House Clears Illegal Aliens for College Aid," *Arkansas Democrat-Gazette*, February 24, 2005, sec. A.

77. Laura Kellams, "Holt Yanks His Bill on Illegal Aliens," *Arkansas Democrat-Gazette*, April 8, 2005, sec. B.

78. Bleed and Wickline, "House Clears Illegal Aliens for College Aid."

Conclusion

1. Jennifer Stump, "Huckabee Announces Hispanic Program at LR Festival," *Arkansas Democrat-Gazette* (Little Rock), May 8, 2000, sec. B.

2. Mike Rodman, "Springdale Up in Arms over Aliens," *Arkansas Democrat-Gazette*, July 24, 1994.

3. Bill Reiter, "Baptist Convention; Welcome Urged for State's Hispanic Influx," *Arkansas Democrat-Gazette*, November 6, 2001, sec. B.

4. Personal interview, summer 2012.

5. Michael McNutt, "Oklahoma's High Court Upholds State's Anti-Illegal Immigration Bill," *Daily Oklahoman* (Oklahoma City), June 15, 2011, http://newsok.com/article/3577093.

6. John Lyon, "Hispanics Have Yet to Make Inroads in Arkansas Politics," *Arkansas News*, January 22, 2012, http://www.nwaonline.com/news/2012/jan/22/hispanics-have-yet-make-inroads-arkansas-politics/.

7. "Youths" were defined as those under the age of eighteen. "Univision Insights: Hispanics Show Double Digit Growth in Maryland, Arkansas, Iowa, Indiana and Vermont According to 2010 Census Data," press release, Univision Communications, Inc., February 11, 2011, http://www.businesswire.com/news/home/20110211006290/en/Univision-Insights-Hispanics-Show-Double-Digit-Growth.

8. Lyon, "Hispanics Have Yet to Make Inroads."

Bibliography

Primary Sources

Arkansas Democrat-Gazette (Little Rock), October 1991–April 2005.
Arkansas Gazette (Little Rock), April 1975–August 1975, May 1980, March 1990–October 1991.
Arkansas Times (Little Rock), September 1980.
Bennett, W. J., Jr., et al. *Center Valley*. Archeological Assessment Report No. 217 / Fort Chaffee Cultural Resource Report No. 17. US Army Corps of Engineers, Little Rock District, July 24, 1995.
Clinton, William. Bill Clinton State Government Project. Unprocessed Papers. William J. Clinton Presidential Library and Museum, Little Rock, Arkansas.
Fernandez, Alina. Papers. Special Collections Department, University of Arkansas Libraries, Fayetteville, Arkansas.
La Vida Nueva (Fort Chaffee, AR), May–June 1980.
Pryor, David Hampton. Papers. Special Collections Department, University of Arkansas Libraries, Fayetteville, Arkansas.
SE Asia Relocation Collection, Artwork/Photographs. Pebley Center, Boreham Library, University of Arkansas–Fort Smith.
Southwest Times Record (Fort Smith, AR), June 1980.
US Bureau of the Census. *Number of Inhabitants, Arkansas*. Washington, DC: US Department of Commerce, 1981.
———. *Detailed Characteristics of the Population, Arkansas*. Washington, DC: US Department of Commerce, 1981.
———. *General Population Characteristics, Arkansas*. Washington, DC: US Department of Commerce, 1990.
———. *General Population Characteristics, California*. Washington, DC: US Department of Commerce, 1990.
———. *Profiles of General Demographic Characteristics, Arkansas*. Washington, DC: US Department of Commerce, 2000.
———. *Profiles of General Demographic Characteristics, California*. Washington, DC: US Department of Commerce, 2000.

———. *American Community Survey, Arkansas.* Washington, DC: US Department of Commerce, 2006.

———. *General Population Characteristics, Arkansas.* Washington, DC: US Department of Commerce, 2010.

US Congress. Eleventh Report of the Preparedness Subcommittee of the Committee on Armed Services. *Investigation of the Preparedness Program.* 82nd Cong., 1st sess., 1951.

Secondary Sources

"Active KKK Groups." *Southern Poverty Law Center.* 2010. http://www.splcenter.org/get-informed/intelligence-files/ideology/ku-klux-klan/active_hate_groups.

Aguirre, B. E. "Cuban Mass Migration and the Social Construction of Deviance." *Bulletin of Latin American Research* 13 (1994): 155–183.

Anderson, William C. "Early Reaction in Arkansas to the Relocation of Japanese in the State." *Arkansas Historical Quarterly* 23 (Autumn 1964): 195–211.

Ansley, Fran, and Jon Shefner, eds. *Global Connections and Local Receptions: New Latino Immigration to the Southeastern United States.* Knoxville: University of Tennessee Press, 2009.

Balogh, Brian. "From Metaphor to Quagmire: The Domestic Legacy of the Vietnam War." In *After Vietnam: Legacies of a Lost War,* edited by Charles E. Neu, 24–55. Baltimore, MD: Johns Hopkins University Press, 2000.

Bartley, Numan V. "Looking Back at Little Rock." *Arkansas Historical Quarterly* 66, no. 2 (2007): 112–124. Originally published in 1966.

———. *The New South, 1945–1980.* Baton Rouge: Louisiana State University Press, 1995.

———. *The Rise of Massive Resistance: Race and Politics in the South during the 1950s.* Baton Rouge: Louisiana State University Press, 1999.

Bass, Jack, and Walter De Vries. *The Transformation of Southern Politics: Social Change and Political Consequence since 1945.* New York: Basic Books, 1976.

Bean, Frank D., Gillian Stevens, and Jennifer Van Hook. "Immigration Welfare Receipt: Implication for Policy." In *America's Newcomers and the Dynamics of Diversity,* edited by Frank D. Bean and Gillian Stevens, 66–93. New York: Russell Sage Foundation, 2003.

Bearden, Russell. "Life inside Arkansas's Japanese-American Relocation Centers." *Arkansas Historical Quarterly* 48 (Summer 1989): 169–196.

"Better Security for Camp Asked as Refugees Flee." *New York Times,* May 28, 1980, 14.

Biven, W. Carl. *Jimmy Carter's Economy: Policy in an Age of Limits.* Chapel Hill: University of North Carolina Press, 2002.

Blair, Diane D. "The Big Three of Late Twentieth-Century Arkansas Politics: Dale Bumpers, Bill Clinton, and David Pryor." *Arkansas Historical Quarterly* 54, no. 1 (Spring 1995): 53–79.

Blair, Diane K., and Joan Roberts. "Acquiescent Arkansas: The 1981 Response to Reaganomics and the New Federalism." *Publius* 12 (1983): 163–174.

Blevins, Brooks. *Hill Folks: A History of Arkansas Ozarkers and Their Image*. Chapel Hill: University of North Carolina Press, 2002.
Boles, John B. *The Great Revival: Beginnings of the Bible Belt*. Lexington: University Press of Kentucky, 1996.
Bolton, S. Charles. "Jeffersonian Indian Removal and the Emergence of Arkansas Territory." *Arkansas Historical Quarterly* 62, no. 3 (2003): 253-271.
Borjas, George J. "Immigration and Welfare: A Review of the Evidence." In *The Debate in the United States over Immigration*, edited by Peter Duignan and L. H. Gann, 121-144. Palo Alto, CA: Hoover Institution Press, 1998.
Borjas, George J., and Lynette Hilton. "Immigration and the Welfare State: Immigrant Participation in Means-Tested Entitlement Programs." *Quarterly Journal of Economics* 111, no. 2 (1996): 575-604.
Borneman, John. "Emigres as Bullets/Immigration as Penetration Perceptions of the Marielitos." *Journal of Popular Culture* 20, no. 3 (1986): 73-92.
Brill, Andrew. "*Brown* in Fayetteville: Peaceful Southern School Desegregation in 1954." *Arkansas Historical Quarterly* 65, no. 4 (2006): 337-359.
Broadway, Michael J. "From City to Countryside: Recent Changes in the Structure and Location of the Meat- and Fish-Processing Industries." In *Any Way You Cut It: Meat Processing and Small Town America*, edited by Donald D. Stull, Michael J. Broadway, and David Griffith, 17-40. Lawrence: University Press of Kansas, 1995.
Brundage, W. Fitzhugh. *The Southern Past: A Clash of Race and Memory*. Cambridge, MA: Belknap Press of Harvard University Press, 2005.
Cacho, Lisa Marie. "'The People of California Are Suffering': The Ideology of White Injury in Discourses of Immigration." *Cultural Values* 4 (2000): 389-418.
Campagna, Anthony. *Economic Policy in the Carter Administration*. Westport, CT: Greenwood, 1995.
Capó, Julio, Jr. "Queering Mariel: Mediating Cold War Foreign Policy and U.S. Citizenship among Cuba's Homosexual Exile Community, 1978-1994." *Journal of American Ethnic History* 29, no. 4 (2010): 78-106.
Carter, Dan T. "Legacy of Rage: George Wallace and the Transformation of American Politics." *Journal of Southern History* 62, no. 1 (February 1996): 3-26.
———. *The Politics of Rage: George Wallace, the Origins of the New Conservatism, and the Transformation of American Politics*. New York: Simon and Schuster, 1995.
Cheng, Wendy. *The Changs Next Door to the Díazes: Remapping Race in Suburban California*. Minneapolis: University of Minnesota Press, 2013.
Cobb, James C. *The Selling of the South: The Southern Crusade for Industrial Development, 1936-1990*. 2nd ed. Urbana: University of Illinois Press, 1993.
Cobb, James C., and William Stueck. "Introduction." In *Globalization and the American South*, edited by James C. Cobb and William Stueck, xi-xvi. Athens: University of Georgia Press, 2005.
Cope, Graeme. "'Honest White People of the Middle and Lower Classes'? A Profile of the Capital Citizens' Council during the Little Rock Crisis of 1957." *Arkansas Historical Quarterly* 61, no. 1 (2002): 37-58.
Cortina, Regina. "MexAmerica and the Global American South." Paper presented at the Navigating the Globalization of the American South conference, University of North Carolina-Chapel Hill, 2005.

Cosgrove, Denis. *Social Formation and Symbolic Landscape*. Madison: University of Wisconsin Press, 1984.
Cossman, Jeralynn S., and Edward L. Powers. "Dynamics of Hispanic Population Growth in Arkansas." *Arkansas Business and Economic Review* 33, no. 4 (2000): 2-8.
Crespino, Joseph. *In Search of Another Country: Mississippi and the Conservative Counterrevolution*. Princeton, NJ: Princeton University Press, 2007.
Critchlow, Donald T. *The Conservative Ascendancy: How the GOP Right Made Political History*. Cambridge, MA: Harvard University Press, 2007.
De Genova, Nicholas. "Migrant 'Illegality' and Deportability in Everyday Life." *Annual Review of Anthropology* 31 (2002): 419-447.
Dillard, Tom W. Book review of *Arkansas and the New South, 1874-1929*, by Carl H. Moneyhon. *Journal of American History* 85, no. 4 (1999): 1601-1602.
Donato, Katharine M., Charles Tolbert, Alfred Nucci, and Yukio Kawano. "Changing Faces, Changing Places: The Emergence of New Nonmetropolitan Immigrant Gateways." In *New Faces in New Places: The Changing Geography of American Immigration*, edited by Douglas S. Massey, 75-98. New York: Russell Sage Foundation, 2008.
Dudas, Jeffrey R. "In the Name of Equal Rights: 'Special' Rights and the Politics of Resentment in Post-Civil Rights America." *Law and Society Review* 39, no. 4 (2005): 723-757.
Egerton, John. *Speak Now against the Day: The Generation before the Civil Rights Movement in the South*. New York: Knopf, 1994.
Engstrom, David. *Presidential Decision Making Adrift: The Carter Administration and the Mariel Boatlift*. New York: Rowman and Littlefield, 1997.
Engstrom, James D. "Industry and Immigration in Dalton, Georgia." In *Latino Workers in the Contemporary South*, edited by Arthur D. Murphy, Colleen Blanchard, and Jennifer A. Hill, 44-56. Athens: University of Georgia Press, 1999.
Erwin, Debora O. "An Ethnographic Description of Latino Immigration in Rural Arkansas: Intergroup Relations and Utilization of Healthcare Services." *Southern Rural Sociology* 19, no. 1 (2003): 46-72.
Fernández, Gastón A. "The Freedom Flotilla: A Legitimacy Crisis of Cuban Socialism?" *Journal of Interamerican Studies and World Affairs* 24, no. 2 (1982): 183-209.
———. "Race, Gender, and Class in the Persistence of the Mariel Stigma Twenty Years after the Exodus from Cuba." *International Migration Review* 41, no. 3 (2007): 602-622.
Fink, Leon. *The Maya of Morganton: Work and Community in the Nuevo New South*. Chapel Hill: University of North Carolina Press, 2003.
Fort Smith Chamber of Commerce. "Frequently Asked Questions." November 8, 2004. http://www.fschamber.com/ goodquestions.asp.
———. "Perfect Homes." November 8, 2004. http://www.fschamber.com/perfect homes.asp.
———. "Top Employers, Fort Smith, Arkansas." October 5, 2008. http://www.fortsmithchamber.org/WhitePapers/WhitePapersDisplay.asp?p1=2043&p2=Y&p9=&Sort.
Foster, Carly Hayden. "The Welfare Queen: Race, Gender, Class, and Public Opinion." *Race, Gender, & Class* 15, no. 3-4 (2008): 162-180.

Franklin, H. Bruce. *Vietnam and Other American Fantasies.* Amherst: University of Massachusetts Press, 2000.
Freyer, Tony A. "Politics and Law in the Little Rock Crisis, 1954-1957." *Arkansas Historical Quarterly* 66, no. 2 (2007): 145-166.
Froelich, Jacqueline, and David Zimmermann. "Total Eclipse: The Destruction of the African American Community of Harrison, Arkansas in 1905 and 1909." *Arkansas Historical Quarterly* 58, no. 2 (1999): 131-159.
Gee, James Paul. *An Introduction to Discourse Analysis: Theory and Method.* New York: Routledge, 1999.
Gilmore, Ruth Wilson. "Fatal Couplings of Power and Difference: Notes on Racism and Geography." *Professional Geographer* 54, no. 1 (2002): 15-24.
Glenn, Evelyn Nakano. *Unequal Freedom: How Race and Gender Shaped American Citizenship and Labor.* Cambridge, MA: Harvard University Press, 2002.
Gobierno del Estado—Zacatecas. "Gral. Pánfilo Natera." September 9, 2008. http://www.zacatecas.gob.mx/Municipios/GpanfilonateraHist.htm.
———. "Gral. Pánfilo Natera—Infraestructura Social Y De Comunicaciones." September 9, 2008. http://www.zacatecas.gob.mx/Municipios/Gpanfilonatera Infra.htm.
———. "Perfil Sociodemográfico." September 9, 2008. http://www.zacatecas.gob.mx/Municipios/GpanfilonateraSoc.htm.
Godfrey, Phoebe. "Bayonets, Brainwashing, and Bathrooms: The Discourse of Race, Gender, and Sexuality in the Desegregation of Little Rock's Central High." *Arkansas Historical Quarterly* 62, no. 1 (2003): 42-67.
Goldberg, David Theo. *The Racial State.* Malden, MA: Blackwell, 2002.
Goldfield, David. "The Changing Continuity of the South." *Reviews in American History* 20, no. 2 (1992): 229-234.
Griffin, Larry J., and Katherine McFarland. "'In My Heart, I'm an American': Regional Attitudes and American Identity." *Southern Cultures* 13, no. 4 (2007): 119-137.
Griffith, David. "*Hay Trabajo*: Poultry Processing, Rural Industrialization, and the Latinization of Low-Wage Labor." In *Any Way You Cut It: Meat Processing and Small Town America,* edited by Donald D. Stull, Michael J. Broadway, and David Griffith, 129-151. Lawrence: University Press of Kansas, 1995.
———. "New Midwesterners, New Southerners: Immigration Experiences in Four Rural American Settings." In *New Faces in New Places: The Changing Geography of American Immigration,* edited by Douglas S. Massey, 179-210. New York: Russell Sage Foundation, 2008.
Guerrero, Perla M. "Chicana/o History as Southern History: Race, Place, and the U.S. South." In *A Promising Problem: The New Chicana/o History,* edited by Carlos Kevin Blanton, 83-110. Austin: University of Texas Press, 2016.
———. "A Tenuous Welcome for Latinas/os and Asians: States' Rights Discourse in Late 20th Century Arkansas." In *Race and Ethnicity in Arkansas: New Perspectives,* edited by John Kirk, 141-151. Little Rock: University of Arkansas Press, 2014.
Guglielmo, Thomas A. *White on Arrival: Italians, Race, Color, and Power in Chicago, 1890-1945.* New York: Oxford University Press, 2004.
Guthey, Greig. "Mexican Places in Southern Spaces: Globalization, Work, and Daily Life in and around the North Georgia Poultry Industry." In *Latino*

Workers in the Contemporary South, edited by Arthur D. Murphy, Colleen Blanchard, and Jennifer A. Hill, 57–67. Athens: University of Georgia Press, 1999.

Gutiérrez, David G. "Sin Fronteras? Chicanos, Mexican Americans, and the Emergence of the Contemporary Mexican Immigration Debate, 1968-1978." In Between Two Worlds: Mexican Immigrants in the United States, edited by David G. Gutiérrez, 175–212. Wilmington, DE: Scholarly Resources, 1996.

———. Walls and Mirrors: Mexican Americans, Mexican Immigrants, and the Politics of Ethnicity. Berkeley: University of California Press, 1995.

Hall, Stuart. "Race, Articulation, and Societies Structured in Dominance." In Sociological Theories: Race and Colonialism, 305–345. UNESCO, 1980.

———. "Re-Thinking the 'Base-and-Superstructure' Metaphor." In Papers on Class, Hegemony, and Party: The Communist University of London, edited by Jon Bloomfield, 44–48. London: Lawrence and Wishart, 1977.

Hallet, Miranda Cady. "'Better Than White Trash': Work Ethic, Latinidad and Whiteness in Rural Arkansas." Latino Studies 10, no. 1–2 (2012): 81–106.

Hancock, Ange-Marie. The Politics of Disgust: The Public Identity of the Welfare Queen. New York: New York University Press, 2004.

Hennessy-Fiske, Molly. "The Town That Didn't Look Away." Los Angeles Times, July 23, 2006, sec. A.

Hernández, Kelly Lytle. Migra! A History of the U.S. Border Patrol. Berkeley: University of California Press, 2010.

Hernández-León, Rubén, and Víctor Zúñiga. "'Making Carpet by the Mile': The Emergence of a Mexican Immigrant Community in an Industrial Region of the U.S. Historic South." Social Science Quarterly 81, no. 1 (2000): 49–66.

Hirschman, Charles, and Douglass S. Massey. "Places and Peoples: The New American Mosaic." In New Faces in New Places: The Changing Geography of American Immigration, edited by Douglas S. Massey, 4–10. New York: Russell Sage Foundation, 2008.

Hufker, Brian, and Gray Cavender. "From Freedom Flotilla to America's Burden: The Social Construction of the Mariel Immigrants." Sociological Quarterly 31, no. 2 (1990): 321–335.

Ignatiev, Noel. How the Irish Became White. New York: Routledge, 1995.

"Immigrants in Arkansas." The Economist, November 3–9, 2007. Podcast, MPEG file (3:04 min).

Inda, Jonathan Xavier. Targeting Immigrants: Government, Technology, and Ethics. Malden, MA: Blackwell, 2006.

———. "The Value of Immigrant Life." In Women and Migration: In the U.S.-Mexico Borderlands, edited by Denise A. Segura and Patricia Zavella, 134–159. Durham, NC: Duke University Press, 2007.

Instituto Nacional de Estadística y Geografia. "Información estadística disponible." September 28, 2008. http://galileo.inegi.gob.mx/CubexConnector/validaDatos.do?geograficaE=32016.

———. "Marco geoestadisco municipal." February 28, 2008. http://galileo.inegi.org.mx/website/mexico/viewer.htm?bsqTable=77&bsqField=CVEMUN&bsqStr=32016&TName=MGM&seccionB=mdm.

Jackson, Peter. "Geography, Race, and Racism." In New Models in Geography, Volume 2: The Political-Economy Perspective, edited by Richard Peet and Nigel Thrift, 176–195. New York: Routledge, 1989.

———. *Maps of Meaning: An Introduction to Cultural Geography*. London: Unwin Hyman, 1989.
Jacobson, Matthew Frye. *Whiteness of a Different Color: European Immigrants and the Alchemy of Race*. Cambridge, MA: Harvard University Press, 1998.
Jacobson, Robin Dale. *The New Nativism: Proposition 187 and the Debate over Immigration*. Minneapolis: University of Minnesota Press, 2008.
Jeffords, Susan. *The Remasculinization of America: Gender and the Vietnam War*. Bloomington: Indiana University Press, 1989.
Johnson, Ben F., III. "After 1957: Resisting Integration in Little Rock." *Arkansas Historical Quarterly* 66, no. 2 (2007): 258-283.
———. *Arkansas in Modern America, 1930-1999*. Fayetteville: University of Arkansas Press, 2000.
Kandel, William A., and Emilio A. Parrado. "Hispanic Population Growth and Public School Responses in Two New South Immigrant Destinations." In *Latinos in the New South: Transformations of Place*, edited by Heather A. Smith and Owen J. Furuseth, 111-134. Burlington, VT: Ashgate, 2006.
———. "Industrial Transformation and Hispanic Migration to the American South: The Case of the Poultry Industry." In *Hispanic Spaces, Latino Places: Community and Cultural Diversity in Contemporary America*, edited by Daniel D. Arreola, 255-276. Austin: University of Texas Press, 2004.
Katznelson, Ira. *When Affirmative Action Was White: An Untold History of Racial Inequality in Twentieth-Century America*. New York: Norton, 2005.
Kelley, Robin D. G. "Foreword." In *Remembering Slavery: African Americans Talk about Their Personal Experiences of Slavery and Emancipation*, edited by Ira Berlin, Marc Favreau, and Steven F. Miller, vii-x. New York: New Press, 2007.
Key, V. O. *Southern Politics in State and Nation*. New York: Knopf, 1949.
Kilpatrick, Judith. "Desegregating the University of Arkansas School of Law: L. Clifford Davis and the Six Pioneers." *Arkansas Historical Quarterly* 68, no. 2 (2009): 123-156.
Kim, Claire Jean. "The Racial Triangulation of Asian Americans." *Politics and Society* 27, no. 1 (1999): 105-138.
Kirk, John A. "The 1957 Little Rock Crisis: A Fiftieth Anniversary Retrospective." *Arkansas Historical Quarterly* 66, no. 2 (2007): 91-111.
Kruse, Kevin M. *White Flight: Atlanta and the Making of Modern Conservatism*. Princeton, NJ: Princeton University Press, 2005.
Lamis, Alexander P. *The Two Party South*. Expanded ed. New York: Oxford University Press, 1990.
Lancaster, Guy. *Racial Cleansing in Arkansas, 1883-1924: Politics, Land, Labor, and Criminality*. Lanham, MD: Lexington Books, 2014.
Lassiter, Matthew D. *The Silent Majority: Suburban Politics in the Sunbelt South*. Princeton, NJ: Princeton University Press, 2006.
Leach, Mark A., and Frank D. Bean. "The Structure and Dynamics of Mexican Migration to New Destinations in the United States." In *New Faces in New Places: The Changing Geography of American Immigration*, edited by Douglas S. Massey, 51-74. New York: Russell Sage Foundation, 2008.
Lewis, George. *Massive Resistance: The White Response to the Civil Rights Movement*. London: Hodder Arnold, 2006.
Lipman, Jana. "A Refugee Camp in America: Fort Chaffee and Vietnamese and

Cuban Refugees, 1975-1982." *Journal of American Ethnic History* 33, no. 2 (2014): 57-87.

Loescher, Gil, and John A. Scanlan. *Calculated Kindness: Refugees and America's Half-Open Door, 1945 to the Present.* New York: Free Press, 1986.

Loewen, James W. *The Mississippi Chinese: Between Black and White.* Long Grove, IL: Waveland, 1971.

———. *Sundown Towns: A Hidden Dimension of American Racism.* New York: Touchstone, 2005.

———. "Sundown Towns and Counties: Racial Exclusion in the South." *Southern Cultures* 15, no. 1 (2009): 22-47.

Lowe, Lisa. *Immigrant Acts: On Asian American Cultural Politics.* Durham, NC: Duke University Press, 1996.

Luibhéid, Eithne. *Entry Denied: Controlling Sexuality at the Border.* Minneapolis: University of Minnesota Press, 2002.

———. "Queer/Migration: An Unruly Body of Scholarship." *GLQ: A Journal of Lesbian and Gay Studies* 14, no. 2-3 (2008): 169-190.

Lutz, Catherine A. *Homefront: A Military City and the American Twentieth Century.* Boston: Beacon, 2001.

Lye, Colleen. *America's Asia: Racial Form and American Literature, 1893-1945.* Princeton, NJ: Princeton University Press, 2005.

MALDEF (Mexican American Legal Defense Fund). "Latinos to Bring Class Action Lawsuit Alleging Racial Profiling by Police in Rogers, Arkansas." March 23, 2001. http://www.maldef.org/news/press.cfm?ID=48.

———. "MALDEF Settles Police Abuse Case in Rogers, Arkansas." November 14, 2003. http://www.maldef.org/news/press.cfm?ID=194.

Markusen, Ann. *Regions: The Economics and Politics of Territory.* Totowa, NJ: Rowman and Littlefield, 1987.

Marrow, Helen B. "Hispanic Immigration, Black Population Size, and Intergroup Relations in the Rural and Small-Town South." In *New Faces in New Places: The Changing Geography of American Immigration,* edited by Douglas S. Massey, 211-248. New York: Russell Sage Foundation, 2008.

Marsden, George M. *Fundamentalism and American Culture.* 2nd ed. New York: Oxford University Press, 2006.

Martini, Edwin. *Invisible Enemies: The American War on Vietnam, 1975-2000.* Amherst: University of Massachusetts Press, 2007.

Massey, Douglas S., Joaquín Arango, Graeme Hugo, Ali Kouaouci, Adela Pellegrino, and J. Edward Taylor. *Worlds in Motion: Understanding International Migration at the End of the Millennium.* Oxford, UK: Clarendon, 1998.

Massey, Douglas S., and Chiara Capoferro. "The Geographic Diversification of American Immigration." In *New Faces in New Places: The Changing Geography of American Immigration,* edited by Douglas S. Massey, 25-50. New York: Russell Sage Foundation, 2008.

Massey, Douglas S., Jorge Durand, and Nolan J. Malone. *Beyond Smoke and Mirrors: Mexican Immigration in an Era of Economic Integration.* New York: Russell Sage Foundation, 2002.

Masud-Piloto, Felix Roberto. *From Welcomed Exiles to Illegal Immigrants: Cuban Migration to the U.S., 1959-1995.* Lanham, MD: Rowman and Littlefield, 1996.

McClain, Paula D., et al. "Racial Distancing in a Southern City: Latino Immigrants' Views of Black Americans." *Journal of Politics* 68, no. 3 (2006): 571–584.
McGirr, Lisa. *Suburban Warriors: The Origins of the New American Right*. Princeton, NJ: Princeton University Press, 2001.
Miller, Brian Stanford. "Car Tags and Cubans: Bill Clinton, Frank White and Arkansas' Return to Conservatism." PhD diss., University of Mississippi, 2006.
Mitchell, Don. *The Lie of the Land: Migrant Workers and the California Landscape*. Minneapolis: University of Minnesota Press, 1996.
Moctezuma Longoria, Miguel. "La experiencia de las remesas comunitarias del club de migrantes El Remolino, Zacatecas. Una experiencia comunitaria binacional." In *Integración Económica y Resistencia Popular en México*, edited by Laura Carlsen, Hilda Salazar, and Timothy A. Wise, 225–245. Mexico City: Miguel Ángel Porrua, 2003.
Molina, Natalia. *How Race Is Made in America: Immigration, Citizenship, and the Historical Power of Racial Scripts*. Berkeley: University of California Press, 2014.
———. "The Power of Racial Scripts: What the History of Mexican Immigration to the United States Teaches Us about Relational Notions of Race." *Latino Studies*, suppl. Race and Blackness in the Latino/a Community 8, no. 2 (2010): 156–175.
Montejano, David. *Anglos and Mexicans in the Making of Texas, 1836–1986*. Austin: University of Texas Press, 1987.
Morales, Rebecca. "Dependence or Interdependence: Issues and Policy Choices Facing Latin Americans and Latinos." In *Borderless Borders: US Latinos, Latin Americans, and the Paradox of Interdependence*, edited by Frank Bonilla, Edwin Meléndez, Rebecca Morales, and María de los Angeles Torres, 1–14. Philadelphia: Temple University Press, 1998.
Moreton, Bethany. *To Serve God and Wal-Mart: The Making of Christian Free Enterprise*. Cambridge, MA: Harvard University Press, 2009.
Morgan, Gordon. *Black Hillbillies of the Arkansas Ozarks*. Fayetteville: Department of Sociology, University of Arkansas, 1973.
"Native American Tribes of Arkansas." *Native Languages of the Americas*. http://www.native-languages.org/arkansas.htm.
Ngai, Mae. *Impossible Subjects: Illegal Aliens and the Making of Modern America*. Princeton, NJ: Princeton University Press, 2004.
Omi, Michael, and Howard Winant. *Racial Formation in the United States: From the 1960s to the 1990s*. 2nd ed. New York: Routledge, 1994.
Parrado, Emilio A., and William Kandel. "New Hispanic Migrant Destinations: A Tale of Two Industries." In *New Faces in New Places: The Changing Geography of American Immigration*, edited by Douglas S. Massey, 99–123. New York: Russell Sage Foundation, 2008.
Passel, Jeffrey S., and Wendy Zimmerman. "Are Immigrants Leaving California? Settlement Patterns of Immigrants in the Late 1990s." Washington, DC: Urban Institute, 2001.
Pastor, Manuel, Jr. "Interdependence, Inequality, and Identity: Linking Latinos and Latin Americans." In *Borderless Borders: US Latinos, Latin Americans, and the Paradox of Interdependence*, edited by Frank Bonilla, Edwin Melén-

dez, Rebecca Morales, and María de los Angeles Torres, 17–34. Philadelphia: Temple University Press, 1998.
Patterson, James T. *Restless Giant: The United States from Watergate to Bush v. Gore.* New York: Oxford University Press, 2005.
Pedraza, Silvia. "Cuba's Refugees: Manifold Migrations." *Cuba in Transition* 5 (1995): 311–329.
———. "Los Marielitos of 1980: Race, Class, Gender, and Sexuality." *Cuba in Transition* 14 (2004): 89–102.
Peña, Susana. "'Obvious Gays' and the State Gaze: Cuban Gay Visibility and U.S. Immigration Policy during the 1980 Mariel Boatlift." *Journal of the History of Sexuality* 16, no. 3 (2007): 482–514.
———. *Oye Loca: From the Mariel Boatlift to Gay Cuban Miami.* Minneapolis: University of Minnesota Press, 2013.
"Politics Key to the Fate of Camp's Last Cubans." *New York Times*, January 4, 1982, sec. A.
Pritchett, Merrill R., and William L. Shea. "The Afrika Korps in Arkansas, 1943–1946." *Arkansas Historical Quarterly* 37, no. 1 (Spring 1978): 3–22.
Radcliff, Maranda. "Fort Chaffee." *Encyclopedia of Arkansas History and Culture.* July 2008. http://www.encyclopediaofarkansas.net/encyclopedia/entry-detail.aspx?entryID=2263.
Ribas, Vanesa. *On the Line: Slaughterhouse Lives and the Making of the New South.* Berkeley: University of California Press, 2016.
Riffel, Brent E. "The Feathered Kingdom: Tyson Foods and the Transformation of American Land, Labor, and Law, 1930–2005." PhD diss., University of Arkansas, 2008.
Rivera Brooks, Nancy. "Area's Rebound Expected to Continue." *Los Angeles Times*, November 26, 1996, pt. D.
Roberts, Alden E. "Racism Sent and Received: Americans and Vietnamese View One Another." *Research in Race and Ethnic Relations* 5 (1988): 75–97.
Roediger, David. *The Wages of Whiteness: Race and the Making of the American Working Class.* Rev. ed. New York: Verso, 1999.
Rojas, James. "The Enacted Environment: The Creation of 'Place' by Mexicans and Mexican Americans in East Los Angeles." Master's thesis, Massachusetts Institute of Technology, 1991.
Rosen, Marjorie. *Boom Town: How Wal-Mart Transformed an All-American Town into an International Community.* Chicago: Chicago Review Press, 2009.
Sánchez, George J. *Becoming Mexican American: Ethnicity, Culture, and Identity in Chicano Los Angeles, 1900–1945.* New York: Oxford University Press, 1993.
Santa Ana, Otto, Juan Morán, and Cynthia Sánchez. "Awash under a Brown Tide: Immigration Metaphors in California Public and Print Media Discourse." *Aztlán* 23 (1998): 137–176.
Schulman, Bruce. *From Cotton Belt to Sunbelt: Federal Policy, Economic Development and the Transformation of the South, 1938–1980.* New York: Oxford University Press, 1991.
Shbikat, Gazi, and Steve Striffler. "Arkansas Migration and Population." *Arkansas Business and Economic Review* 33, no. 3 (2000): 1–5.
Shefner, Jon, and Katie Kirkpatrick. "Introduction: Globalization and the New

Destination Immigrant." In *Global Connections and Local Receptions: New Latino Immigration to the Southeastern United States*, edited by Fran Ansley and Jon Shefner, xv–xl. Knoxville: University of Tennessee Press, 2009.

Smith, Barbara Ellen. "Across Races and Nations: Social Justice Organizing in the Transnational South." In *Latinos in the New South: Transformations of Place*, edited by Heather A. Smith and Owen J. Furuseth, 235–256. Burlington, VT: Ashgate, 2006.

Smith, C. Calvin. "The Response of Arkansans to Prisoners of War and Japanese Americans in Arkansas, 1942–1945." *Arkansas Historical Quarterly* 53 (Autumn 1994): 340–366.

Smith, Doug. "We're Coming Here to Pick the Country Up." *Arkansas Times*, January 24, 2008, 10–11, 17–18.

Smith, Heather A., and Owen J. Furuseth. "Making Real the Mythical Latino Community in Charlotte, North Carolina." In *Latinos in the New South: Transformations of Place*, edited by Heather A. Smith and Owen J. Furuseth, 191–216. Burlington, VT: Ashgate, 2006.

Smith, Neil. "Contours of Spatialized Politics: Homeless Vehicles and the Production of Geographical Scale." *Social Text* 33 (1992): 54–81.

———. *Uneven Development: Nature, Capital, and the Production of Space*. New York: Blackwell, 1984.

Southern Poverty Law Center. "Arkansas Hate Map." 2010. http://www.splcenter.org/get-informed/hate-map#s=AR.

Stepick, Alex. *Pride against Prejudice: Haitians in the United States*. Needham Heights, MA: Allyn and Bacon, 1998.

Stockley, Grif. *Daisy Bates: Civil Rights Crusader from Arkansas*. Jackson: University Press of Mississippi, 2005.

Striffler, Steve. *Chicken: The Dangerous Transformation of America's Favorite Food*. New Haven, CT: Yale University Press, 2005.

———. "Neither Here nor There: Mexican Immigrant Workers and the Search for Home." *American Ethnologist* 34, no. 4 (2007): 674–688.

———. "We're All Mexicans Here: Poultry Processing, Latino Migration, and the Transformation of a Class in the South." In *The American South in a Global World*, edited by James L. Peacock, Harry L. Watson, and Carrie R. Matthews, 152–163. Chapel Hill: University of North Carolina Press, 2005.

Stuesse, Angela. *Scratching Out a Living: Latinos, Race, and Work in the Deep South*. Berkeley: University of California Press, 2016.

Sturken, Marita. *Tangled Memories: The Vietnam War, the AIDS Epidemic, and the Politics of Remembering*. Berkeley: University of California Press, 1997.

Tang, Eric. "A Gulf Unites Us: The Vietnamese Americans of Black New Orleans East." *American Quarterly* 63, no. 1 (2011): 117–149.

Thomas, Jo. "Troops Ordered to Arkansas Camp after Refugee Riot." *New York Times*, June 3, 1980, A1.

Tindall, George B. *The Emergence of the New South, 1913–1945*. Baton Rouge: Louisiana State University Press, 1967.

Torres, Maria de los Angeles. *In the Land of Mirrors: Cuban Exile Politics in the United States*. Ann Arbor: University of Michigan Press, 1999.

Torres, Rebecca M., E. Jeffrey Popke, and Holly M. Hapke. "The South's Silent

Bargain: Rural Restructuring, Latino Labor and the Ambiguities of Migrant Experience." In *Latinos in the New South: Transformations of Place*, edited by Heather A. Smith and Owen J. Furuseth, 37–68. Burlington, VT: Ashgate, 2006.

US Immigration and Customs Enforcement. "Delegation of Immigration Authority Section 287(g) Immigration and Nationality Act." October 28, 2009. http://www.ice.gov/pi/news/factsheets/section287_g.htm.

Wainer, Andrew. "The New Latino South and the Challenge to Public Education: Strategies for Educators and Policymakers in Emerging Immigrant Communities." Los Angeles: Tomás Rivera Policy Institute, University of Southern California, 2004.

Warwick, Sabin. "The White Place: A Good Home and Little Isolation in Northwest Arkansas." *Arkansas Times*, February 3, 2005, sec. A.

Wasem, Ruth Ellen. "U.S. Immigration Policy on Haitian Migrants." *CRS Report for Congress*, January 21, 2005. trac.syr.edu/immigration/library/P960.pdf.

Webb, Clive. "A Continuity of Conservatism: The Limitations of *Brown v. Board of Education*." *Journal of Southern History* 70, no. 2 (2004): 327–336.

———, ed. *Massive Resistance: Southern Opposition to the Second Reconstruction*. New York: Oxford University Press, 2005.

Weise, Julie M. *Corazón de Dixie: Mexicanos in the U.S. South since 1910*. Chapel Hill: University of North Carolina Press, 2015.

———. "Mexican and Mexican-Americans in the Mississippi Delta, 1908–1939." Unpublished paper, 2006.

———. "Mexican Nationalisms, Southern Racisms: Mexicans and Mexican Americans in the U.S. South, 1908–1939." *American Quarterly* 60, no. 3 (2008): 749–778.

Whayne, Jeannie M. "Dramatic Departures: Political, Demographic, and Economic Realignment." In *Arkansas: A Narrative History*, edited by Jeannie M. Whayne, Thomas A. DeBlack, George Sabo, and Morris S. Arnold, 372–400. Fayetteville: University of Arkansas Press, 2002.

Whayne, Jeannie M., Thomas A. DeBlack, George Sabo, and Morris S. Arnold. *Arkansas: A Narrative History*. Fayetteville: University of Arkansas Press, 2002.

Wilhoit, Francis M. *The Politics of Massive Resistance*. New York: George Braziller, 1973.

Wilson, Bobby M. *America's Johannesburg: Industrialization and Racial Transformation in Birmingham*. Lanham, MD: Rowman and Littlefield, 2000.

Winders, Jamie. "Bringing Back the (B)order: Post-9/11 Politics of Immigration, Borders, and Belonging in the Contemporary US South." *Antipode* 39, no. 5 (2007): 920–942.

———. "Changing Politics of Race and Region: Latino Migration to the US South." *Progress in Human Geography* 29, no. 6 (2005): 683–699.

———. "New Directions in the Nuevo South." *Southeastern Geographer* 51, no. 2 (2011): 327–340.

———. "Re-Placing Southern Geographies: The Role of Latino Migration in Transforming the South, Its Identities, and Its Study." *Southeastern Geographer* 51, no. 2 (2011): 342–358.

———. "Representing the Immigrant: Social Movements, Political Discourse,

and Immigration in the US South." *Southeastern Geographer* 51, no. 4 (2011): 596–614.
Woodruff, Nan Elizabeth. *American Congo: The African American Freedom Struggle in the Delta*. Cambridge, MA: Harvard University Press, 2003.
Woods, Clyde. *Development Arrested: The Blues and Plantation Power in the Mississippi Delta*. New York: Verso, 1998.
Woodward, C. Vann. *Origins of the New South, 1877–1913*. 2nd ed. Baton Rouge: Louisiana State University Press, 1971.
———. *The Strange Career of Jim Crow*. 3rd rev. ed. New York: Oxford University Press, 2002.
Wright, Gavin. *Old South, New South: Revolutions in the Southern Economy since the Civil War*. New York: Basic Books, 1986.
Wyatt, Clarence R. "The Media and the Vietnam War." In *The War That Never Ends: New Perspectives on the Vietnam War*, edited by David L. Anderson and John Ernst, 266–269. Lexington: University Press of Kentucky, 2007.
Zellner, Wendy. "Hiring Illegals: The Risks Grow." *Business Week*, May 13, 2002, 94–96.

Index

Page numbers in italics refer to figures. First-name-only entries are pseudonyms.

Adkins, Homer Martin, 53–54, *55–56*
affirmative action, 78
agriculture industry, 10, 28–29, 31–37, 40, 53–54, 56, 112–114, 123, 134–135, 141, 161. *See also* poultry industry
"alien citizens," 15
aliens. *See* "illegal aliens"
Americans for an Immigration Moratorium (AIM), 153, 170–171, 173
Ammons, Shannon, 38–39
Anchondo-Rascon, Amador, 140
Ansley, Fran, 46–47
anti-immigrant legislation, 26, 171, 173, 175, 179–180
Arguelles, Lourdes, 81
Aristide, Jean-Bertrand, 161
Arkansas Agricultural Experiment Station, 35
Arkansas Best, 134
Arkansas Democrat-Gazette, 3, 20, 153, 159, 164, 171
Arkansas Friendship Coalition (AFC), 179–180
Arkansas Gazette, 20, 60, 119, 157
Arkansas Poultry Federation, 119, 120
Arkansas State Police (ASP), 74, 76, 88, 97, 100, 103, 169
Arkansas Taxpayer and Citizen Protection Act, 175

Arvest Bank, 150
assimilation, 8, 14–16, 50, 59, 63, 65, 109, 132, 147, 150, 165, 170, 174, 177
Atkinson, Drexel, 157

Baker, Ray, 129
Baldor Electric, 134
balsero crisis, 161–162
Baran, Melinda, 115–116
Barling, Arkansas, 56, 74, 76, 95, 96, 103, 105
Batchelor, Fines F., Jr., 98
Benham, Paul, Jr., 117–118
Berkshire, F. W., 160
Berlin Crisis, 57
Berra, Joe, 167
Bible Belt, 34, 61, 177
Blevins, Brooks, 3, 38, 174
Blossom, Virgil T., 43
Boozman, John, 175
Border Patrol. *See* US Border Patrol
Borneman, John, 80–81
Brainerd, A. T., 89
Brantley, Max, 43
Bravo, Ruben Tormo, 93
Brown v. Board of Education, 41–42, 44, 59, 77
Buchanan, Patrick, 173
Buddhism, 62

Bumpers, Dale, 96–97, 104
Bush, George H. W., 118, 160, 161, 162
Bush, George W., 36, 168, 175

Cambodian immigrants, 66, 132, 133, 195n62
Campagna, Anthony, 79
Camp Chaffee, Arkansas, 52. *See also* Fort Chaffee, Arkansas
Camp Dermott, Arkansas, 55
Camp Jerome (later Camp Dermott), Arkansas, 53, 55
Camp Monticello, Arkansas, 55
Camp Pendleton, California, 60
Camp Robinson, Arkansas, 55
Camp Rohwer, Arkansas, 53, 54, 55
capitalism, 12, 31
carta de escoria ("dreg" letter), 89
Carter, Billye and Don, 90
Carter, Dan, 77
Carter, Jimmy, 76, 79, 85–86, 91, 96–97, 102, 104–105, 107, 109
Casey, Thomas R., 97
Castro, Fidel, 5, 16, 18, 51, 74, 79–80, 82, 162
"Castro agents," 93–94, 96
Catholic Church, 34, 62, 91
Cauthron, Bill, 88, 90
Central Intelligence Agency (CIA), 92
Chaffee—Resettlement, Consolidation report, 82
Charleston, Arkansas, 43–44
Cheng, Wendy, 13, 50
Chinese Exclusion Act (1882), 13
Chinese immigrants, 11, 14, 132, 172
Christianity, 36–39; Baptist Church, 34, 36, 59, 118, 178; Catholic Church, 34, 62, 91; and charity, 18, 24, 51–52, 59–60; Christian School movement, 58–59, 79; and consumption, 39; Cumberland Presbyterian Church, 34; and Latina/o immigrants, 178; and Mariel Cuban refugees, 17, 74–79, 91, 109; Religious Right, 58–59, 76, 78; and slavery, 17, 51; Southern Baptist Convention, 58, 76, 78, 91; and

Vietnamese refugees, 1, 5, 17–18, 58–63, 84, 109
citizenship, 9, 14–15, 61, 63, 69, 86, 94, 150, 168, 175, 181; alien citizens, 15; naturalized citizens, 15, 139, 152, 154; noncitizens, 14; substantive citizenship, 15
Civiletti, Benjamin R., 107–108
Civil Rights Act (1964), 38, 59, 77
Civil War, 27, 37, 41–42
Clark, Steve, 98, 100–102, 105–107, 116
class, 8, 12, 21–24, 30, 63, 80, 173; managerial class, 133; middle class, 5, 22, 31–32, 38–39, 43, 80, 129, 133; and mobility, 25, 113, 142–143, 146; planter class, 31; upper class, 21, 39, 62, 80, 116, 129; working class, 10, 17, 21–24, 30, 39, 43, 51, 77, 80, 112–116, 125–129, 133, 143, 160–163
Clinton, Bill, 1–2, 25, 30, 76, 84, 87, 88, 90, 96–98, 100–108, 116–118, 157, 161–162
Cobb, James C., 31–33, 46
Cold War, 66, 81, 93
Colombian immigrants: Gretel (Colombian immigrant), 110, 144–145, 147
communism, 1, 5, 8, 17–18, 51, 68, 72, 75–76, 79–81, 83–84, 89, 95, 99, 103–104, 109; anti-communist movement, 65, 75, 78, 89, 104
Comprehensive Employment and Training Act (CETA), 86
Congressional Black Caucus, 85
Congressional Immigration Reform Caucus, 175
construction industry, 10, 36, 39, 40, 45, 114, 134, 143
Cook, Howard, 164
Copley, Steve, 179–180
corridor of prosperity, 3, 33, 36–41
cotton industry, 27, 35, 120
criminals and criminality: and documentation status, 5, 16–18, 110, 153, 154, 160–161; and Latina/o immigrants, 152–155; and Mariel

Cuban refugees, 18, 24, 51, 75–76, 79–83, 89, 93–94; and racialization, 25, 51, 75–76, 79–83, 89, 93, 152–155, 171, 173
Crosland, David, 81
Cuba, 80, 82–83, 89, 93, 161, 194; Back Door Policy, 74. *See also* Castro, Fidel
Cuban Adjustment Act (1966), 104
"Cuban/Haitian entrant (status pending)" designation, 25, 76, 100, 104, 109
Cuban-Haitian Task Force (CHTF), 82, 85, 91, 105
Cuban refugees and exiles: *balsero* crisis, 161–162; and camp tensions, 88–96; and "Castro agents," 93–94, 96; and Christianity, 17, 74–79, 91, 109; Clinton's press statement on, 1–2, 84, 88; as "communists, criminals, and homosexuals," 5, 17, 18, 24, 51, 75–76, 79–83, 89, 92–94, 99, 109; and economic recession, 79, 86; Enrique (Cuban immigrant), 146–147; and federal government, 83–87, 96–103; Fort Chaffee uprising (June 1, 1980), 5, 74–76, 88, 93–96, 99–101; as "illegal aliens," 25, 110, 114; Joint Security Plan for the Cuban Entrants Processing Center Resettlement Operation, 104–106, 108; and legal status, 103–108; Mariel boatlift, 57, 81–82, 91, 103, 109, 121, 157; and place, 17–18; and racialization, 11, 80, 87, 90; and state assistance to federal government, 84–87; waves of, 80

Daly, Joe, 91
Danville, Arkansas, 48, 61, 191n106
Davis, Jeff, 29, 37
Deferred Action for Childhood Arrivals (DACA), 22
De Genova, Nicholas, 15, 152, 154, 162
DeHart, Dave, 195n62
De La Torre, Alberto and Bertha, 166

DeLay, Gunner, 154, 175
DeLuca, Ben, 137–138
democracy, 161
Democratic Party, 1, 31–33, 37–38, 58, 60, 76–78, 90, 104, 174, 176
demographics, 30, 33–34, 39, 47, 49, 51, 83, 99, 113, 115, 131–132; Arkansas (1980–2000), 120–123; La Blanca, Zacatecas (Mexico), 123–125
Department of Health and Human Services (DHHS), 91–92
Department of Homeland Security, 169
Department of Justice (DOJ), 81, 88, 97, 100–101, 139, 141
desegregation, 2, 29, 40–45, 60, 118. *See also* segregation
discrimination, 32, 117, 119, 147–149, 167, 178
Do, Thuan Van, 68–69
Dominican immigrants, 162
drug use and drug dealing, 89, 92, 129, 164, 171
Drummond, James, 97–100
Du Bois, W. E. B., 9
Dudas, Jeffrey, 77–78
Duke, David, 118
Dumas Clarion, 61

economic geography, 11–12
Educational Council for Foreign Medical Graduates (ECFMG) exam, 69–70, 71
Egerton, John, 32
Eidenberg, Gene, 84, 97, 104
Eisenhower, Dwight D., 38, 41
Elliot, Joyce, 176
English as a second language (ESL), 150, 175. *See also* language
Engstrom, David, 104
Equal Rights Amendment, 58, 79
ethnic studies, 11–12

Falwell, Jerry, 58, 78
Family, Life, America, and God (FLAG), 59, 79
Faubus, Orval, 41, 44–45, 60

Fayetteville-Springdale-Rogers Metropolitan Statistical Area (MSA), 121–122, 134
Federal Bureau of Investigations (FBI), 92, 100, 139
Federal Emergency Management Agency (FEMA), 82, 88, 89, 91, 94, 97, 100, 102
Federal Motor Carrier Act, 36
Fernandez, Gastón, 83
Filipino immigrants, 14
Fink, Leon, 46
food stamps, 64, 87, 172, 195n50, 199n71. *See also* social welfare
Forbes, Ralph, 206n30
foreignness, 5, 14, 15, 40, 59, 63–64, 99, 153, 155–156, 169
Fort Bragg, North Carolina, 57
Fort Chaffee, Arkansas, 53; during Berlin Crisis, 57; establishment of, 40, 52; as Cuban refugee center, 1–2, 5, 7, 40, 74–110; as Southeast Asian refugee center, 1–2, 40, 49–50, 52–73; uprising of June 1, 1980, 5, 74–76, 88, 93–96, 99–101; during World War II, 40, 53
Fort Chaffee Task Force Situation Reports (SITREP), 88
Fort Indiantown Gap, Pennsylvania, 60, 75, 104
Fort McCoy, Wisconsin, 75, 104
Fort Smith, Arkansas, 1, 40, 48, 56, 57, 63, 95, 122, 126–135, 139, 142, 144–146, 148, 163, 175, 181
Franklin, Benjamin, 169–170
Freeze, Jack, 1, 108–109
Froelich, Jacqueline, 37
Frolic Footwear, 63–64

Garlington, Gordon, 179–180
Gates, Carroll L., 171
Gates, E. S., 157
Gavalis, Joseph, 137
Gentlemen's Agreement (1907), 14
Georgia-Pacific Company, 134
Gerber, 134, 142
Gladden, John, 166

Glenn, Evelyn Nakano, 15
globalization, 46–47, 113
Godfrey, Phoebe, 44–45
Golden Living, 134
Goldfield, David, 33
Goldwater, Barry, 38
"good ol' boys" system, 26, 179, 180
Gramscian notion of common sense, 11
Griffen, Wendell, 118
Guam, 62, 66
Guatemalan immigrants, 46, 140, 145, 146, 158

Haitian immigrants, 84–87, 92, 102, 110, 160–162. *See also* "Cuban/Haitian entrant (status pending)" designation
Hallet, Miranda Cady, 48
Hammerschmidt, John Paul, 38, 96, 174
Hancock, Ange-Marie, 87
Hapke, Holly M., 128
Harland, Leland, 64
Harp, Doug, 88
Harrison, Arkansas, 2, 28, 29, 38, 57, 189n64
Hatch Act, 35
Hazard Analysis and Critical Control Point (HAACP), 141
Helton, Laura E., 47
Hernández, Kelley Lytle, 160
Hipple, Jim, 159–160
Hispanic Assimilation Program, 177
Hmong immigrants, 132
Holmes, Christian R., 105
Holt, Jim, 175
homophobia, 81
homosexuality, 5, 17, 18, 24, 75, 76, 79–83, 92, 99, 109
Hopson, Mark D., 141
Hot Springs, Arkansas, 115–116, 171–172
Huckabee, Mike, 17, 51, 154, 176–178
Human Rights Watch, 141, 149
Hunt, Johnnie Bryan, 36, 49
Huntington, Samuel P., 173–174

Hutchinson, Jeremy, 169
Hutchinson, Tim, 38, 169, 174

"illegal aliens," 171–173, 176, 177–178; and Cuban refugees, 25, 110, 114; and Latina/o immigrants, 14–15, 17–18, 25, 51, 109–110, 135–138, 152–157, 159–160, 162–164, 166–169; and Mexican immigrants, 14–15, 17, 135–138, 156; and poultry industry, 3, 17, 135–138, 152–157, 159–160, 162–163; and public space, 163–164, 166–169; and racialization, 17–18, 25, 51, 152–156
Illegal Immigration Reform and Immigrant Responsibility Act (1996), 168–169, 179
illegality, 15, 18, 25, 48; spatial illegality, 25, 153–155, 162, 163–166, 168, 174
Immigration Act (1917), 14
Immigration Act (1924), 14
Immigration and Customs Enforcement (ICE), 169
Immigration and Nationality Act (1952), 14, 81, 107–108, 168
Immigration and Naturalization Service (INS), 81, 85, 91–92, 94, 107–108, 114, 136–141, 155, 159–160, 168; Electronic Verification Program, 141, 150
Inda, Jonathan Xavier, 16, 154, 164, 171, 173
Indian Removal Act (1830), 27
indigenous peoples, 7, 27, 34, 170–172
internment camps, 14, 53–60, 177
Irvin, Tommy, 134

Jackson, Jesse, 85, 118
Japanese American internment, 14, 53–55, 58–60, 177
J. B. Hunt, 36
Jenny Lind, Arkansas, 89–90, 98, 103
Jim Crow policies, 41, 48, 120
Johnson, Don, 138

Johnson, Lyndon, 84–85
Johnson, Phil, 159
Johnson, Viney, 116
Jones, Jimmie "Red," 88
Justin, C. L., 156–157

Kandel, William, 10
Katznelson, Ira, 32
Keck, Tim, 167
Kell, William E., 100
Kelley, Robin D. G., 30–31
Kennedy, Edward, 85
Kennemore, Dick, 160–162
Kennon, Gary, 167
Key, V. O., 37
Kidd, Ron, 138
Kim, Claire Jean, 12
King, James, 85
Kirk, John A., 41, 43
Kraft-Planters, 134
Ku Klux Klan, 38, 39, 53, 118, 188n64

La Blanca, Zacatecas (Mexico), 123–128, 134–135, 139, 143
Lagomarcino, John P., 84–86
Lam, Van Thatch, 1
language, 11, 14, 19–22, 62, 63, 66, 68, 73, 87, 131, 132, 148, 150, 156, 173–175
Laotian immigrants, 23, 63, 121, 131–133, 191–192n106
Latina/o immigrants, 2–5, 7–8, 177–182; and Arkansas demographics, 38–39; and discrimination, 143–149, 155; and diversity, 143–149; and "illegal aliens," 14–15, 17–18, 25, 51, 109–110, 135–138, 152–157, 159–160, 162–164, 166–169; and nativism, 170–175; and Nuevo South, 8–11, 22, 45–48; and poultry industry, 45, 47–48, 112–115, 126–127, 133–143, 148–151, 162; and public space, 163–169; and racialization, 11, 13–17, 23, 25–26, 39, 50–52, 73, 152–167, 171, 174–175, 181; and racism, 26, 46, 132, 143–144, 147–148, 167; and teen

pregnancy, 72. *See also* Mexican immigrants
La Vida Nueva (camp newspaper), 20-21, 93-94
Ledbetter, Sam, 176
Leverette, Allen, 179-180
Lewellen, Roy C. "Bill," 119, 120
Lewis, Dave, 91
Lewis, Roy, 158
Lipman, Jana, 50, 192n4
Little Rock, Arkansas, 49, 63, 115-116, 129, 159-160; Cinco de Mayo Festival, 177; and school desegregation, 2, 40-45, 60, 118
Little Rock Nine, 2, 40-45, 60, 118
Long, Jesse L., 98-100
Lopez, Miguel and Nora Virginia, 167
Lowe, Lisa, 13-14
Luibhéid, Eithne, 83
Lye, Colleen, 13-14
lynching, 2, 28-29, 37, 58

MacCoon, John, 141
Mariel Cubans. *See* Cuban refugees and exiles
Marsden, George, 58-59, 78-79
Martinez, Moraisa, 92
massive resistance, 59, 77, 115, 118
Matthews, Phil, 63
McAda, Bill, 89-91, 95, 97
McCarran-Walter Act (Immigration and Nationality Act), 14, 81, 107-108, 168
McClellan, John L., 60
McCoy, Dana, 165-166
McCuen, Bill, 116
McWilliams, Brian, 95
meat-processing industry, 7, 10, 35-36, 112. *See also* poultry industry
Mexican American Legal Defense Fund (MALDEF), 166-168
Mexican American War, 133
Mexican immigrants, 2, 4, 7, 8, 10, 11, 72-73; Andrea (Mexican immigrant), 122-128, 143, 206n49; and Arkansas demographics, 120-121, 133; and Christianity, 51; Genoveva (Mexican immigrant), 110, 145-156; Gustavo (Mexican immigrant), 110, 144-145, 147; as "illegal aliens," 14-15, 17, 110, 135-138, 156; Javier (Mexican immigrant), 122-128, 138-139, 143; Jesús (author's father, Mexican immigrant), 127-128, 138-139, 143; and Nuevo South, 45-48; and poultry industry, 112-113, 115, 135, 137-146; and public space, 163-167; and racialization, 14-17, 25, 39, 152-167, 171, 174-175, 181; Ricardo (Mexican immigrant), 148-149; Rodolfo (Mexican immigrant), 206n49
military police (MP), 74, 76, 88-89, 95, 200n77
Miller, Julieanne, 163
Mississippi Delta Plans, 9-10, 30-31
Mitchell, Mable, 116
"model minorities," 16, 50-51, 181
Mohl, Raymond, 46
Molina, Natalia, 13, 131
Moral Majority, 51, 58, 61, 76, 78
Moreton, Bethany, 37
Morris, Dan, 153, 170-171, 173
Moseley, Jack, 89

National Governors' Association, 76, 84-86, 102
National Guard, 41, 56-57, 76, 88, 90, 172
Native American peoples, 7, 27, 34, 170-172
nativism, 7, 13, 65, 69, 154, 160, 166, 169-175, 177
Negrete, Juan, 158
New Deal, 30-32
New Right, 77-78
New South, 8-11, 30-33, 180-182
Ngai, Mae, 14-15, 152, 154, 162
Nixon, Richard, 77
no checan papeles (not checking papers), 4, 7, 128, 134-139
North Little Rock, Arkansas, 116, 129
Northwest Arkansas Times, 61

Nuevo South, 22, 180-181; field of, 45-48; framework of, 8-11

Obama, Barack, 22
Occupational Safety and Health Administration, 142
OK Foods, 134
Omi, Michael, 12
Operation SouthPAW, 136-137
Osborne, Rick, 70
Osceola, Arkansas, 159-160, 162, 163
OXFAM, 143

Pagan, John, 119-120
"parolee" status, 104, 106, 192n4
Patterson, James T., 79
Peterson, Coleman, 39, 44
Peterson, Rana, 44
Peterson Farms, 149-150
Pico Rivera, California, 123-129, 133
place: place-making, 17-19; and race, 4, 7-8, 11-17, 47-52, 131, 153
plantation bloc, 9-10, 26, 27-28, 30-31, 33-35, 179-182
Plunkett, Bob, 95-96
Popke, E. Jeffrey, 128
Populist Party (People's Party), 37
Posse Comitatus Act (18 USC section 1385), 98, 101, 102, 106
poultry industry, 3, 7, 10, 17, 21, 126-127, 149-151, 163, 181; history of, in Arkansas, 28, 35-36, 112-115; and legislation, 36, 119-120; and Nuevo South, 45, 47-48; OK Foods, 134; and social networks, 47, 127-128, 134-135; Tyson Foods, 5, 6, 10, 35-36, 39-40, 112-114, 134-136, 139-141, 143, 149, 159, 179-180; and undocumented workers, 134-43; working conditions, 139-143. *See also* Tyson Foods
prayer in schools, 58, 59, 79
President's Commission on Civil Rights, 38
prisoners of war (POWs), 52-56
Pritchard, Bill, 176

Proposition 187 (California), 173
Proposition 200 (Arizona), 173, 175, 214n73
Protect Arkansas Now, 175
Pryor, David, 1-2, 49, 60, 69-71, 84, 96-97, 156
public schools, 29, 40-45, 58, 78, 86, 115, 129-132, 144-145, 175; Fabian (public school employee), 2, 155
Puerto Rican immigrants, 121, 133, 195n50; Celia (Puerto Rican immigrant), 146-147
Pugh, Arthur, 160, 162

racial cleansing, 2, 7, 23, 28-29, 57, 177
racial formation, 11-17, 47, 50, 133, 182
racialization, 11-17; and criminality, 25, 51, 75-76, 79-83, 89, 93, 152-155, 171, 173; and Cuban refugees, 11, 80, 87, 90; and "illegal aliens," 17-18, 25, 51, 152-156; and Latina/o immigrants, 11, 13-17, 23, 25-26, 39, 50-52, 73, 152-167, 171, 174-175, 181; and place, 11-17, 47-48; and Vietnam refugees, 11, 18, 49-51, 58-59, 63-65, 72-73; and yellow peril, 63-65
racial profiling, 148, 167-168
racial projects, 11, 12, 50
racial scripts, 13, 131
racial terror, 23, 28-29, 51, 131-132
racial triangulation, 12-13
racism, 9, 31, 71, 171-172, 174-175, 178; anti-Asian racism, 13, 51, 59, 71, 192n7; anti-Black racism, 17, 23, 28, 38, 49, 51, 57, 71-72, 90, 99, 177; anti-Latina/o racism, 26, 46, 132, 143-144, 147-148, 167; anti-Semitism, 49; and Ku Klux Klan, 38, 39, 53, 118, 188n64; and legislative redistricting, 115, 117-118; and Populist Party, 37; structural racism, 115; sundown towns, 2, 7, 29, 58, 177
Rafinski, Karen, 115

Ragsdale, C. B., 54
Reagan, Ronald, 77, 85, 87, 104
recession, economic, 7, 65, 79, 86, 112, 126, 128
Reconstruction, 9, 30-31, 38, 115, 119, 174. *See also* Second Reconstruction
Rector, William F., 42
redistricting, 115-118, 178
Refugee Act (1980), 103-104, 109
Refugee Education Assistance Act (REAA), 102
religion. *See* Buddhism; Christianity
Religious Leaders for Racial Justice, 118
Religious Right, 58-59, 76, 78
republicanism, 174
Republican Party, 24, 31, 36-39, 77, 87, 169, 172-176, 177; Washington County (Arkansas) Republican Women, 172-173
Rheem, 134, 142
Ribas, Vanesa, 143
Riccio, Dorothy, 82
Rich, Rudy, 81
Riffel, Brent E., 141
Robertson, Pat, 58, 78
Robinson, Ray, 97
Robison, James, 58, 78
Rodman, Mike, 164
Roediger, David, 30
Rogers, Arkansas, 2, 29, 38, 149-150, 153, 159, 165-170, 174-175, 181; demographics of, 121-122. *See also* Fayetteville-Springdale-Rogers Metropolitan Statistical Area (MSA)
Rojas, James, 212n35
Roosevelt, Franklin D., 30
Russell, Ron, 119

Salvadoran immigrants, 2, 22, 48, 94, 110, 125, 129, 133, 144-146, 155
Sampier, John, 150-151, 153, 170, 174-175
Sánchez, George, 160
scales, analytic, 4, 12, 16, 17, 153, 154

Schaffer, Archie, 136
school busing, 42, 58, 78
Schrag, Peter, 169-170
Schulman, Bruce, 30, 32
Second Reconstruction, 59, 77. *See also* Reconstruction
segregation: and cotton industry, 27; and Democratic Party, 37; and education, 40-45, 115, 118, 120, 178; Jim Crow, 41, 48, 120; and Latina/o immigrants, 145-147; and massive resistance, 59, 77, 115, 118; and Second Reconstruction, 59; self-segregation, 82, 145-146; and sexuality, 82; and whiteness, 75, 77
September 11, 2001, attacks of, 168
service industry, 10, 37, 114, 126, 134
Shefner, Jon, 46-47
Shek, Gim, 64
Siemens, Doug, 136
slavery, 9, 17, 27, 30-31, 33-35, 51, 77, 115, 177
Smith, Alecta Caledonia Melvina, 28
Smith, A. Lee, 171-173
Smith, Neil, 12
Smith, William French, 104
social positioning, 48, 178
social services, 31, 86
social welfare, 16, 32, 64, 77, 87, 154, 172, 195n50, 199n71
SouthPAW. *See* Operation SouthPAW
space, public, 48, 154-156, 163-169, 212n35
spatial illegality, 25, 153-155, 162, 163-166, 168, 174
Springdale, Arkansas, 2, 22, 29, 35, 164, 166, 169, 175, 181; demographics of, 121-122; First Baptist Church of, 36, 59. *See also* Fayetteville-Springdale-Rogers Metropolitan Statistical Area (MSA)
states' rights, 2, 5, 29, 40-45, 51, 59-63, 77-78
States' Rights Party, 38
Statue of Liberty, 62

Striffler, Steve, 112, 135, 141, 149
Stueck, William, 46
Stuesse, Angela C., 47, 143
sundown towns, 2, 7, 29, 58, 177
supermajority districts, 116–117

Tabor, Jessee F., 3–4, 135–136, 160
Tan Dan (camp newspaper), 20
Tang, Eric, 50
Thai immigrants, 132
Tidball, Bill, 88
Title XX, 86
tobacco industry, 35
Tolan, J. H., 53
Torres, Rebecca M., 128
Trail of Tears, 9, 30
Tran, Hoa Thi Kim, 66–68
Trane, 134
tranquilidad, 128
Traugh, Bill, 82
Trinh, Hong Thi Cam, 69
Truman, Harry, 37–38
Tucker, Jim Guy, 137
Turner, Jerry, 66–69
Tyson, John, 35–36, 40, 112, 113
Tyson Foods, 5, 6, 10, 35–36, 39–40, 112–114, 134–136, 139–141, 143, 149, 159, 179–180

unemployment, 3, 61, 63–64, 75, 79, 87, 126–127, 129, 135, 156, 171, 211n15
United States Catholic Conference (USCC), 91
University of Arkansas: Fayetteville campus, 35, 38, 44, 132, 144; Fort Smith campus, 66
University of Arkansas Medical Center, 70
US Border Patrol, 3, 108, 110, 135–137, 155, 159–161, 163, 168
US Department of Agriculture (USDA), 139, 141

Valdez, Victor, 94
Van Buren, Arkansas, 29, 110, 144, 163

Vasquez Ruiz, Francisco, 82–83
Vietnamese refugees, 4–5, 7–8, 19–21, 24–25, 75, 99, 101, 109–110; and Arkansas demographics, 121; and Christianity, 1, 5, 17–18, 58–63, 76, 84, 109; and economic anxiety, 61, 63–65, 75, 79, 87; and education, 131; and Fort Chaffee, Arkansas, 1–2, 40, 49–50, 52–73; and legal status, 106; as "model minority," 16, 181; as "parolees," 192n4; and racialization, 11, 18, 49–51, 58–59, 63–65, 72–73; and states' rights, 59–63. *See also* "yellow peril"
Vietnam War, 18, 51, 58, 64–65, 78
violence, 16, 99, 100, 119; anti-Back violence, 2, 7, 50, 57; lynching, 2, 28–29, 37, 58; murder, 2, 28–29, 57–58, 75; racial violence, 2, 7–8, 16, 28, 50; and Second Reconstruction, 59, 77; state-sanctioned violence, 2, 7–8, 57
Voting Rights Act, 59, 77

Walker, John W., 116
Wallace, George, 77
Walmart, 5, 36–39, 144, 158, 179
Walton, Sam, 36, 37, 40, 112
War Relocation Authority, 53–54
Webb, Clive, 77
Weise, Julie M., 10, 48
Weiss, Judy, 82
welfare. *See* social welfare
Whirlpool, 134, 142
White, Frank, 57, 87, 108
white flight, 115–116
whiteness, 8, 17, 24, 30, 51–52, 71, 77, 99, 122, 132
Williams, Frank, 54
Wilson, Pete, 87
Winant, Howard, 12
Winders, Jamie, 47
Wolf, Karen, 164–166
Womack, Steve, 151, 154, 167, 174–175
Wood, Doug, 117
Woods, Clyde, 9, 26, 30–31

Woodward, C. Vann, 9, 31
worker safety, 141–142
World War II: Fort Chaffee during, 40, 52–57; internment camps, 14, 52–60, 177; and military-industrial complex, 30; and poultry industry, 35, 113

xenophobia, 7, 64, 69, 108

Yell County Record, 61
"yellow peril," 5, 14, 16, 18, 24; history of concept, 184n16, 192n7; and racialization, 50, 52, 59, 63–65, 70, 72

Zacatecas (Mexico), 123–128, 134–135, 139, 143
Zimmermann, David, 37

www.ingramcontent.com/pod-product-compliance
Lightning Source LLC
Chambersburg PA
CBHW021854230426
43671CB00006B/381